IMAGES
of America

MORRISTOWN

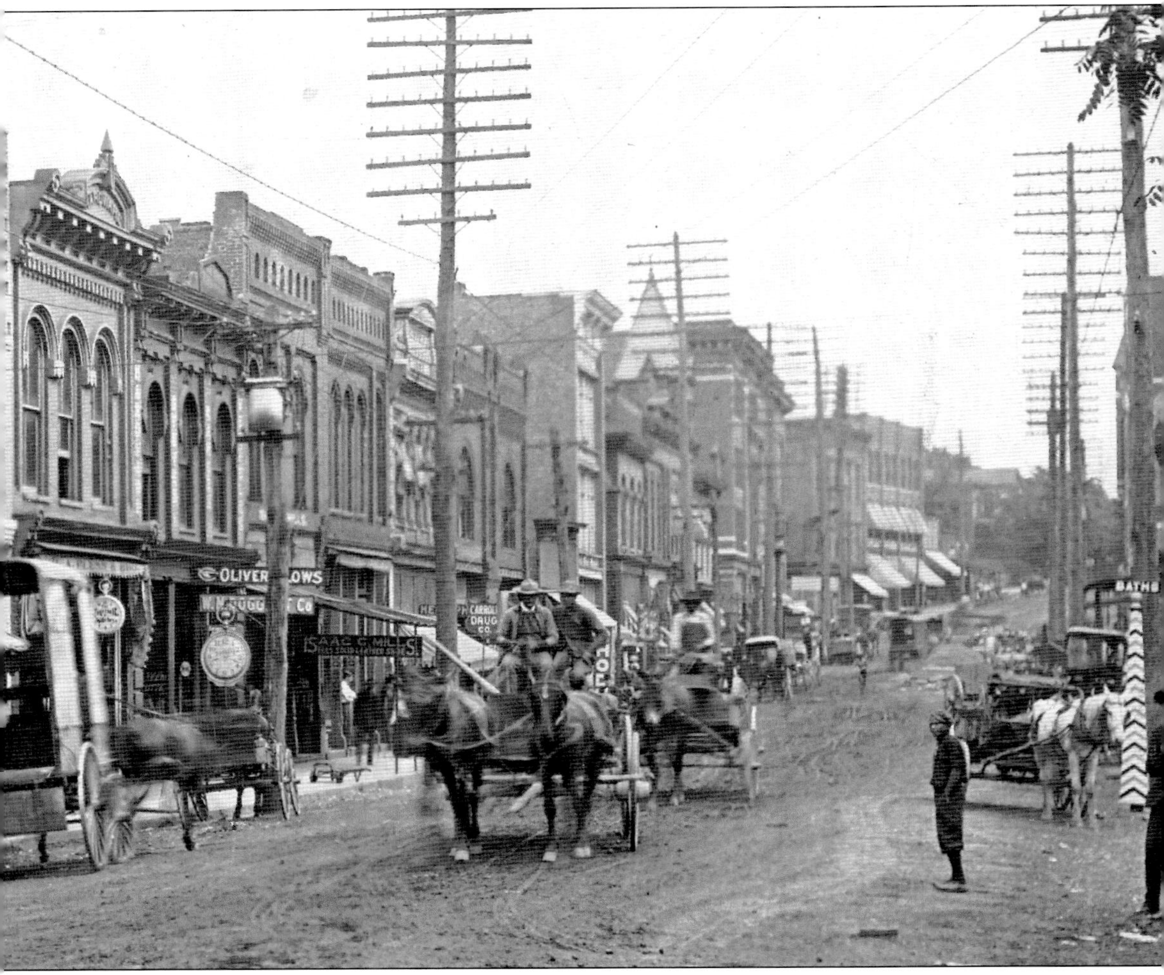

This view of Main Street around 1906 was taken near the corner of Main and Henry Streets looking eastward. Main Street would not be paved until 1916, and horsepower then meant the real thing. Automobiles did not become commonplace for several more years. Some of the businesses at that time were, from left to right starting with second building, D.A. Pless (jewelry), W.N. Doggett Company (hardware), Isaac C. Mills (shoes), Helm-Phillips Company (clothing), and Carroll Drug Store. (Courtesy of the Rose Center.)

On the Cover: Main Street is seen looking west from Cumberland Street on November 8, 1952. It was a bustling downtown business district that was the heartbeat of the local economy. Notice the popularity of neon signs, which illuminated the business district. (Courtesy of the Tennessee State Library and Archives.)

IMAGES *of America*

MORRISTOWN

Larry Michael Hobby

ARCADIA PUBLISHING

ISBN 978-0-7385-9434-7

Published by Arcadia Publishing
Charleston, South Carolina

Printed in the United States of America

Library of Congress Control Number: 2012951307

For all general information, please contact Arcadia Publishing:
Telephone 843-853-2070
Fax 843-853-0044
E-mail sales@arcadiapublishing.com
For customer service and orders:
Toll-Free 1-888-313-2665

Visit us on the Internet at www.arcadiapublishing.com

There are two lasting gifts we can give our children; one is roots, the other wings.

Dedicated to Ghable Isabella Hobby and memory of Aislyn Maria Hobby

Contents

ACKNOWLEDGMENTS

First and foremost, I would like to thank the staff of the Rose Center who have generously shared their vast collection of photographs from the Hal Noe Historical Collection, for without these, this project may have not been possible. Unless otherwise noted, all images appearing in this series are courtesy of the Rose Center or the author.

I also would like to give a special thanks to the volunteers of the Hamblen County Archives and especially to Cindy Lane. Cindy was encouraging and supportive, and her help with writing, research, and fact-checking image text made this book such a success. Thanks to Jennifer Dempster Frey for her editorial and proofing skills that cover for my writing inadequacies. Thanks to Carol Henderson and Amy Maxey at Camera Castle, Inc., for their support and their attention to detail with scanning some very difficult images.

A big thanks to my editors, Elizabeth Bray and Liz Gurley at Arcadia Publishing, for their constant support and letting me help preserve part of Morristown and Hamblen County history for future generations.

Others who contributed photographs are: Edie Burns; Davy Anne Charles; Wanda and Ginger Cowan; Julian B. Culvern; Eddie R. Davis; Celya Harrell Fields; Bobbie Finney; Diane Fox; James "Jeff" Goodson; David Harrell; Danny Hryhorchuck; Jeffrey Allen Hurd; the late Frank Gracey Jarrell, WPA clerk; the late Evelyn Bryan Johnson; James Haywood Julian; Cindy Lane; Steve Litz; Billie D. Loveday; Blanche Murray; Paul Ollis; Shelia Carroll Purkey; Wayne Ratcliff; Minnie Robertson; Norma Samsel; Joe Senter; Doris Livingston Stump; James D. Susong; Harve Turner; David Whittington; Frances Williams; Tina Simmons Wilson; and Ellis Winstead. Other people and organizations that contributed were the Blazers Barber Shop, Bill Haskins of the Bulls Gap Railroad Museum, Camera Castle, Inc., C.M. McClung Historical Collection, Goodson Brothers Coffee, the Henry Street Post Office, the Library of Congress, Morristown Chamber of Commerce, Museum of Fine Arts of Boston, Ratcliff Mfg., LLC, Stetzer Funeral Home, Tennessee State Library and Archives, and the National Archives.

Thanks to all participants for making *Morristown* a success. Unfortunately, not all submitted images could be used due to space restrictions. All efforts were made to ensure the accuracy of information, which was sometimes made difficult by conflicting oral and written histories.

INTRODUCTION

Morristown is sheltered in the Tennessee Valley between the Great Smoky Mountains and the Clinch Mountains. Today, it is known as part of the "Lakeway Area" or the "Land between the Lakes" because of the location of its two beautiful reservoirs. The Tennessee Valley Authority created both Cherokee and Douglas Reservoirs in the 1940s to meet emergency energy demands at the height of World War II. These waterways, combined with its beautiful terrain and a state park, make this area an outdoor enthusiast's paradise.

One of the first European settlers to the area was a farmer named Gideon Morris. In 1787, Morris was granted tracts of land by North Carolina that was located in Washington, Greene, and Hawkins Counties. He probably settled on portions of these grants, which were included in Jefferson County and what is now Hamblen County. Gideon Morris was listed as one of the signers of the petition to annex Watauga to North Carolina in 1775 and served in Col. William Christian's expedition against the Indians. The settlement founded by Morris became known as Morristown. Other early settlers were the McFarland, Riggs, Crockett, and Outlaw families. Many people living in the area today are direct descendants of these early settlers.

Morristown is the county seat of Hamblen County, the third smallest county in Tennessee, and it officially became a city in 1855. Main Street in the city was the dividing line between Jefferson and Grainger Counties. Morristown had continued growth because two important early travel routes intersected at this main thoroughfare. One of the travel routes was a major stagecoach route connecting Baltimore to Knoxville, and the other was a trail possibly created by buffalo looking for a salt lick near Powell's River.

The Civil War brought turmoil to Morristown as it did to most of the nation. The town was controlled by both the Union and the Confederate armies at different times during the conflict, simply because of the easy access of the rail. Several battles were fought in this area, including the Battle of Morristown and Gilliam's Stampede. Approximately 90 men, mostly Confederates, lost their lives, and many were buried in unmarked graves in different locations throughout the county.

Due to the addition of the East Tennessee, Virginia Railroad before the Great War in 1856, the city was able to mend its wounds and grow rapidly after the war and became an important commercial center. The areas strategic location aided Morristown's agricultural and industrial development. The railroad companies recognized this advantageous city and turned Morristown into a railroad hub. Morristown was a child of the railroad. The county's founding coincides with the coming of the iron horse to East Tennessee. Morristown had rapid development after the war, and this extensive expansion led to the forming of Hamblen County in 1870.

Like most Tennessee counties, the creation of Hamblen County came as an answer to the need of its people. In that day and time, both transportation and communication were limited. Also, the geography of the county seats of Jefferson and Grainger Counties presented problems for those who had a need to attend court in their respective counties. Morristown continued to be divided by Main Street, with Jefferson County on the south side of Main Street and Grainger County to the north side. The county was formed after the Civil War from parts of Jefferson, Grainger, and eventually Hawkins Counties. To secure the recommendation of state senator William Green of Hawkins County, he was given the privilege of naming the new county. Senator Green chose to name the county after his grandfather, Hezekiah Hamblen.

Morristown has had its share of unforgettable people and unbelievable events. Take for instance Ambrose Gaines Stuart, better known as "Uncle Am" Stuart. As a kid, he learned to play the fiddle from picking up a number of tunes from Civil War soldiers who passed through the area in the 1860s. He is thought to be the first Tennessean to commercially record country music in June 1924. Stuart gained regional fame in the early 1900s with recordings that would later prove influential in the development of early country music.

Other well-known locals include two men who received Congressional Medals of Honor for their heroism in World War I, who have a building named in their honor; a local entrepreneur from 100 years ago, still known through the Southeast only by his initials; and the creator of the American Flying Machine, which was patented on August 14, 1877, when the Wright brothers were only children; they all called Morristown home. An important event in the town's history was an appropriations bill passed by Congress and later signed by Pres. Franklin D. Roosevelt on July 31, 1940. This bill required the acquisition of 45,158 acres of land and the relocation of 875 families and 51 cemeteries, which changed the entire landscape of Morristown.

The Morristown community had its beginnings in commerce and transportation. Those aspects, when combined with its geography, have made it a desirable place to settle. Over time it has changed from Indian Territory to a railway hub and later to a tourist stop. Throughout its history, however, Morristown has never lost its small-town appeal.

There is a lot to be said for living in a small town. Major influences and big-time personalities have stemmed from humble beginnings, never made possible without their small-town roots. The photographs in this volume will chronicle the community's long and fascinating history. We live in the shadows of the history of those who came before us. This book is dedicated to all men and women who were progressive believers in the future of Morristown. Through their silent footprints, we have inherited this beautiful and well-documented city.

One

Workin' for a Livin'

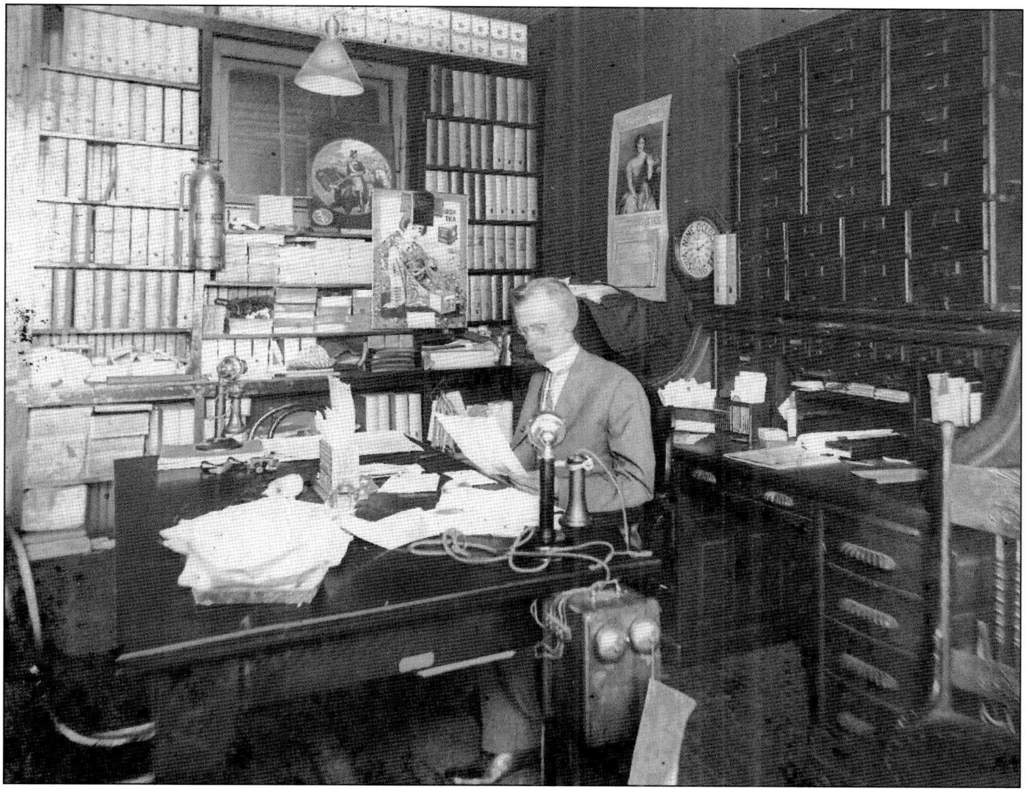

James Franklin Goodson, born in Franklin, North Carolina, made Morristown his adopted home after the family exhausted its money while traveling to Indiana. Goodson first went into a partnership with W.K. Blair in 1882, calling their wholesale grocery Goodson and Blair, which was later succeeded by Goodson and Legg, and finally Goodson, taking full control over the business, changed the name to the J.F. Goodson Wholesale Groceries. Today, his famous JFG brands can be found throughout the Southeast. James Franklin Goodson, shown here working at his desk, was elected Morristown's mayor from 1895 to 1897 and president of the Morristown Board of Trade. One of Morristown's most progressive citizens, Goodson was instrumental in overseeing the establishment of the county fair and the municipal water system. (Courtesy of James "Jeff" Goodson.)

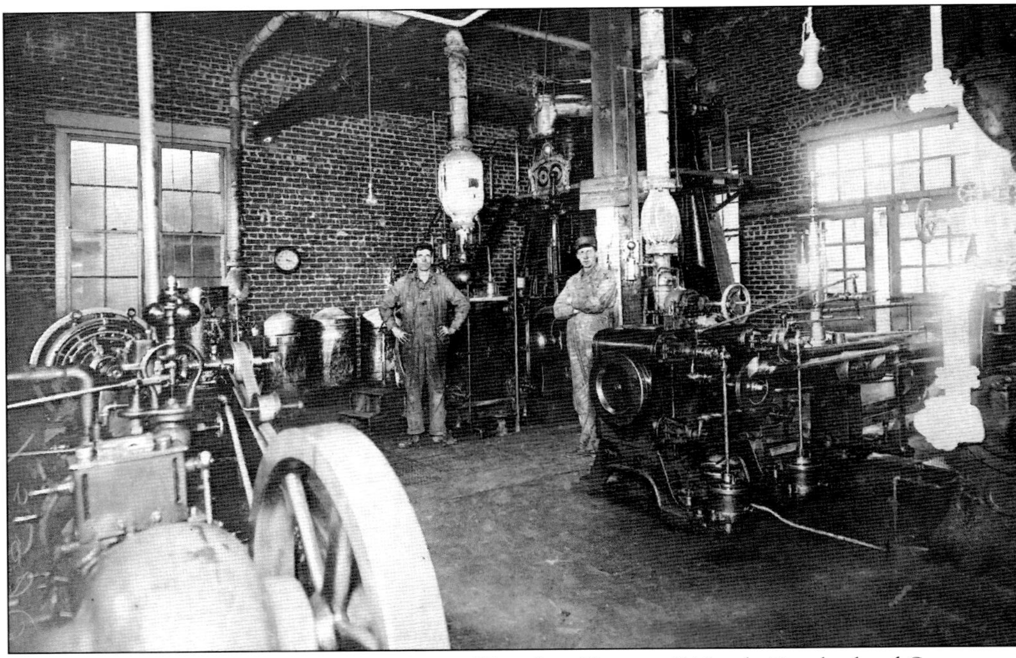

Morristown Power Plant's engine room on Cherokee Drive, off North Cumberland Street, was erected in 1900. The facility was Morristown's first dynamo, with a plant on Turkey Creek. This plant was abandoned when a more modern plant was built on the Holston River with steam turbines. This facility was sold to Tate Springs, giving the famous spa its first electric lights.

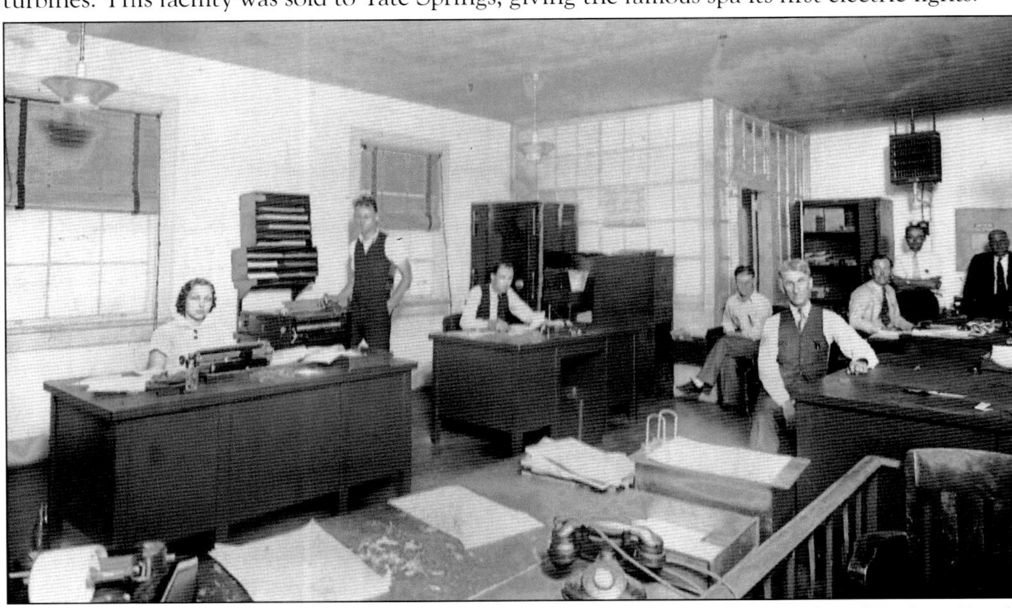

Lea Rayburn established Morristown Knitting Mill in 1927 along the banks of Turkey Creek. In 1952, Rayburn's daughter and son-in-law, Lea Aileen and G. Wayne Smith, purchased the company, and they changed the name to Lea-Wayne Knitting Mills. This image was taken in the 1940s in the Morristown Knitting Mill office. The young man sitting in the background of this picture with legs crossed is G. Wayne Smith. (Courtesy of Ratcliff Mfg., LLC.)

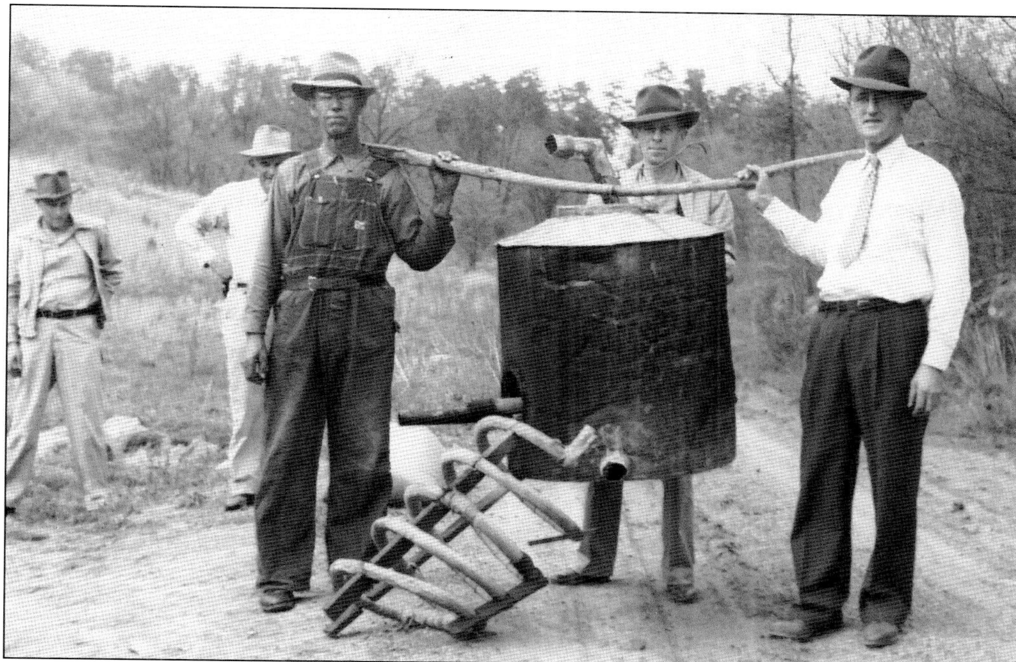

Ben Hooper Shaver, who served as Hamblen County sheriff from 1946 to 1948, poses with an illegal moonshine still that the sheriff's department discovered in rural Hamblen County. In spite of federal laws outlawing the making of untaxed liquor, moonshining continued to be a lucrative cottage industry for Appalachian corn farmers and rural distillers.

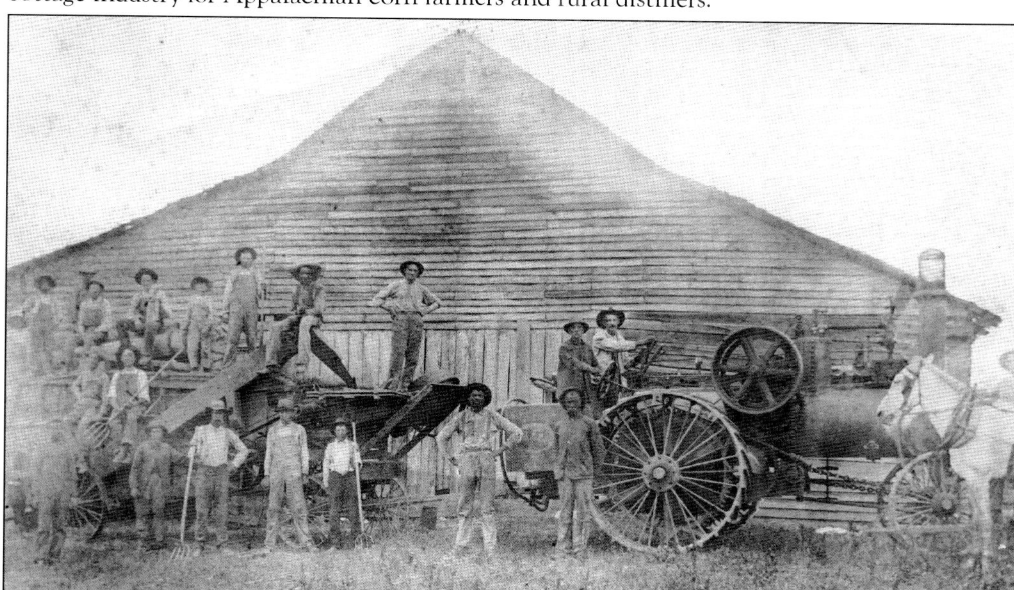

David J. Purkey, a Native American of the Kituwah tribe, is standing in middle with his hands on hips with his wheat-thrashing machine. He is believed to be the first one in Morristown who processed grain fields for farmers in the area. David married Ethel Lily Jones Barbie and had five children. (Courtesy of Shelia Carroll Purkey.)

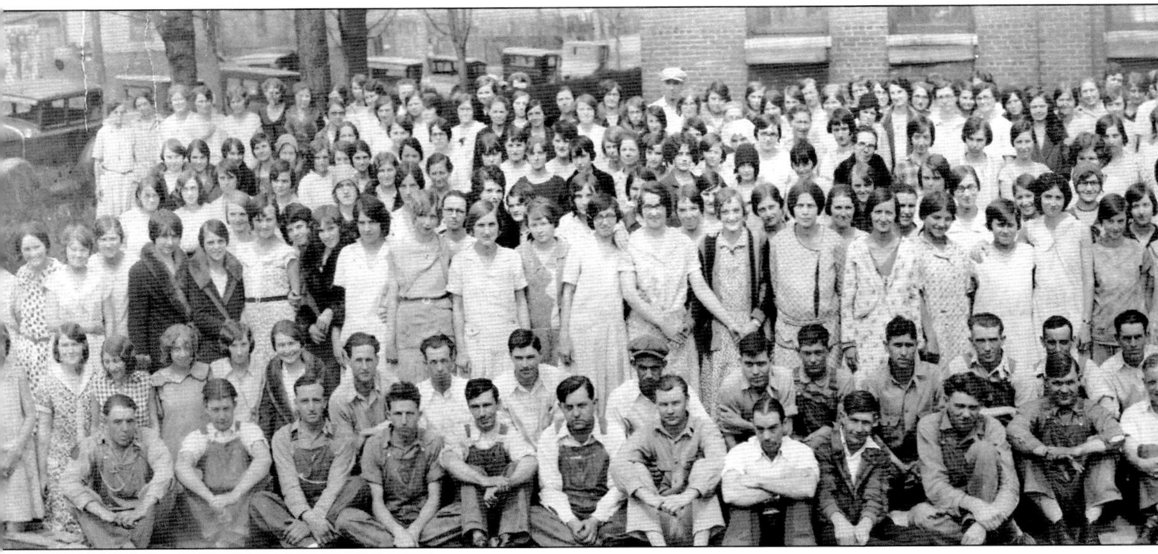

The image above shows the employees of the Charles H. Bacon Company on April 4, 1930. Pictured below are the employees of the Morristown Knitting Mill in April 1930. Both images

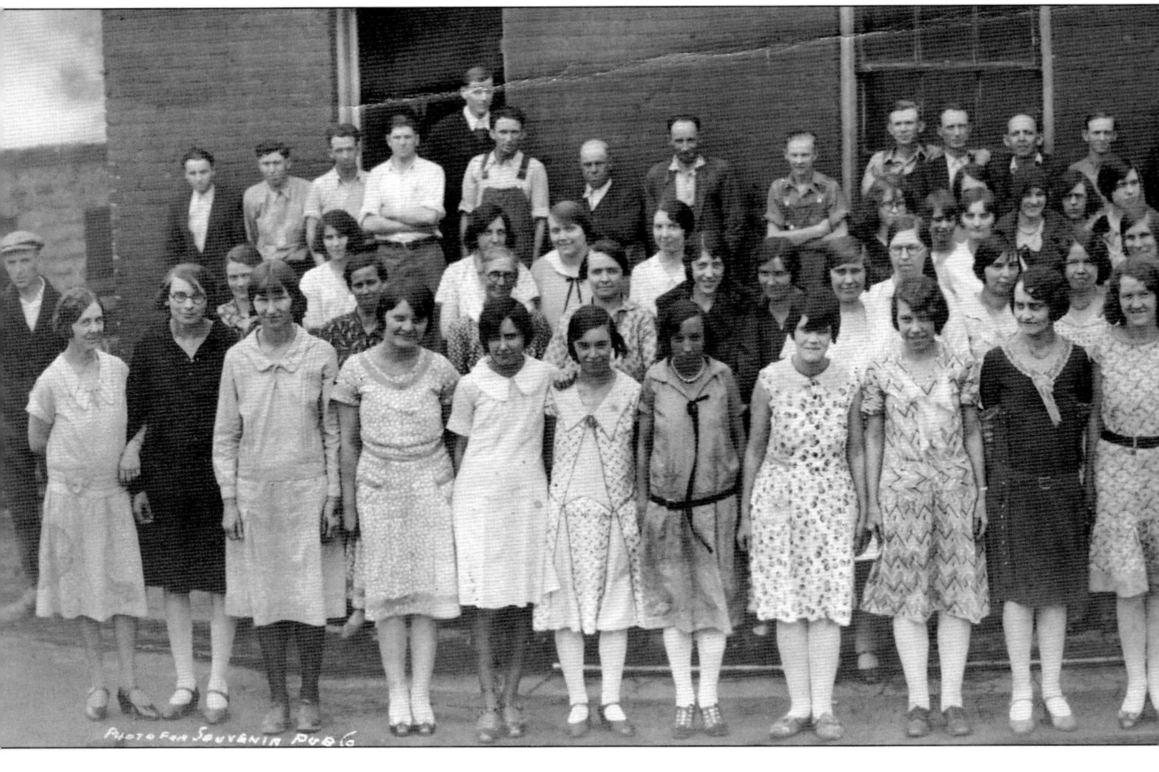

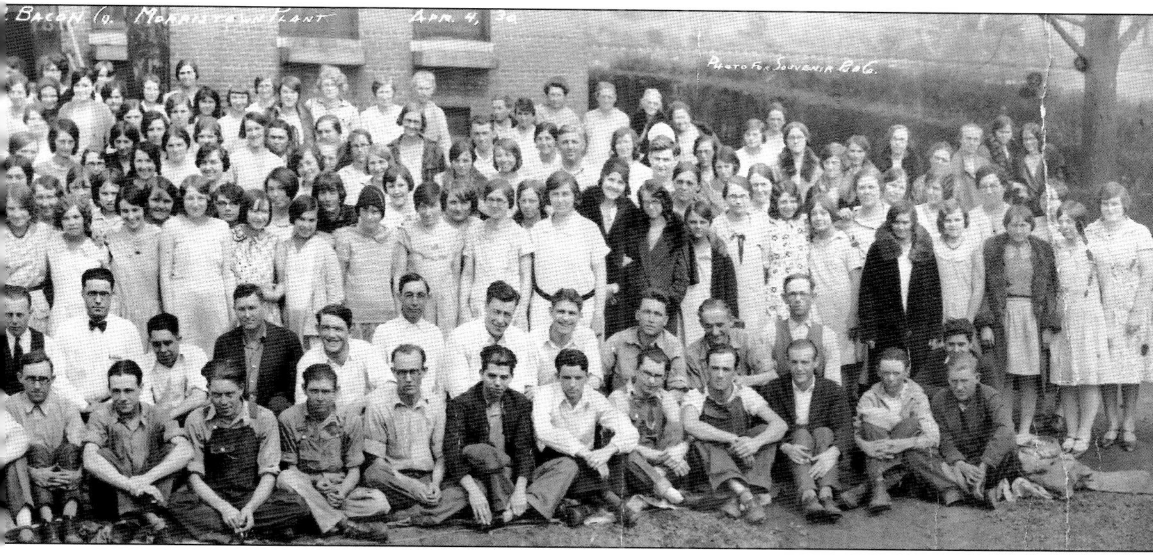

of local hosiery manufacturers were taken by Souvenir Publishing Company and are typical of employee group shots of the period. (Both, courtesy of Ellis Winstead.)

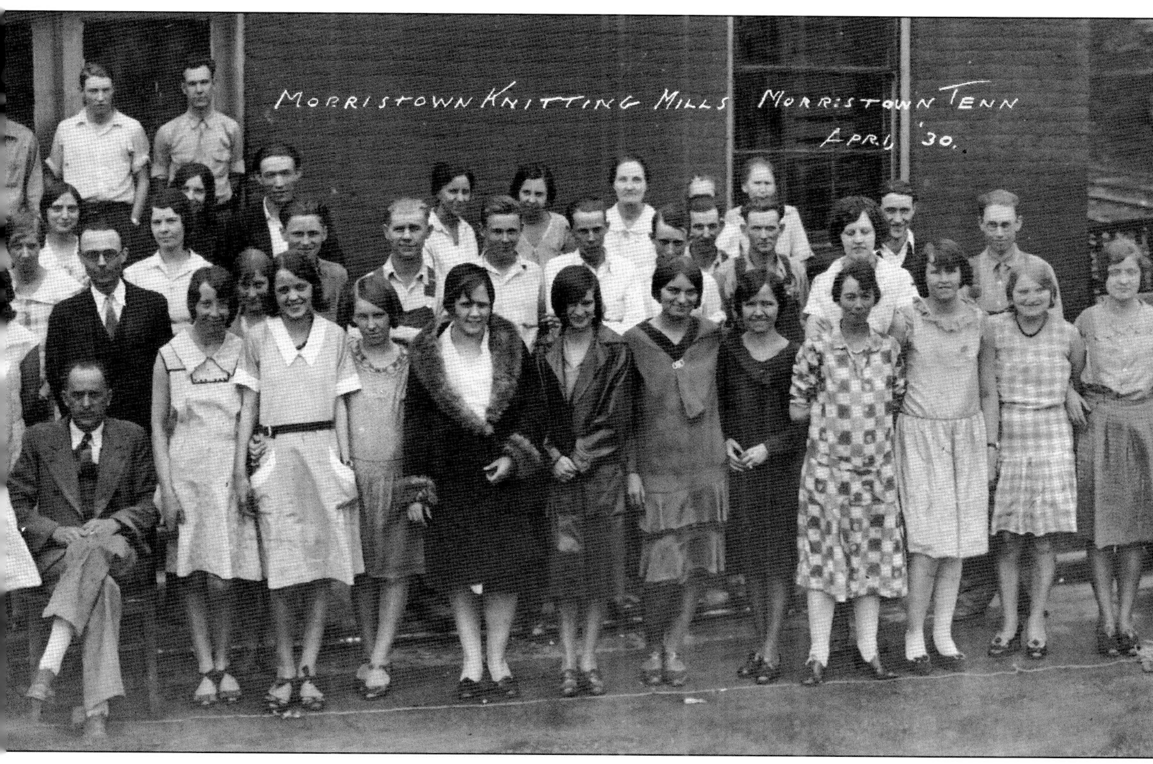

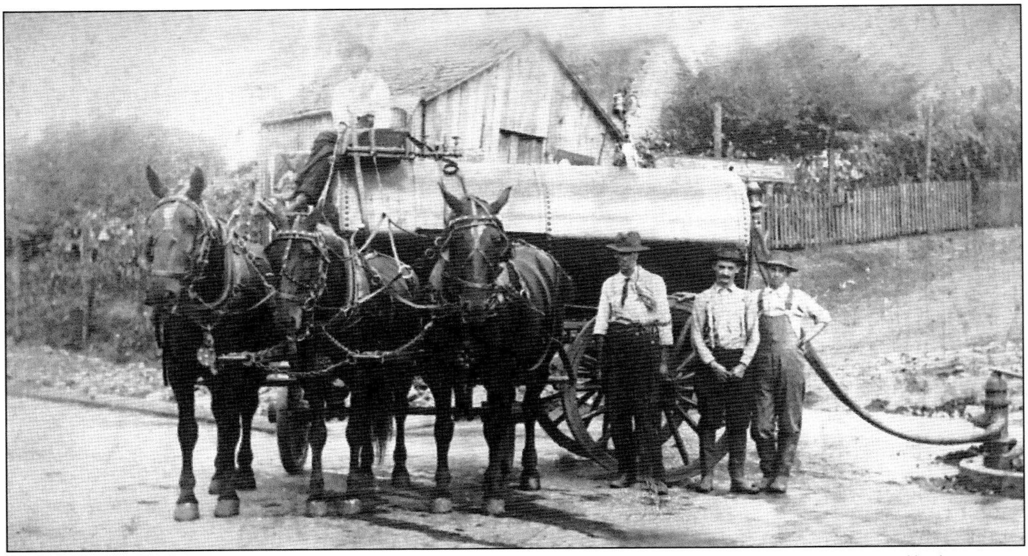

The same horses that pulled the water wagon for street washing also served to pull the city's only fire truck. Upon ringing of the fire bell over city hall, the driver, Mr. Buchanan, would quickly unhitch the trio, hurry to the fire hall, and hitch them to the fire truck. This method was used for several years prior to the purchase of the first motorized truck in 1916. The street department workers shown standing with wagon are, from left to right, Walter Akers, Tal Boatman, and Jim Boatman.

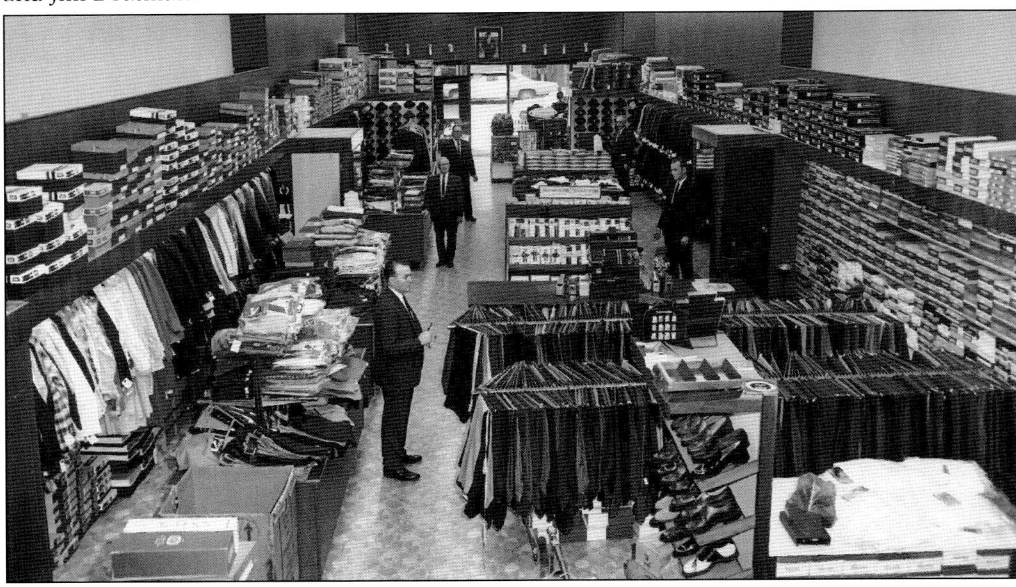

This is the interior of the Rogers Men's Clothing Store with employees being identified as, from front to back, (left side) Bill Ramsey, Claude A. Rogers, and C.D. Cruze; (right side) A.V. Combs and Bob Sawyers. Robert Marion Rogers started the business when the family moved to Morristown in 1897, and he purchased the stock of McFarland and Moffitt, continuing the business under the name of Julian & Rogers until Rogers and Julian dissolved their partnership. The store continued operation for many years as R.M. Rogers & Company and was a favorite men's clothing store for many. (Courtesy of the Hamblen County Archives.)

WCRK was founded in 1947 and has been serving the community since. Radio host Inglebert Patterson, shown here, was host of the program *Party Line*.

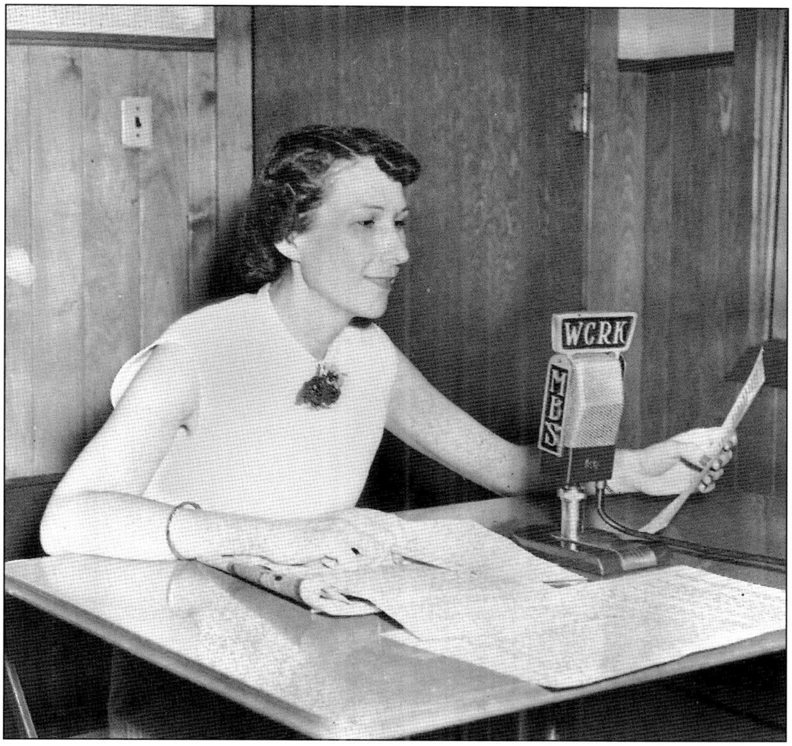

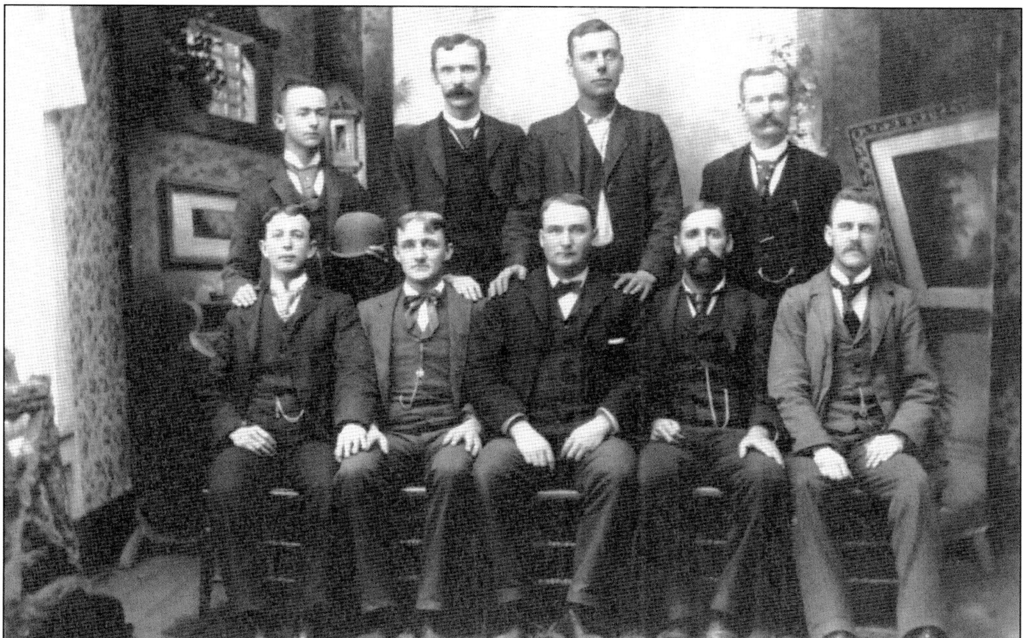

This photograph of well-known Morristown businessmen was taken around 1890. They are, from left to right, (first row) Lodie Holmes, I.C. Mills, John Stubblefield, Will Moffett, and George W. Baker; (second row) Mr. Evans, Mr. McGhee, Mr. O'Neill, and John McCord.

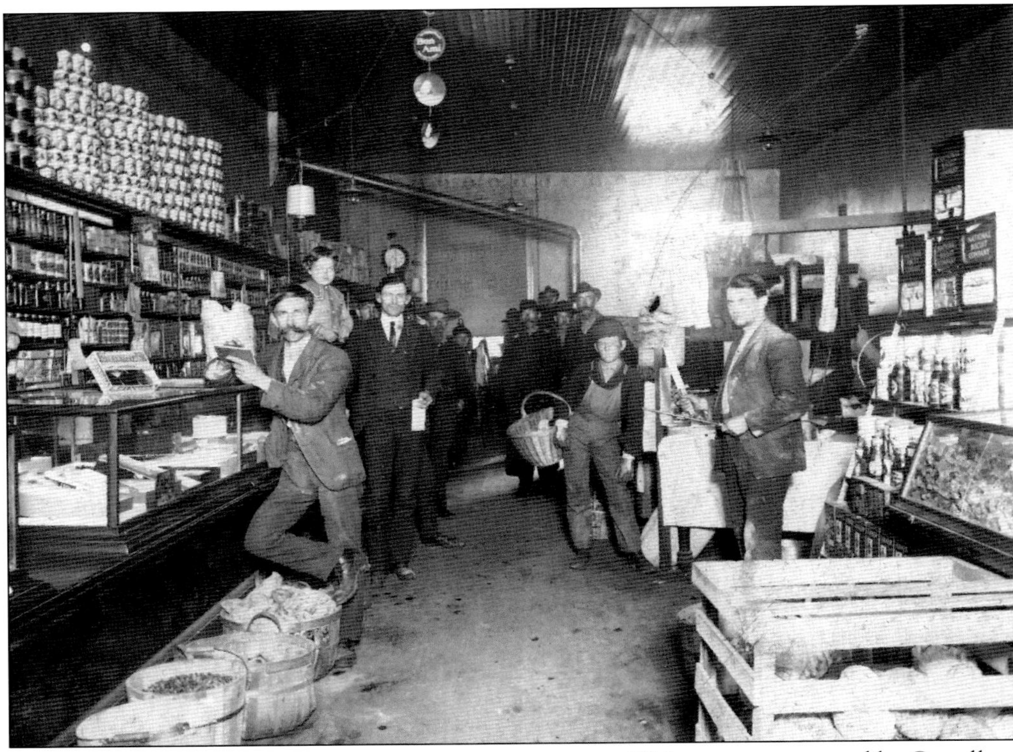

This grocery, operated by Cassell & McGimpsey, occupied one of the two downtown buildings erected by Judge James George Rose. The man (left) leaning on counter is Charles Cassell. Men standing around the heating stove in the rear indicate this photograph was made in colder weather.

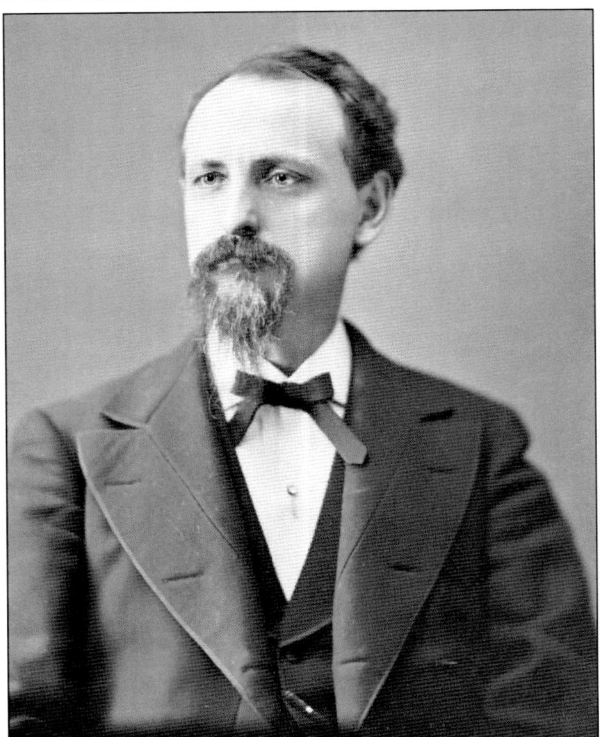

William McFarland was a leading influence on the local community. McFarland, admitted to the bar in 1861, engaged in the practice of law in 1865 in Dandridge, Morristown, and Greeneville. Appointed as judge of the county court in 1870, McFarland was also elected to the 44th Congress, where he served from March 4, 1875, to March 3, 1877. McFarland was also elected mayor of Morristown for four terms and was a member of the board of education. (Courtesy of Library of Congress, Brady-Handy Photograph Collection.)

Adams Quillian Horton was born and raised in Chickamauga, Georgia. Horton moved to Morristown in 1926 and managed the Doughty-Stevens Funeral Home, which had been purchased from Clay Hall. The following year, Horton purchased the interest of the Doughty-Stevens and changed the name to Horton Funeral Home of Morristown. A veteran of World War I, he served 33 months with a cavalry attached to a hospital unit and saw extensive service. (Courtesy of the Morristown Chamber of Commerce.)

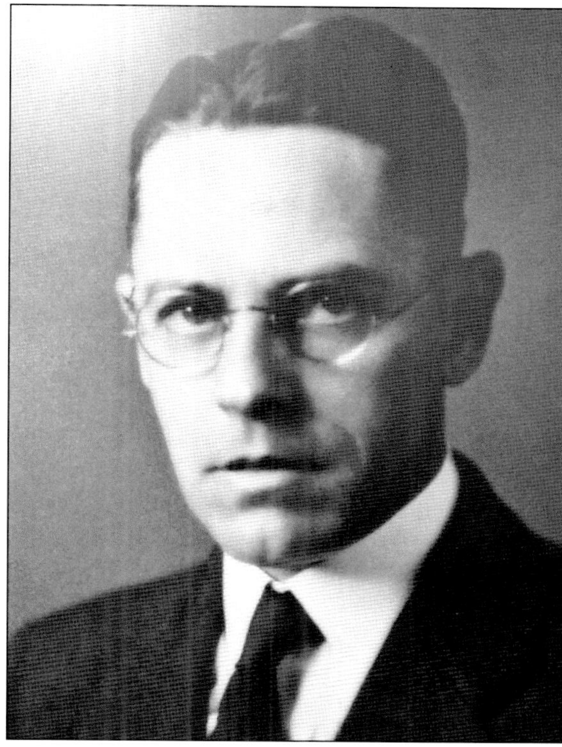

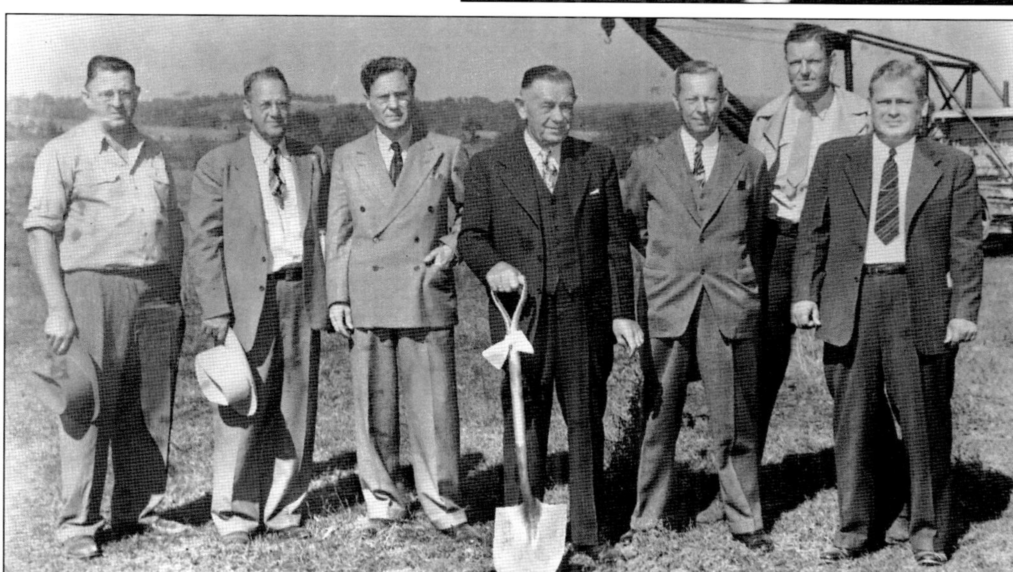

Ground-breaking for the Lowland Rayon Filament Plant in October 1946 marked the first company construction away from the Enka Site in Buncombe County, North Carolina. Breaking ground are Dr. A.J.L. Moritz, Enka's technical vice president (with shovel); P. Paul Kriek, Enka's chief engineer (third from left); Jan Heykoop, the first manager of the Tennessee operations (third from right); and officials of H.K. Ferguson Company, the firm that built the original rayon facilities at both the Enka and Lowland locations. (Courtesy of Paul Ollis.)

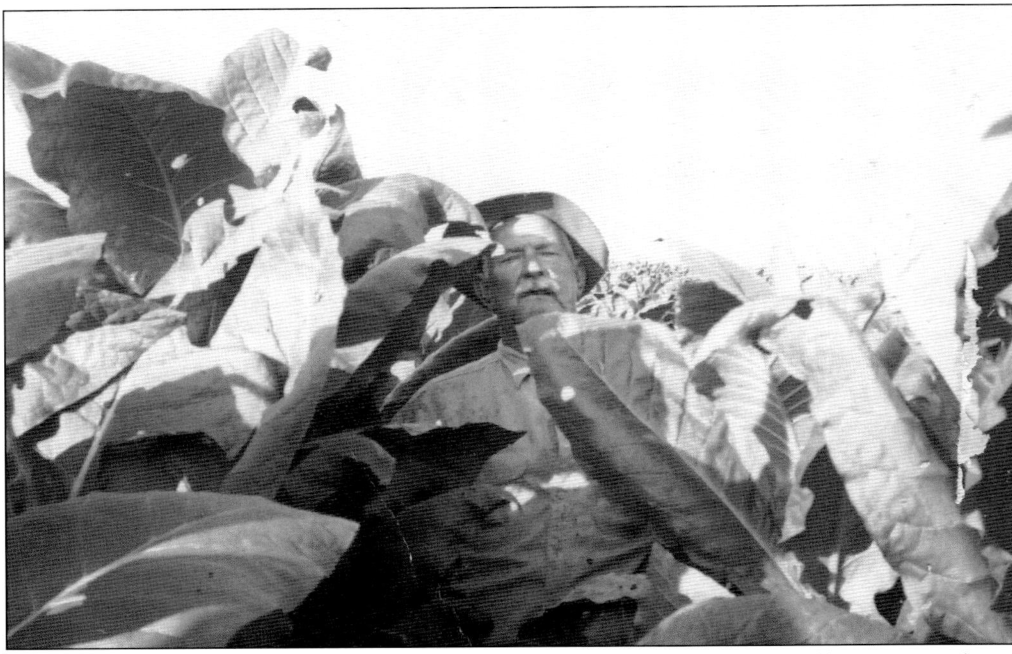

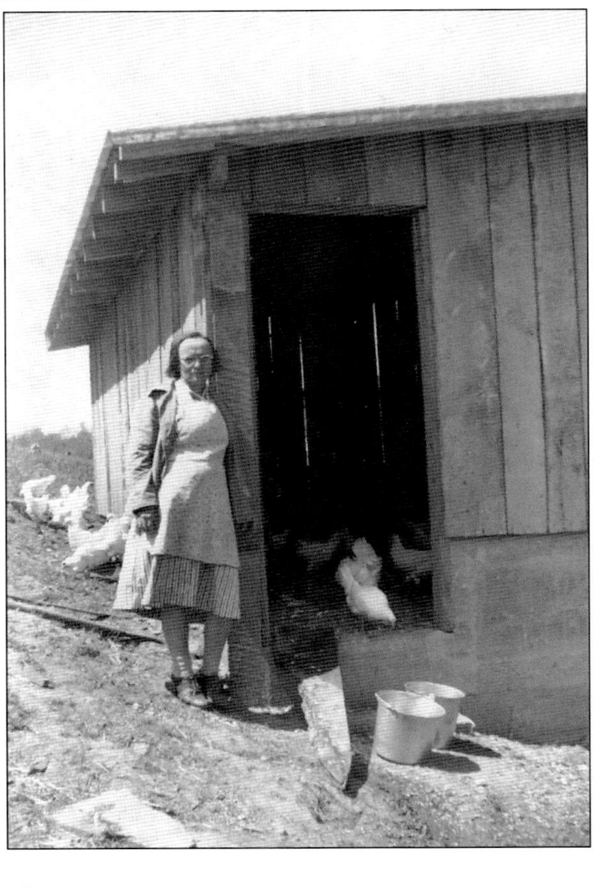

Samuel "Sam" Walker Cowan, shown here standing in his tobacco patch, was the son of George W. Cowan and Nancy Cassell. Sam moved to Tennessee in 1891 and took up residence in the Kidwell's Ridge community. He married Louisa Ivy in 1894, and the couple had four children: Cuba C., A.A. "Guss," Gladys, and Elsie Cowan. (Courtesy of Wanda and Ginger Cowan.)

Ada V. Rhoades (1912–1998), shown here feeding her chickens, is representative of many who raised livestock and vegetable gardens in order to feed their families. Ada was the daughter of Milburn Clasby Marshall and Della Mae Brewer Marshall. In 1934, she married Lewis Frank Rhoades. Together, they struggled to build their house and barn on Slop Creek Road (located in eastern Hamblen County) during the war, when building supplies were either difficult to find or were rationed. The couple had three children: Bobbie Jewell, Donald Lewis, and Jerald Dean. (Courtesy of Cindy Rhoades Lane.)

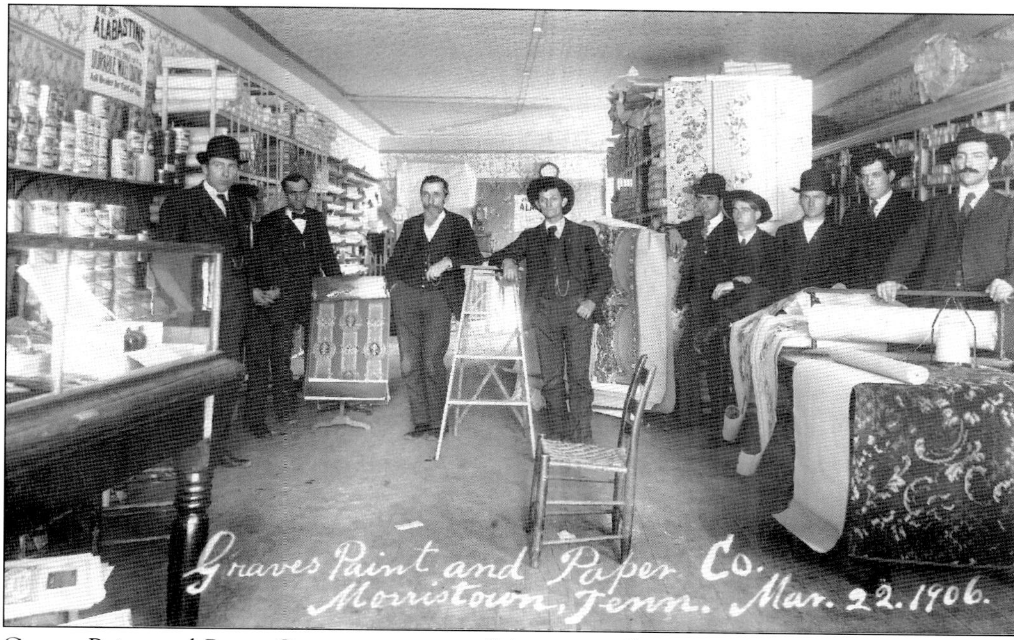

Graves Paint and Paper Company was a well-known wallpaper and pa.nt merchant located downtown on the corner of West Main Street and Peavine Alley. Pictured on March 22, 1906, are, from left to right, Charlie Graves, Harris Havely, owner J.P Graves (middle), Sam Kelley, ? Graves, Henry Merrimam, and three unidentified.

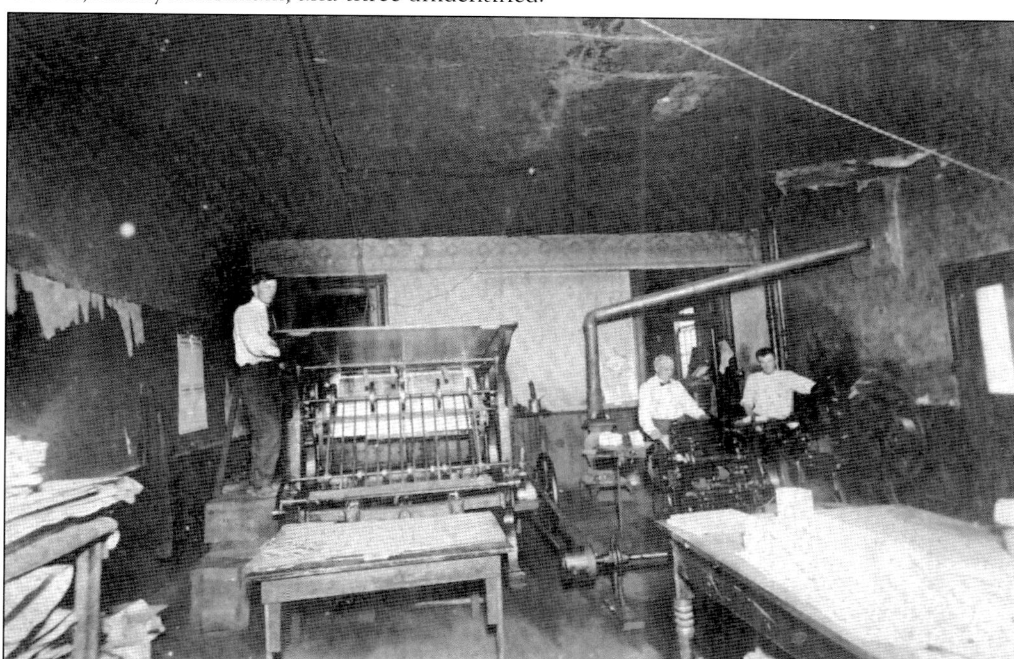

Taken around 1912, this picture shows the interior of the *Morristown Sun*. From left to right are Lee Waddell, Edward Minot Hardy (owner), and Hal A. Noe. Their slogan was "It shines for all." Operation began in 1908 and ceased in 1956.

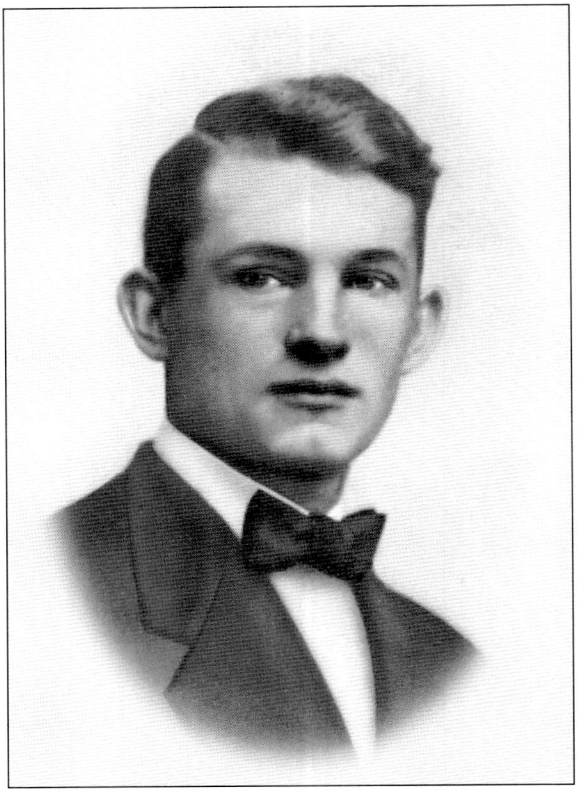

Ralph Edward Julian, shown as a young man, was best known as the owner and pharmacist of Roberts and Turner Drug Store. This firm became the longest continuously open retail business in Morristown history. Originally founded by T.G. McGee in 1867, it became Roberts and Turner in 1897 and kept that name for 76 years until it closed in 1973. (Courtesy of James Haywood Julian.)

Mollie Simmons is shown in 1958 working the old cord board in the South Central Bell Building, where she served as both local and long distance operator. South Central Bell was located on the corner of Second North and Henry Streets until June 18, 1958, when it closed for a new Main Street office. Mollie started working for the company in 1952 and retired after 39 years of service. (Courtesy of Tina Simmons Wilson.)

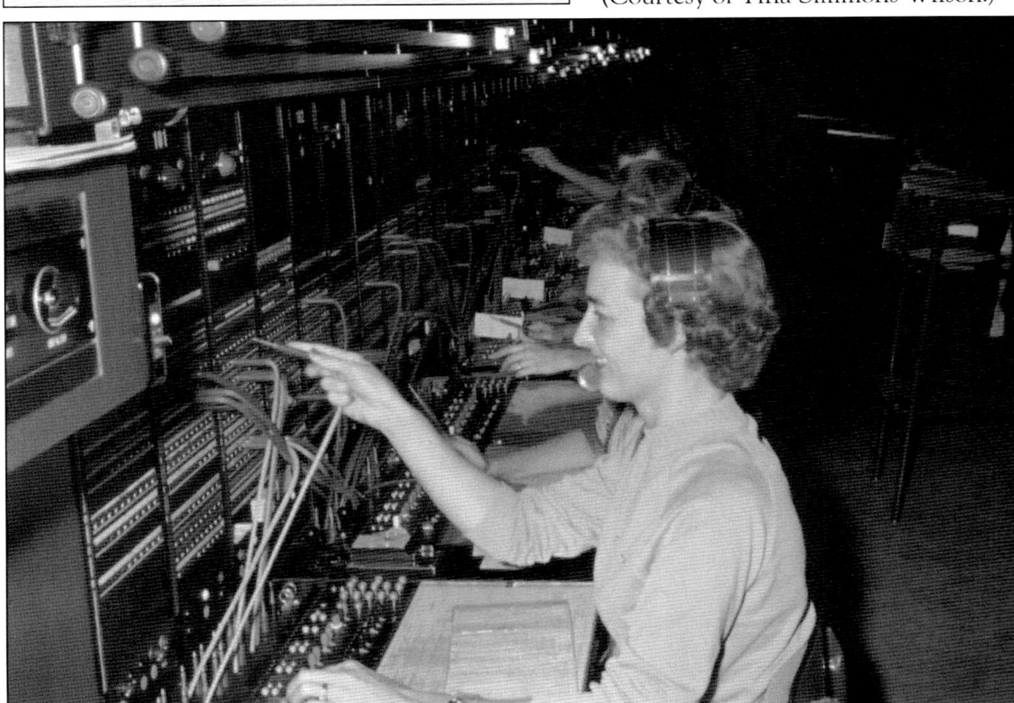

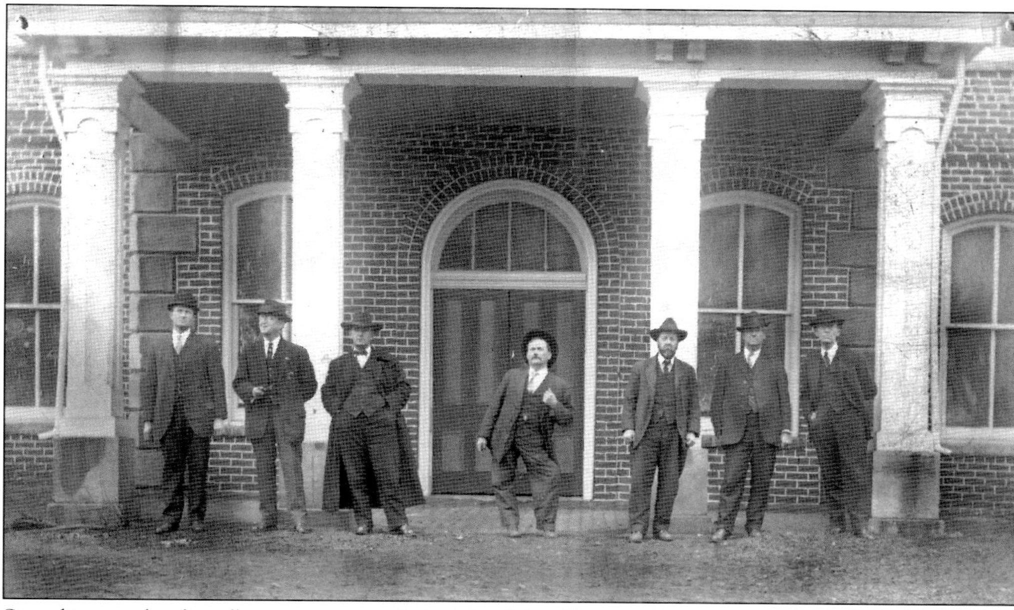

Standing at the first-floor entrance of the Hamblen County Courthouse around 1912 are, from left to right, county officials W.F. Silvers (trustee), J.G. Templin (county court clerk), Will Felknor (sheriff), C.B. Lee (circuit court clerk), Mack Allen (clerk and master), unidentified, and J.J. Thompson (register of deeds).

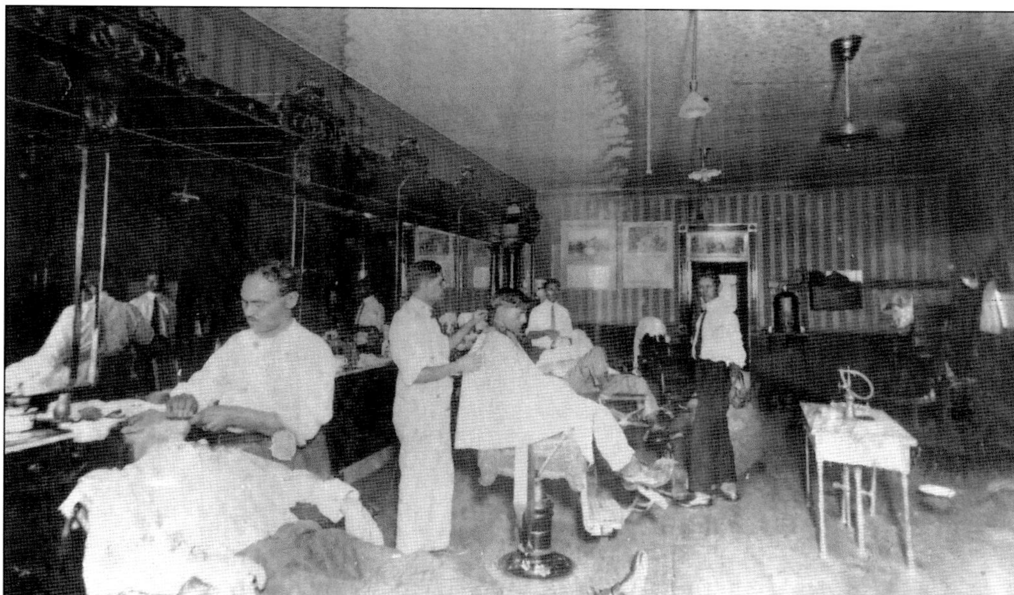

This is the interior of Walkers Barber Shop in the 1920s. The three barbers shown here are, from left to right, Robert "Bob" Walker, Tobe Dwin, and Henry Walker. The barbershop was in the present location of the law office of Danny Hryhorchuck. Notice the water pump table (right). It drew water directly from Turkey Creek, which ran underneath the shop. The room in the front of the shop was a bathroom where locals could bathe before getting a cut or shave. (Courtesy of Danny Hryhorchuck.)

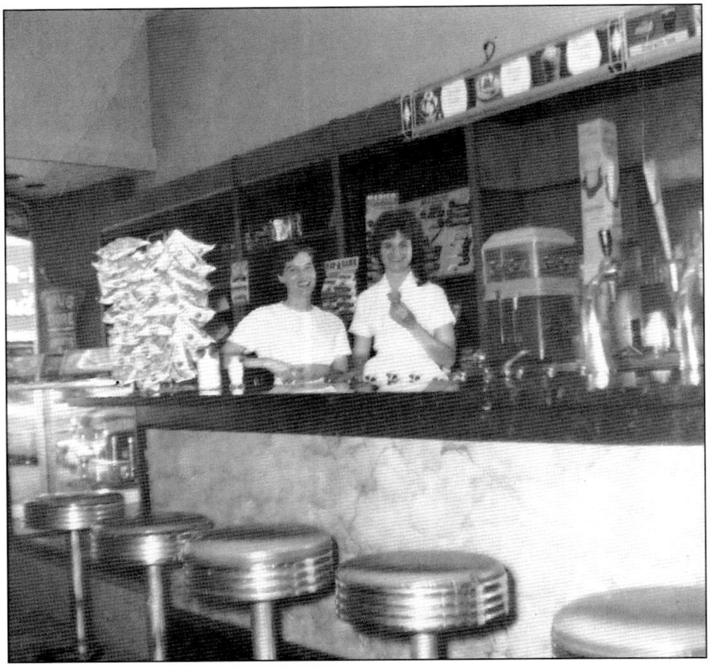

The lunch counter at Roberts and Turner Drug Store was a favorite spot for patrons over the years. Roberts and Turner, like other drugstores of the time, was a place where one could get several conveniences, such as lunch, sodas, and ice cream. The identities of the ladies working the counter are unknown. (Courtesy of James Haywood Julian.)

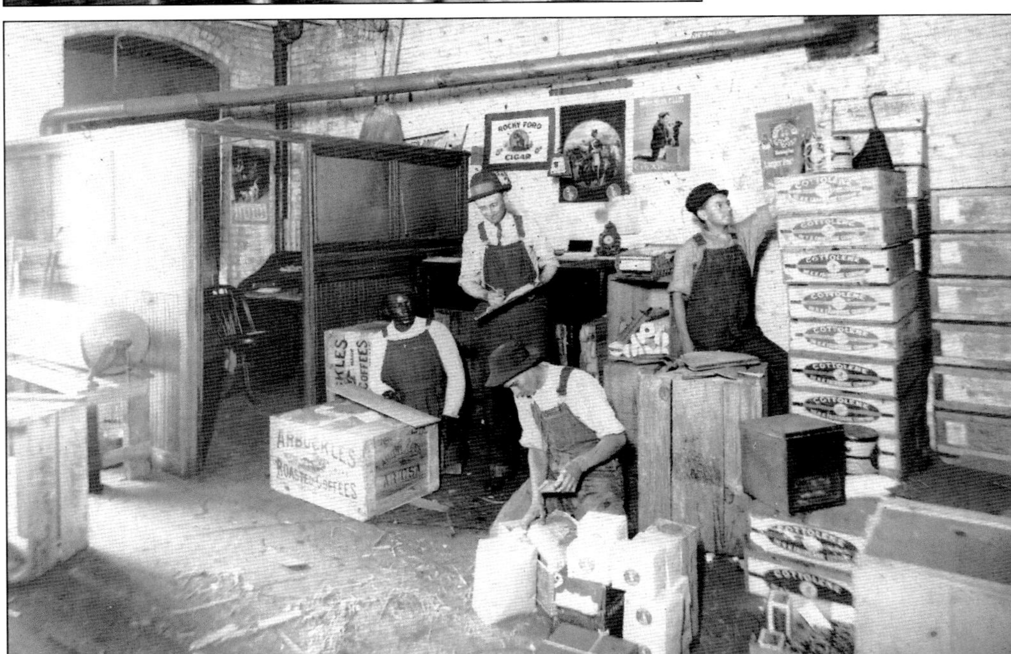

James Goodson distributed coffee that he bought from the Arbuckle Coffee Company (later to become Maxwell Coffee in New York), but he was not pleased with its quality. Goodson decided to approach his supplier in New York for raw materials to test his skill at making a better coffee. Supplied with green coffee beans, Goodson set about roasting his own blend, calling it JF Goodson Special, which led to the regionally popular JFG Coffee Company. Shown are some unidentified employees of the J.F. Goodson Wholesale Groceries. (Courtesy of James "Jeff" Goodson.)

Two

GIMME THAT OL' TIME RELIGION

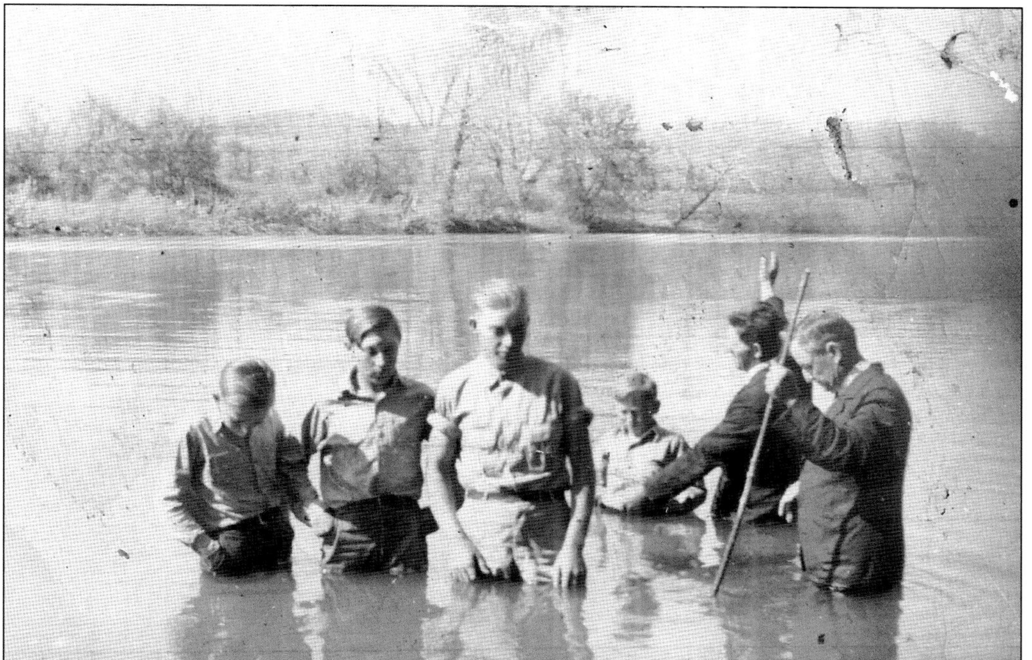

Before baptistries were installed in climate-controlled church buildings, baptisms were performed in lakes and rivers. On May 5, 1940, this photograph was taken on the Holston River, when Kidwell's Ridge Baptist Church baptized four young men who became lifelong members of the church. Pictured are, from left to right, Tip Mayes, J.C. Mayes, Dennis ?, Jimmy Mayes, Steven Green, and unidentified. The Holston River had not yet been flooded to create Cherokee Lake. (Courtesy of Billie D. Loveday.)

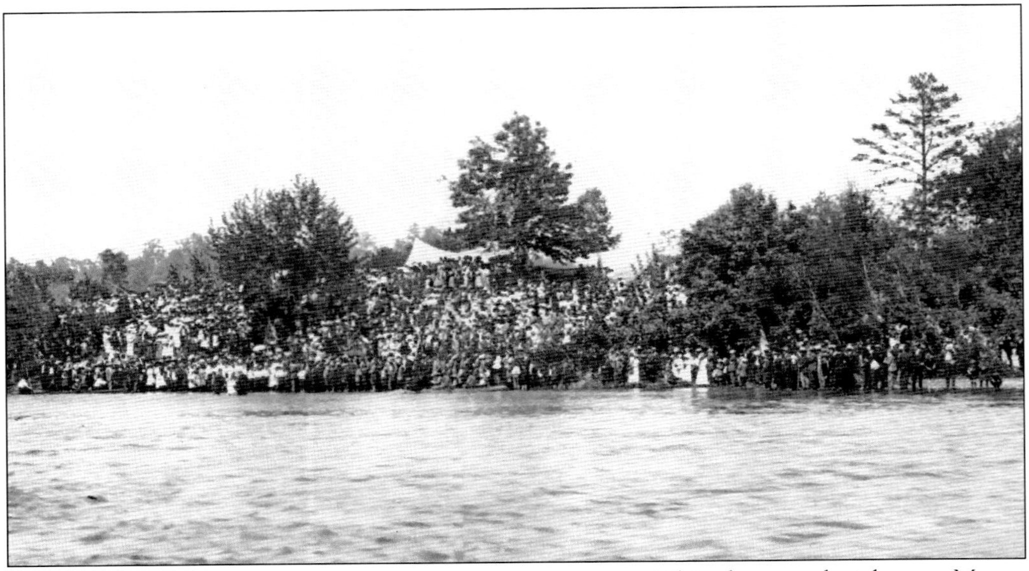

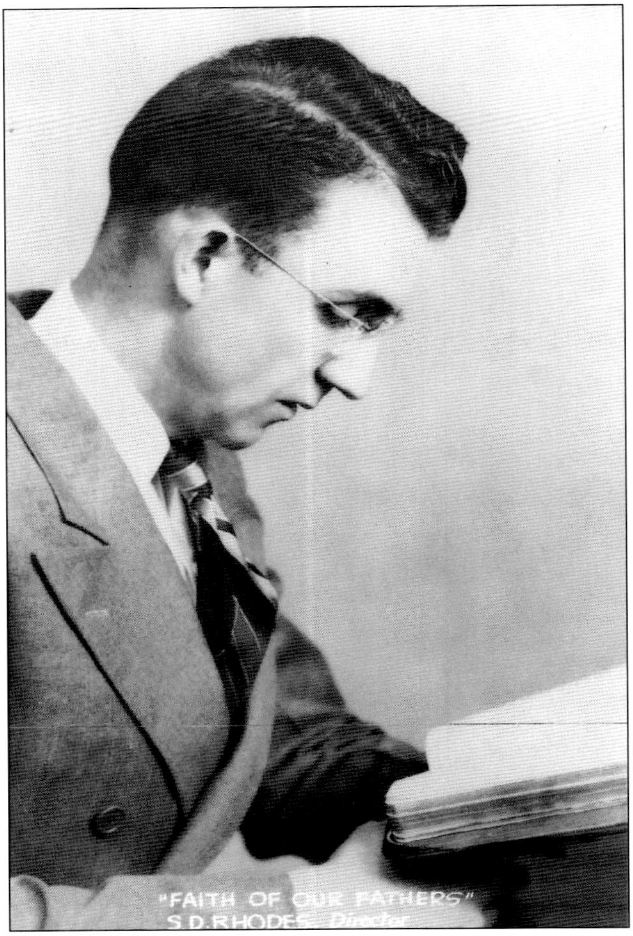

This photograph, taken on May 11, 1913, on the Holston River, shows 5,000 people gathered to witness the 65-minute baptism of 97 souls by Dr. Spencer Tunnell of the First Baptist Church of Morristown. According to research by the late Juanita Loving, church membership grew from 165 to nearly 800 during the nine years that Dr. Tunnell was pastor at First Baptist Church.

Rev. S.D. Rhodes (1916–2005) was a well-respected minister in Hamblen County and surrounding areas. He started preaching at the age of 17 and pastored two churches in North Carolina before coming to Morristown. Beginning in 1943, Reverend Rhodes served as pastor of Calvary Baptist Church for over 16 years. He also served in the following churches: White Oak Grove, Central Baptist, Robertson Creek Baptist, and Holt's Baptist. (Courtesy of Billie D. Loveday.)

Rev. William Harvey Smith founded the First Presbyterian Church of Morristown in May 1867. Prior to this, he served in churches all over East Tennessee, including 10 years at St. Paul Presbyterian Church. During his 50 years of ministry, Reverend Smith performed over 340 marriages and traveled over 35,000 miles. Reverend Smith died on April 21, 1911, at the age of 92. All churches in town suspended their regular Sunday morning services in order to attend his funeral. (Courtesy of Davy Anne Charles.)

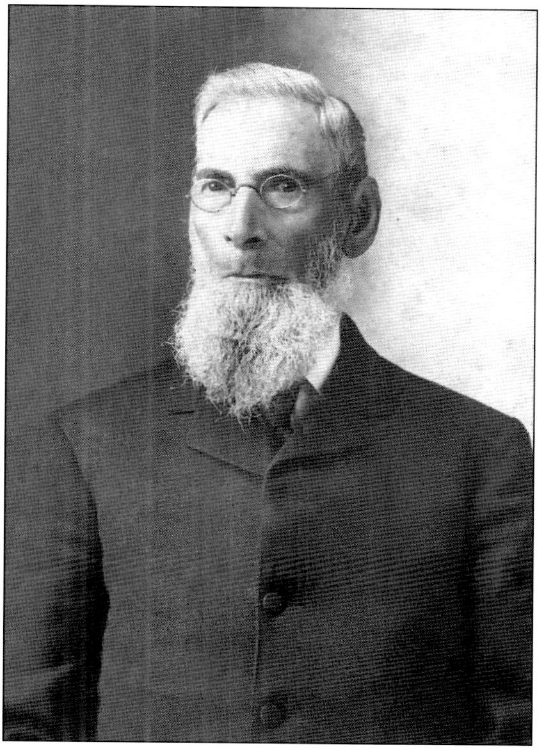

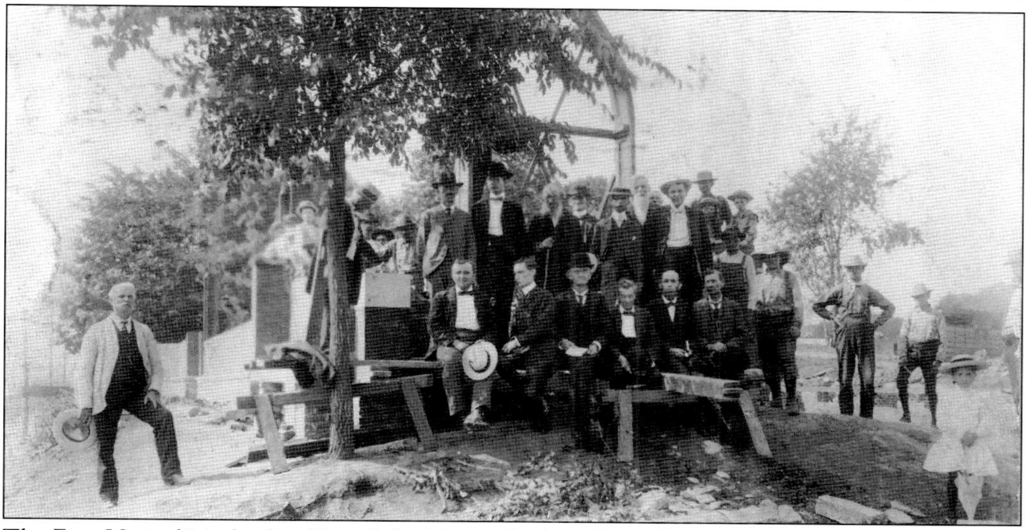

The First United Methodist Church building, which still stands today at the intersection of East First North and Cumberland Streets, was begun in 1902 with the laying of the cornerstone. Some of those present to celebrate were, from left to right, (first row) William Sylvester Myers, Dr. Joseph A. Baylor (pastor), Dr. R.N. Price, Judge James G. Rose, Dr. Andrew J. Bruner, and Marion Roberts; (second row) Rev. Rufus M. Hickey (behind tree), J.J. Wilkinson, Mike C. McCanless, Dr. Thomas J. Speck, John Loop, A. Scruggs, George A. Rowe, and A.W. Lotspeich. Also, notice the newly constructed door frame visible in the background. At a total cost of $20,500, the new church building was dedicated on October 4, 1903.

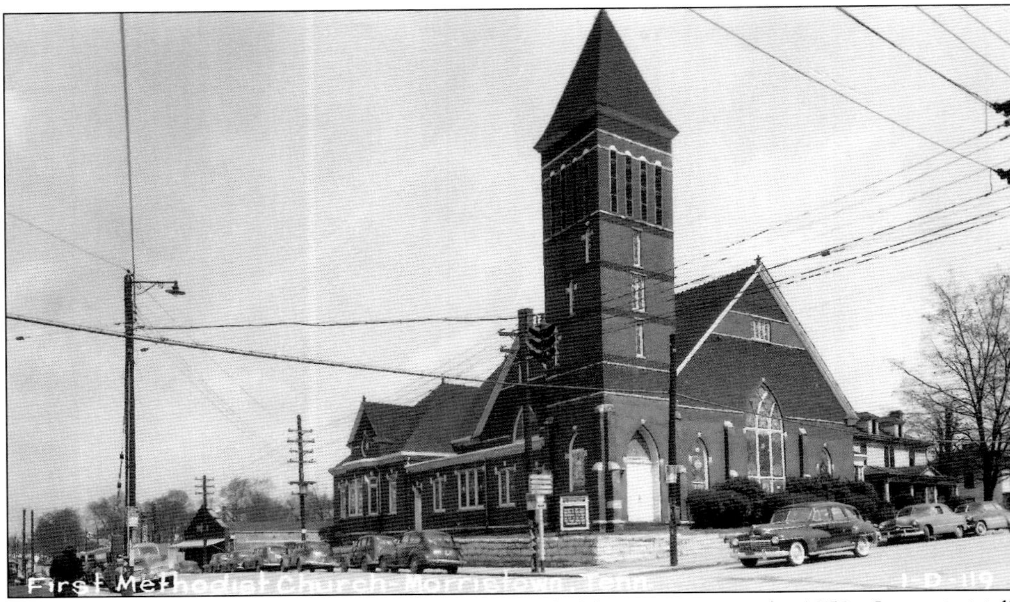

The First Methodist Church of Morristown began holding services in the 1850s. It was initially known as the First Methodist Episcopal Church, South, and was listed on a four-point circuit with Mossy Creek (now Jefferson City), Liberty Hill, and Rogersville.

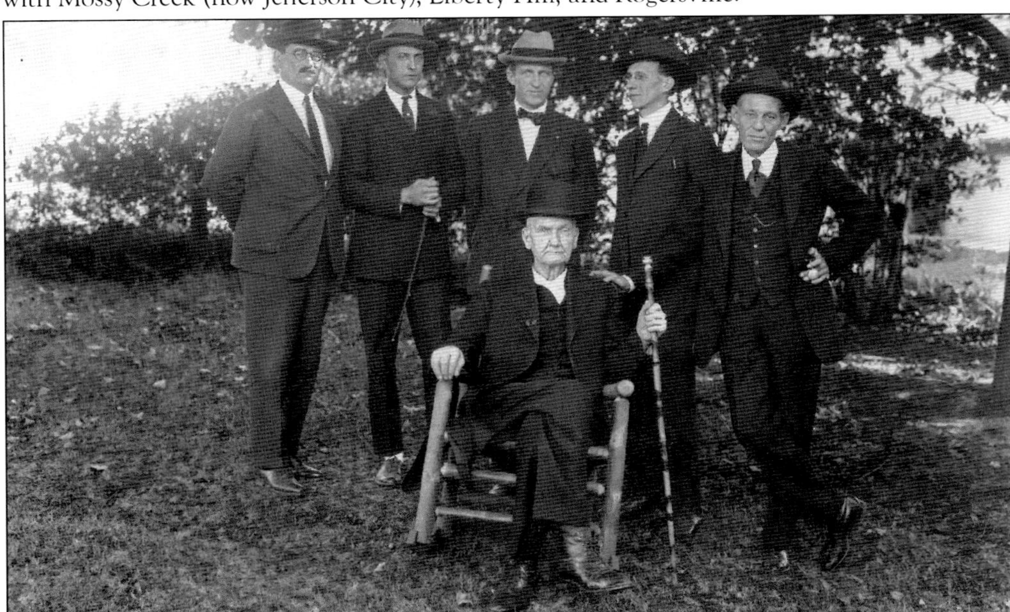

In preparation for the annual conference to be held in Morristown in 1922, the First Methodist Episcopal Church, South, selected five members to the board of stewards. Standing are, from left to right, D.A. Pless, James Dosser, Lynn Sheeley, J.W. Arnold, and Harry F. Trobaugh. Retired Methodist minister Dr. R.N. Price is seated in front. Dr. Price, noted author of *Holston Methodism*, served as pastor of the First Methodist Episcopal Church from 1870 to 1872 and 1888 to 1891. Dr. Price and his family resided on First North Street in a home that is now site of the Women's Club House.

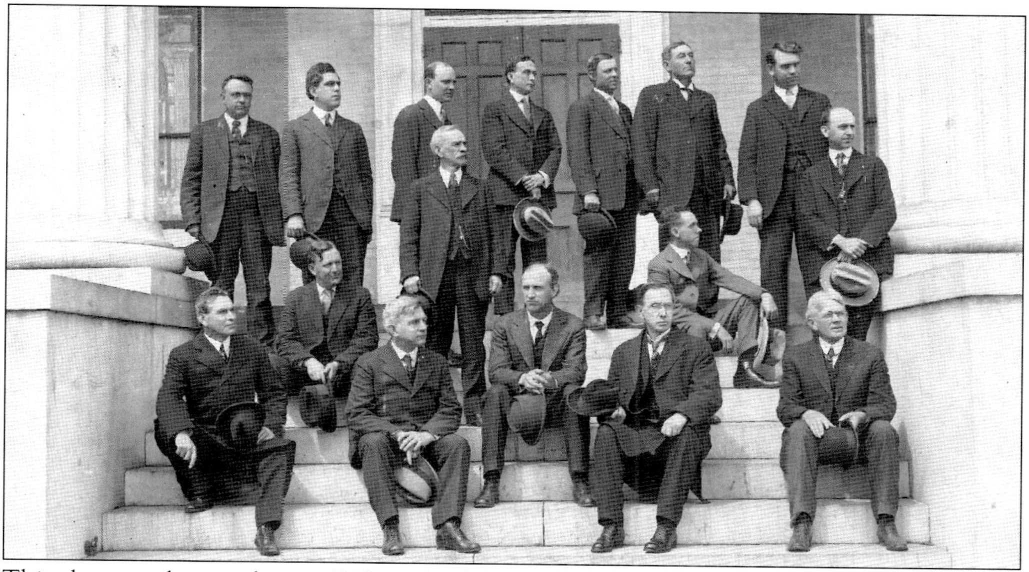

This photograph was taken in 1915 on the front steps of the First Baptist Church of Morristown. From left to right are (sitting) Rev. Spencer Tunnell (pastor, First Baptist Church), H. Roy Reams (Baptist layman), Rev. Lynn Walker (pastor, First Presbyterian Church), Rev. R.L. Stapleton (pastor, Centenary Church), Rev. R.M. Standefer (pastor, Methodist Episcopal Church, South), Gus B. Helm (Baptist layman), and J.D. Hasson (Presbyterian layman); (standing) J.O. Christmas (Centenary layman), J.H. Peoples (First Baptist layman), Sullins Dosser (later Methodist minister), Robert Marion "R.M." Rogers (Methodist Episcopal Church, South, layman), Robert L. Holmes (Presbyterian layman), Arthur H. Proctor (Centenary layman), John Mathes (Baptist layman), Dan T. Rogers (city school superintendent), and J.O. Phillips (Baptist layman).

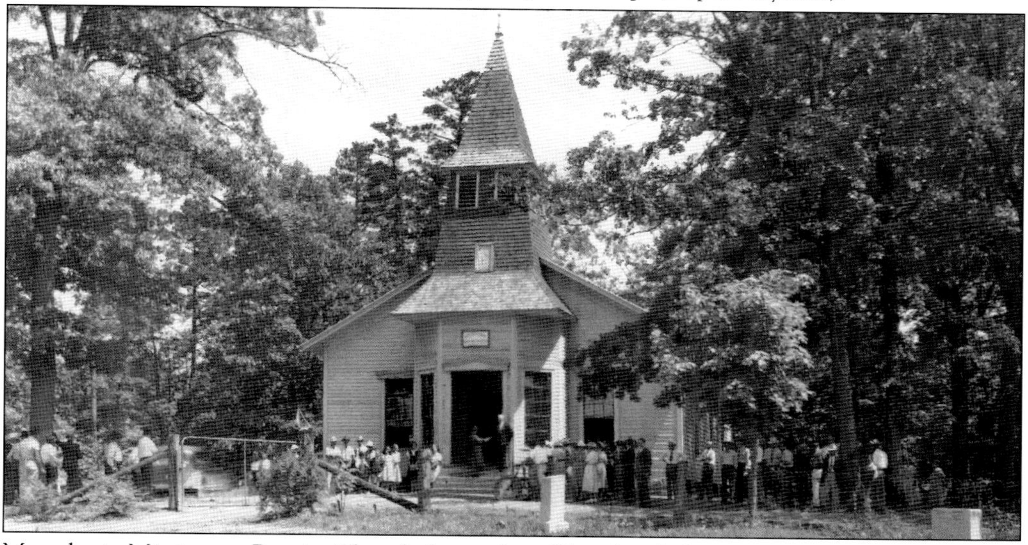

Macedonia Missionary Baptist Church, located on Cherokee Lake, was organized on December 23, 1865. Services were originally held in the Macedonia School building. An agreement was entered on October 1, 1872, for C.C. Johnston to erect a church building for $500, with the church providing the materials. The building was completed in June 1873. The belfry was added in 1910. (Courtesy of Doris Livingston Stump.)

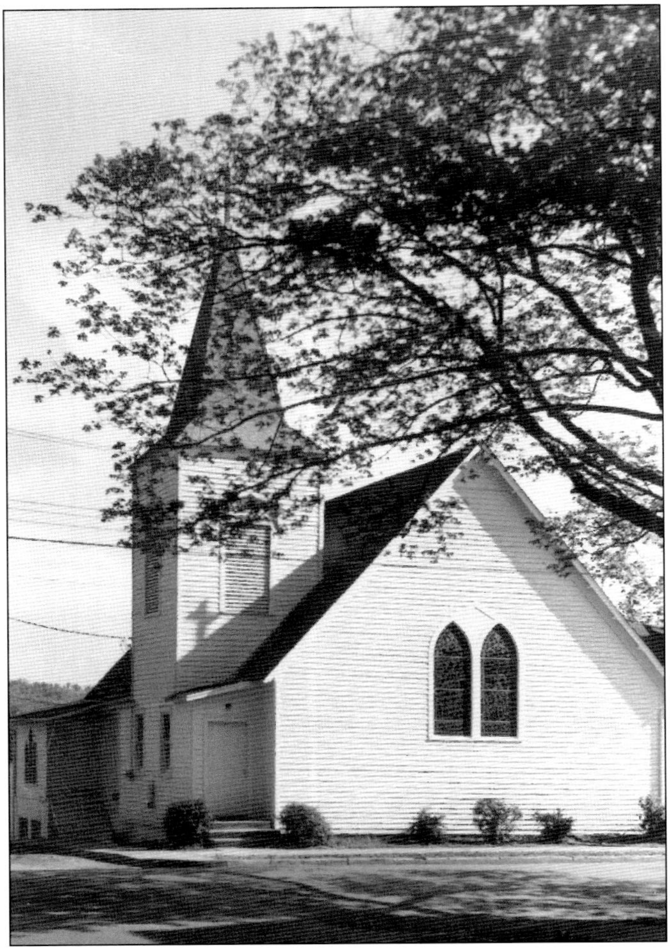

All Saints' Episcopal Church, founded by Rev. E.J. Killefer and five charter members in 1887, erected this frame structure around 1900 and occupied it until 1975. The name of the church has changed twice. Originally, it was named Well's Memorial Mission Church, and in 1900, the name changed to St. Anne's. Finally, in 1906, the church became known as All Saints' Episcopal. (Courtesy of Diane Fox.)

For two weeks in June 1922, Rev. William Ashley "Billy" Sunday held a revival in Morristown. He was considered one of the greatest evangelists of his time. Thousands came from all over East Tennessee, and the railroad ran special trains from Knoxville, Asheville, and Bristol for the occasion. Reverend Sunday poses here (standing behind the two men on first step), with the Kiwanis Club on June 9, 1922. This photograph was taken on the steps of the Mitchell Hotel.

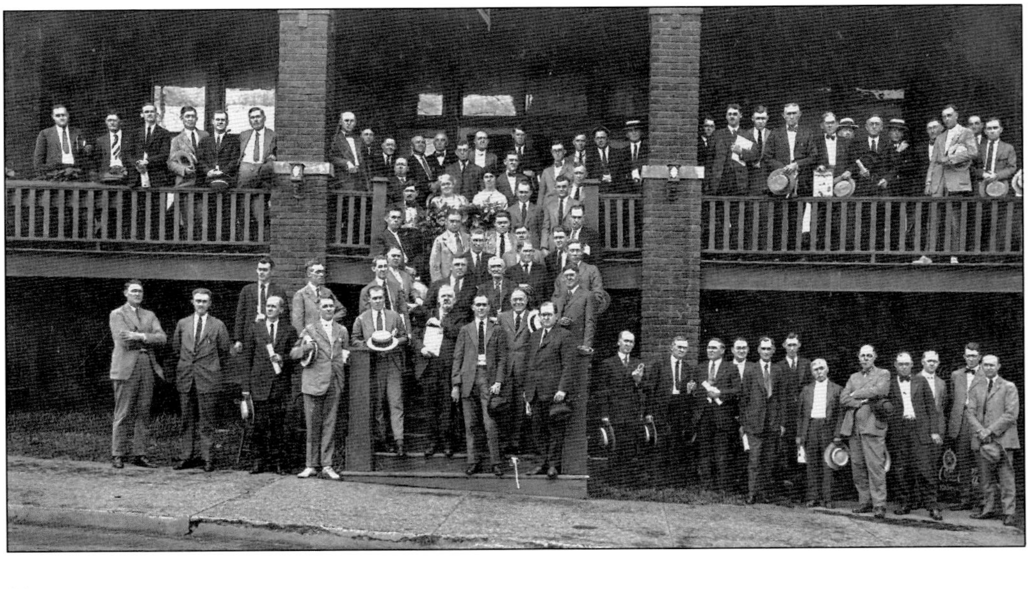

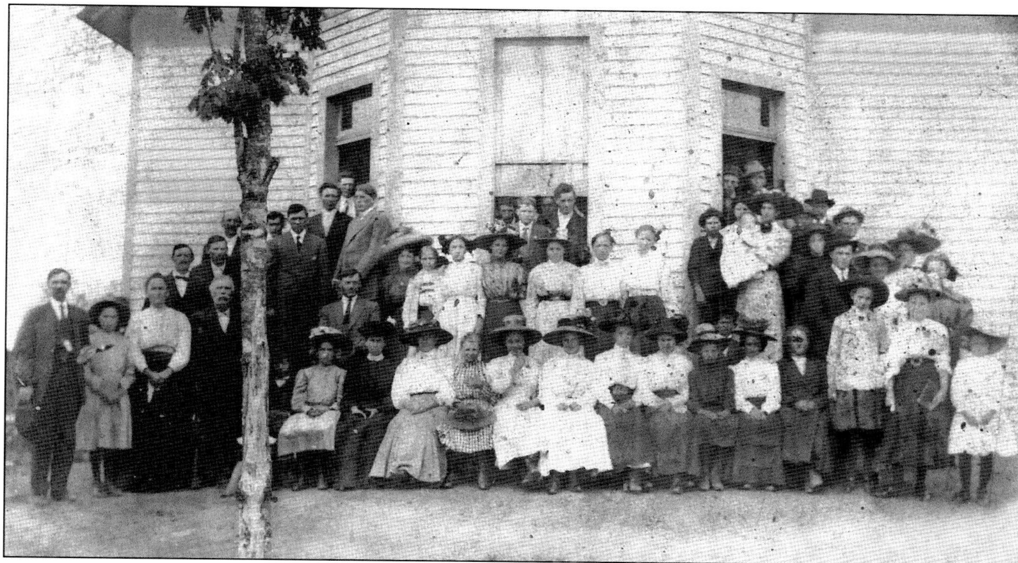

Kidwell's Ridge Baptist Church was organized on Saturday, January 1, 1848, with 58 charter members. Many of those members are buried in the church cemetery, and their descendants help make up the present-day membership. This image, taken around 1911, shows the congregation in front of the newly completed church building, which replaced an older structure.

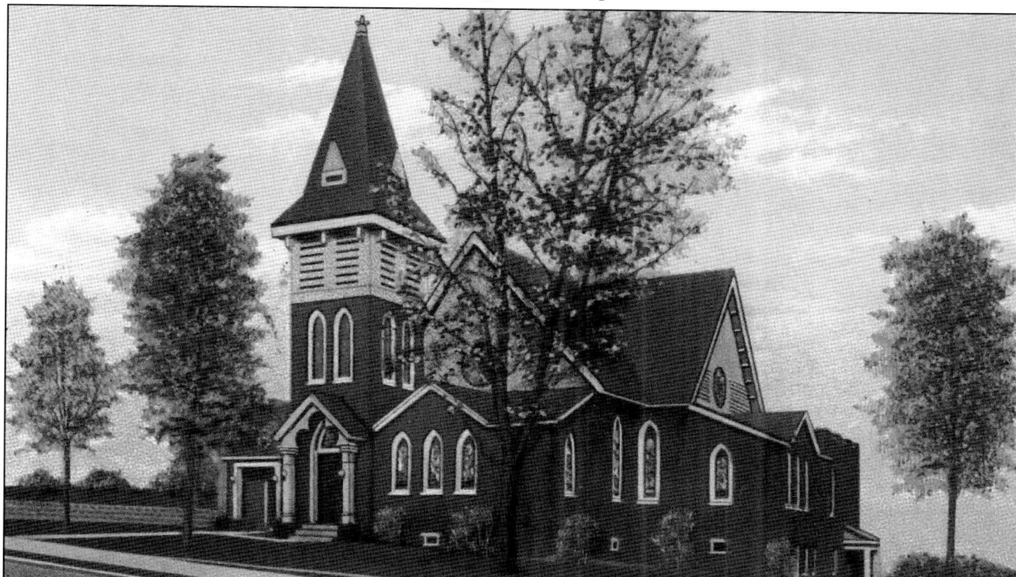

Centenary Methodist Episcopal Church, now Centenary United Methodist, was founded in October 1881 by Dr. Judson Sudbourgh Hill, along with eight charter members. That same year, Dr. Hill founded Morristown Normal and Industrial College (later known as Morristown College). For the three years that Dr. Hill served as pastor of Centenary Methodist, he preached on Sundays and taught school Monday through Friday. Dr. J.J. Robinette replaced Dr. Hill and led the growing congregation in 1886 to erect this building on the corner of West First North and Jackson Streets. Once completed, the congregation no longer had to use the First Presbyterian Church and their homes for services.

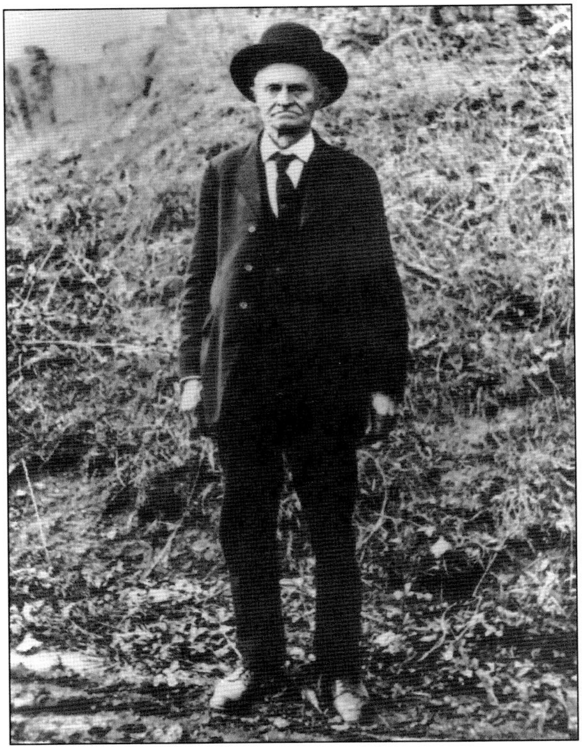

Melville Milton Murrell (1855–1933) became a Methodist preacher when he was 27 years old. When he died at the age of 77, he was considered one of the oldest and most highly respected ministers in East Tennessee. The photograph below shows Murrell preaching to a crowd. Before being called into the ministry, young Melville loved watching birds and had a passion for flying. On August 14, 1877, over 30 years before the Wright brothers' initial flight, he was granted a patent for his flying machine. Reverend Murrell soon traded his flying passion for a lifelong passion of the ministry. Though he never lost an interest in aviation, he no longer actively pursued it. Another interesting fact about Reverend Murrell is that he never drove a car.

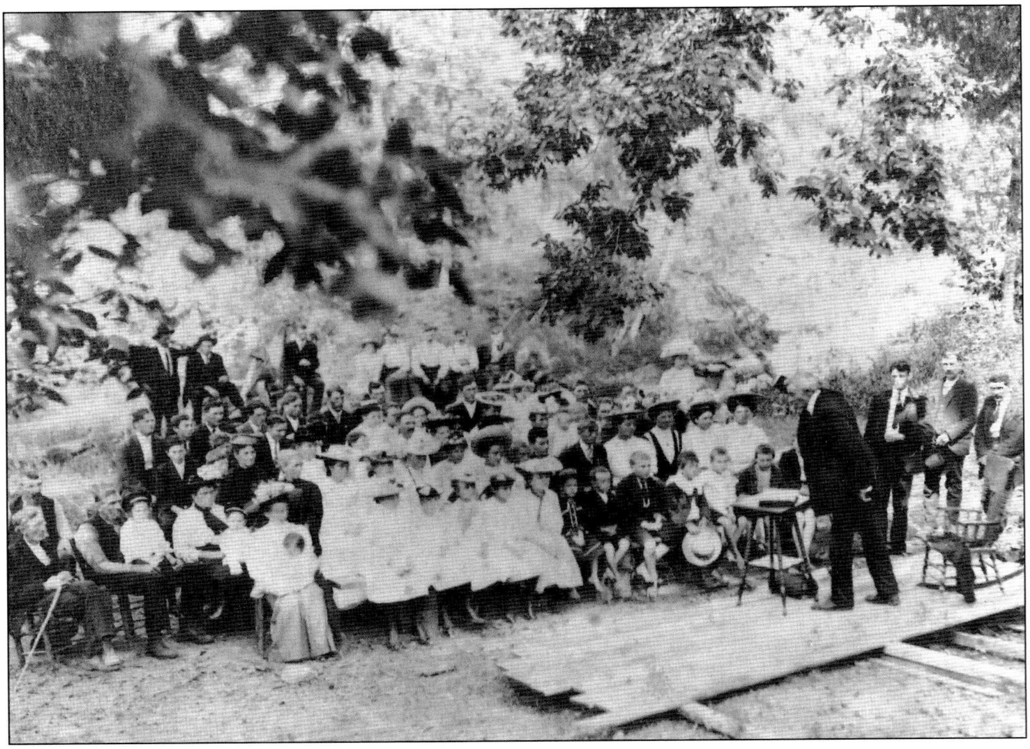

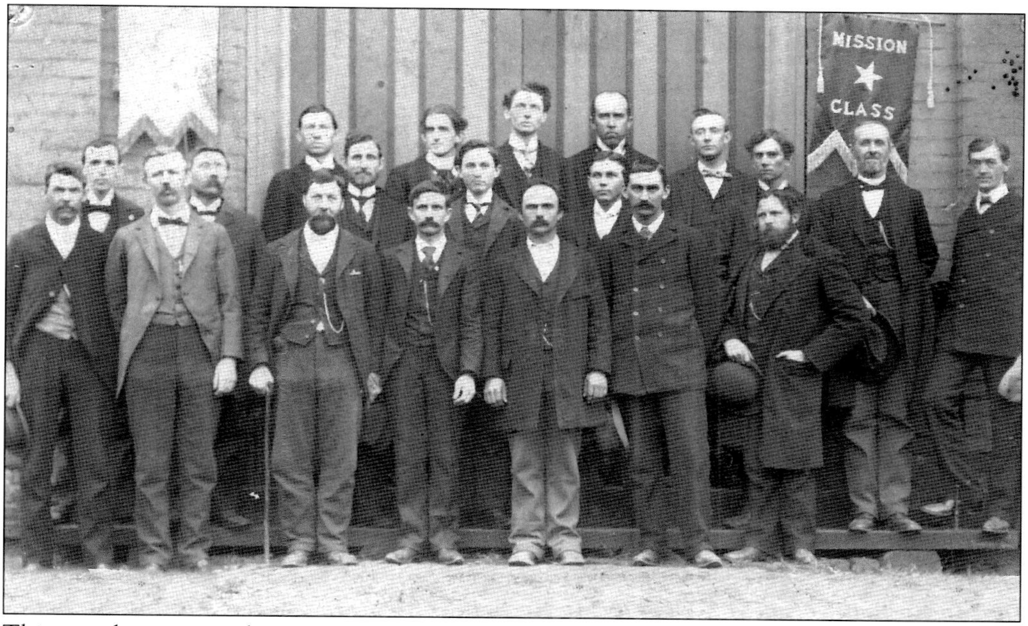

This was the mission class of First Baptist Church. They are standing in front of the church building, which was erected in 1871. The class was taught by Col. T.M. Reeves.

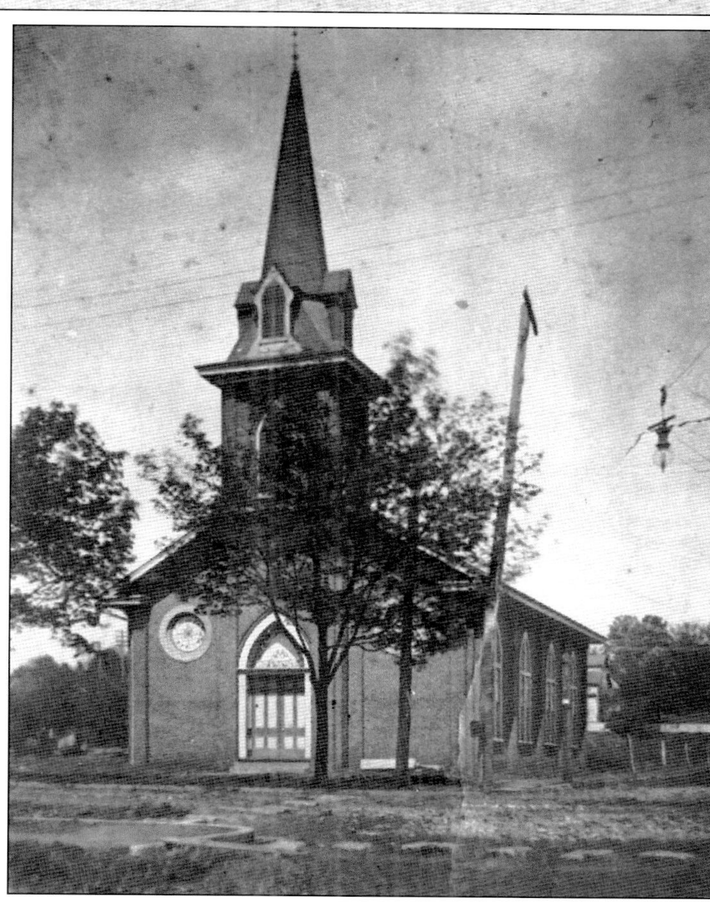

On May 18, 1867, under the leadership of Rev. William Harvey Smith and 26 charter members, First Presbyterian was founded. This building, located on Main Street, was erected on a lot donated to the church by Robert M. Barton, who was an elder in the church. It was dedicated on June 5, 1870.

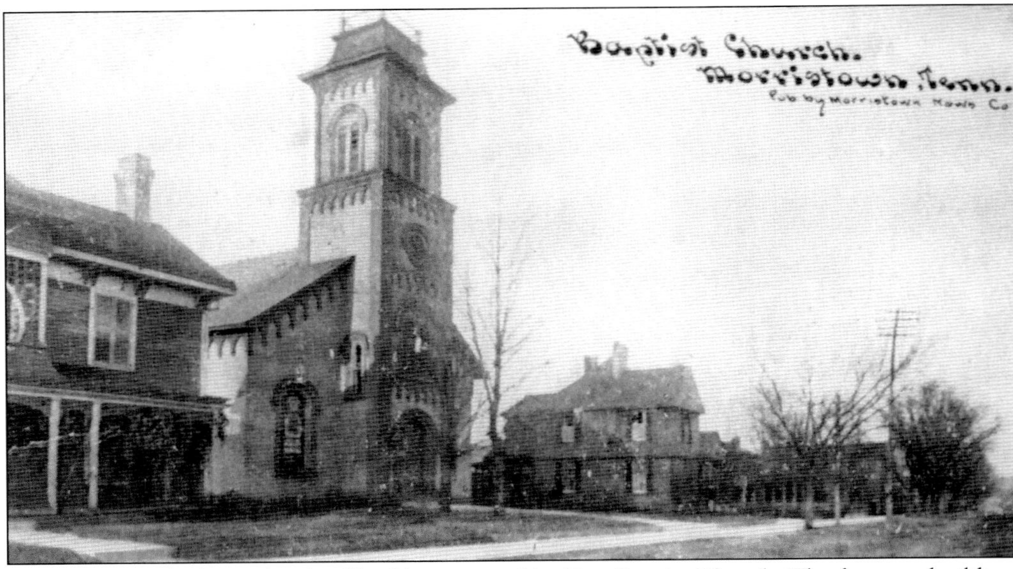

This photograph shows the third building erected by First Baptist Church. The first two buildings were located on North Cumberland Street, but this was the first building erected on the northwest corner of Main and Jackson Streets. When completed in 1871, it cost approximately $10,000 and was considered one of the finest Baptist church buildings in East Tennessee. It was demolished in 1913 to make room for a larger sanctuary, pictured below.

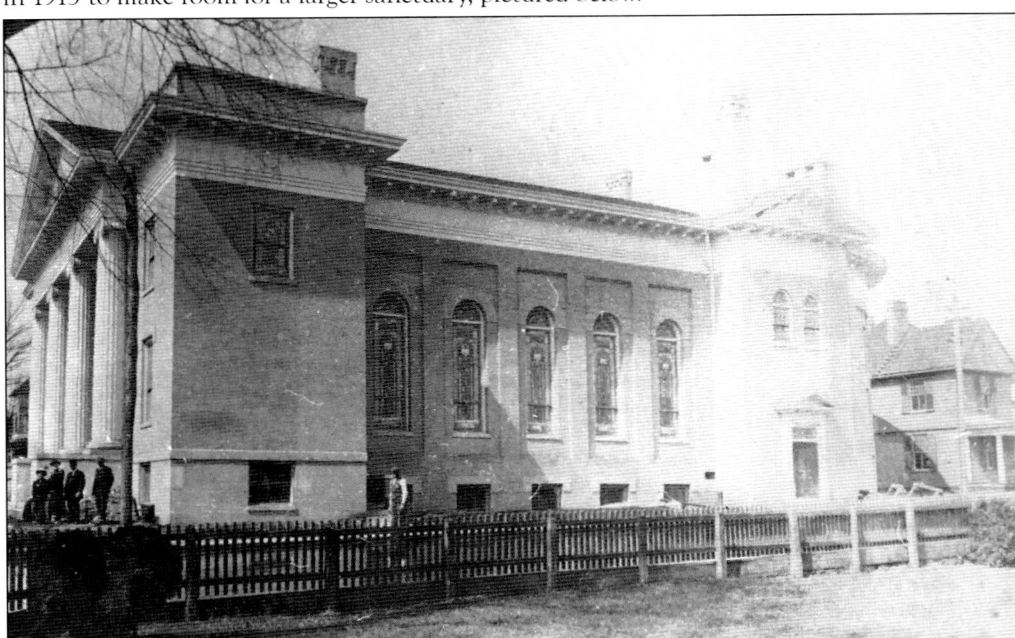

First Baptist Church erected this brick building in 1913 at a cost of $45,000. It replaced the 1871 brick structure (above), which the congregation had outgrown. The house (right) located behind the church building was used as the parsonage. The picket fence (foreground) surrounded the home of Maj. John Murphy, the present-day site of Mayes Family Services. Due to structural issues, this newer sanctuary was torn down in December 2011.

Three

Foundations Past and Present

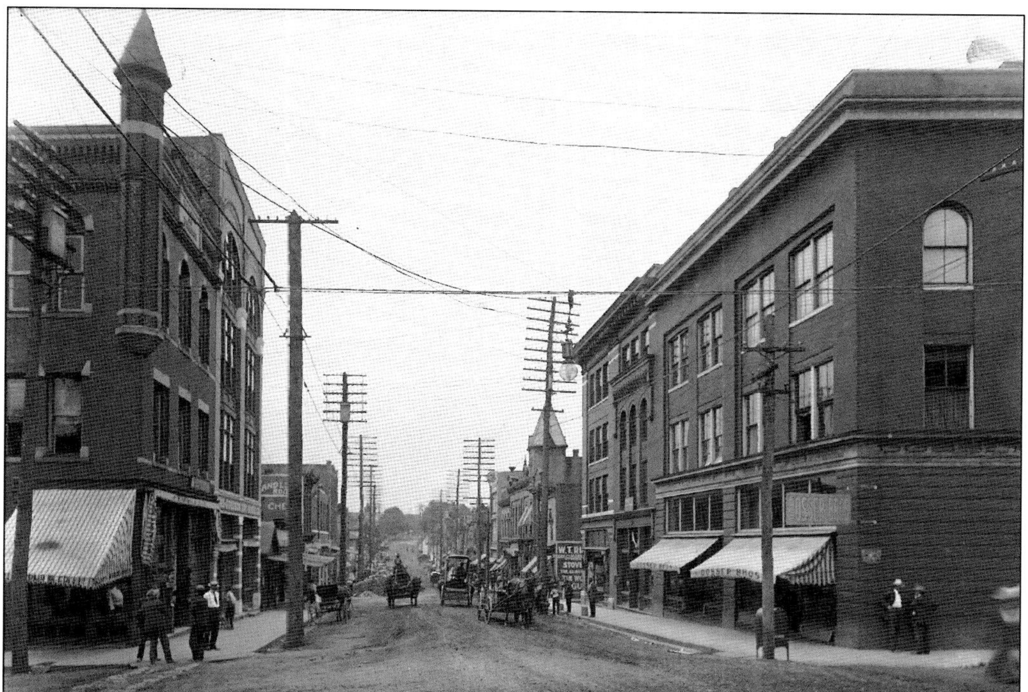

Standing at the intersection of Main and Cumberland Streets and looking westward, this was the scene in downtown Morristown during the early 1900s. A few of the local businesses pictured are Dosser Brothers (first right), J.W. Arnold and Company (first left), and Mims-Goodson Dry Goods (second left). J.W. Arnold and Company moved from this location in January 1910, so this photograph was taken before they moved. Notice the dirt streets. Main Street was the first paved road in Morristown, and it was not paved until 1916. (Courtesy of C.M. McClung Historical Collection.)

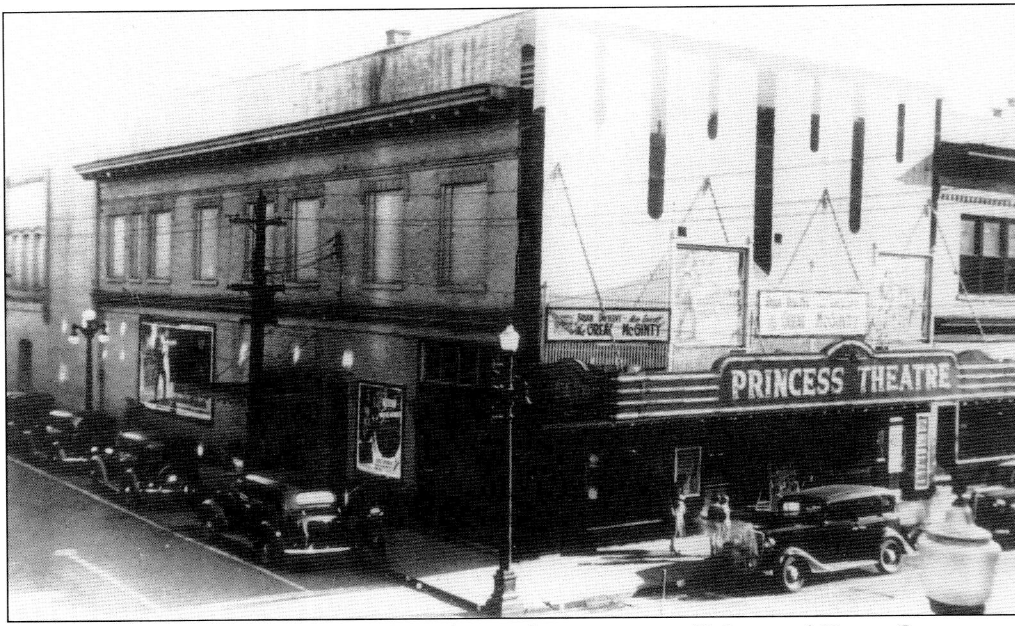

The Princess Theatre, once located on the southwest corner of Main and Henry Streets, was playing *The Return of Frank James* and *The Great McGinty* in this September 1940 photograph. The Princess first opened on October 18, 1915, and could accommodate huge crowds, as it had seating for over 600 people. The theater closed on April 7, 1983, with *The Outsiders* being the last showing. In October 1995, the building was demolished. The Java Garden, a coffee and sandwich shop, now resides on this site.

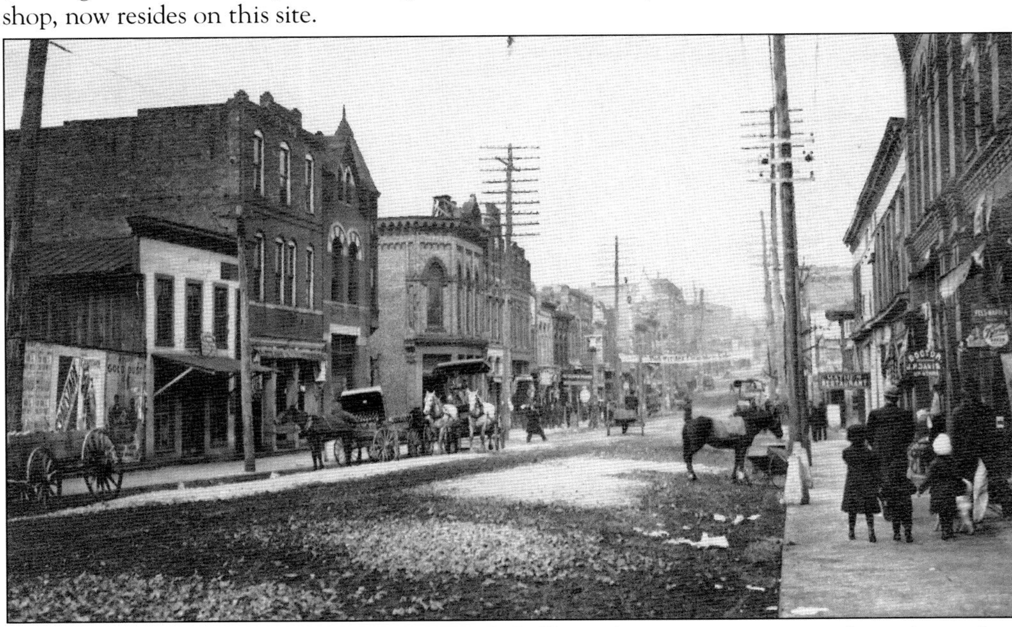

This was downtown Morristown in January 1912. Horse-drawn carriages were the main mode of transportation during this time. Automobiles had only been introduced to the area about four years earlier and were not only in short supply but very much a luxury. (Courtesy of the Tennessee State Library and Archives.)

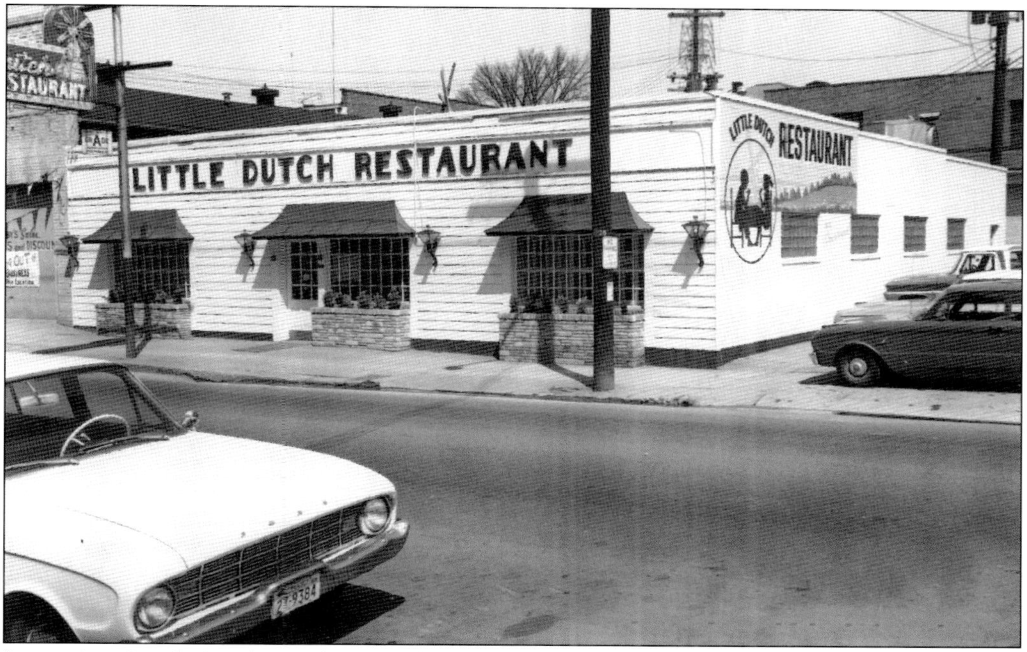

Located on South Cumberland Street, the Little Dutch Restaurant has been serving the public for over 73 years. It was founded in 1939 by Frank and Mattie Lorino and quickly became known as the best place to eat in Morristown. This photograph was taken around 1965. Frank and Mattie ran the business from 1939 until Frank passed away in 1970. Mattie sold the business to George Angelopoulas in 1974. George and his wife, Nina, are still serving it up in downtown Morristown 38 years later. (Courtesy of the Hamblen County Archives.)

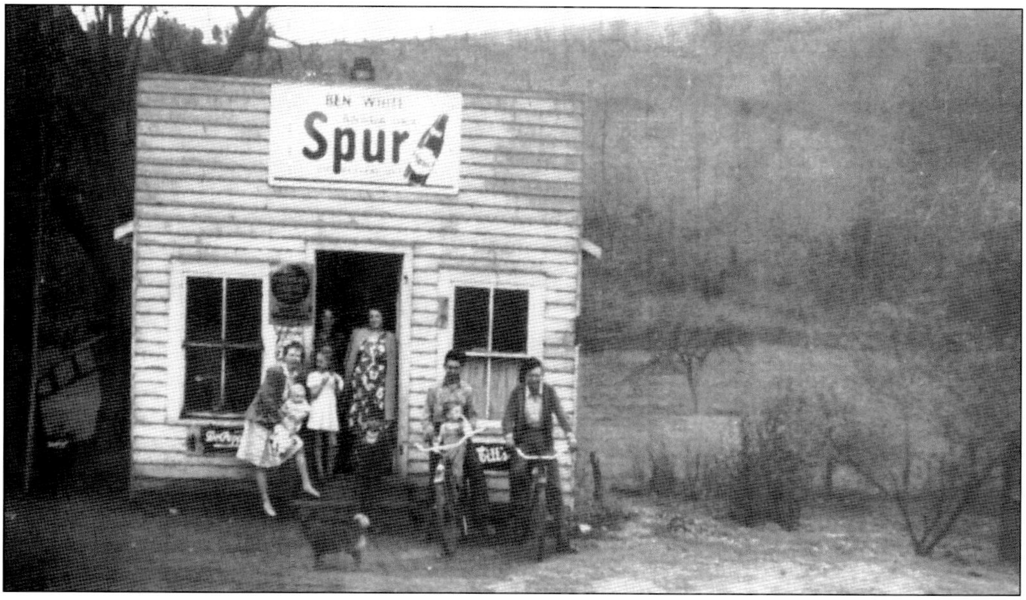

The Spur was a small general store located alongside the railroad on Sulphur Springs Road. Ben White built it around 1942, and his wife, Lucy, ran it until around 1959. This building, which was converted into a private residence, is still standing today. (Courtesy of James D. Susong.)

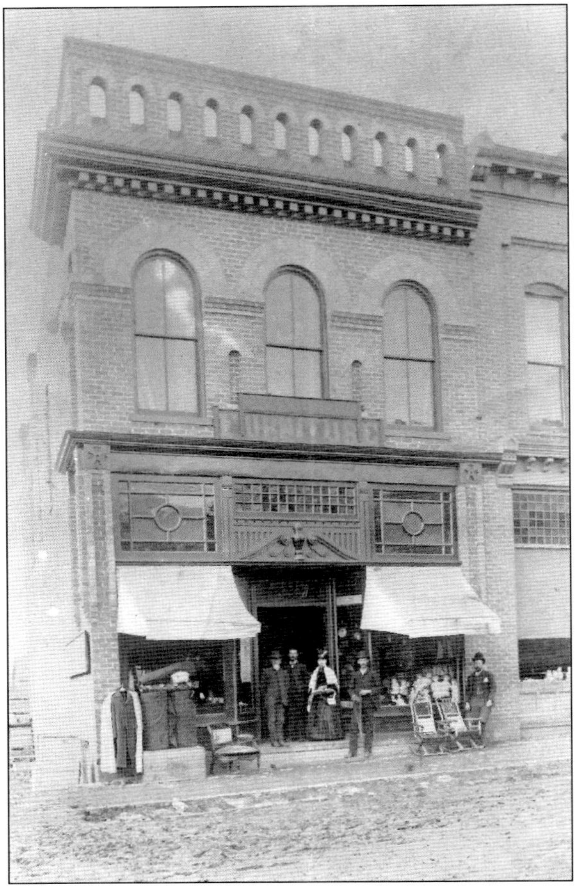

Sidewalk sales are a thing from the past, as can be seen in this 1886 photograph of the Craig, Holley, and Craig Furniture and Merchandise Store, located on the north side of Main Street. It is believed that one of the owners, James W. Holley, is standing second from right. Through the years, this building was also home to Carriger and Berry Men's Store and Thrifty Shops. Today, the building stands vacant.

This two-story brick home of William Porter Jarnagin (1841–1909) once stood on Jarnagin Avenue. William Jarnagin, a wealthy and well-traveled man, donated land for a cemetery on February 3, 1902, and it was named the Emma Jarnagin Cemetery for his mother, Emmaline Riggs Jarnagin. The layout and design of the cemetery was inspired by a French cemetery that William Jarnagin visited during one of his excursions abroad. William never married and never had children. His executor, J.W. Jarnagin, sold the 514-acre estate at public auction on August 17, 1910, for $23,000 to T.S. Myers and Frank Fulkerson.

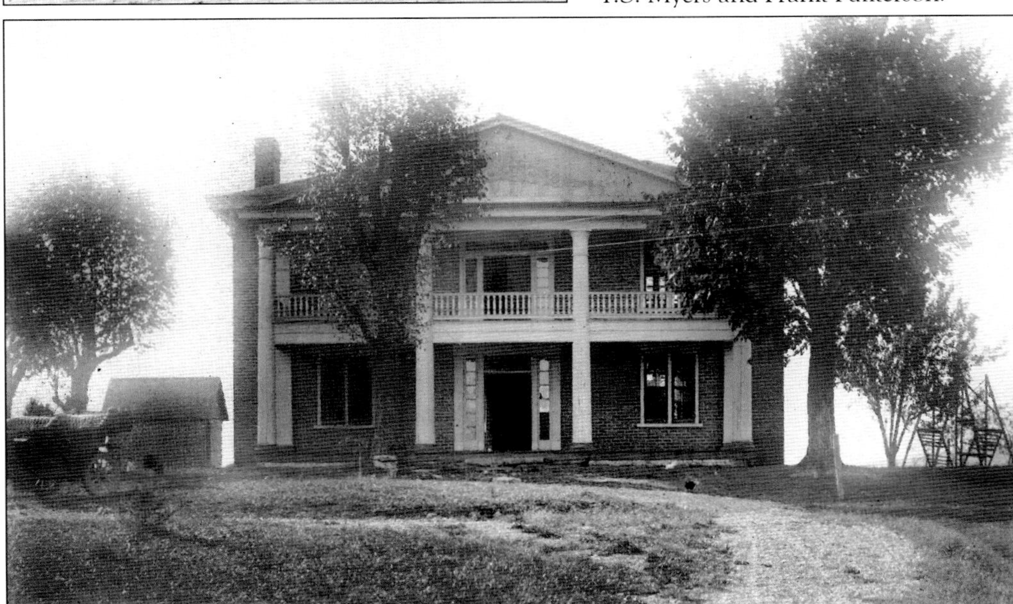

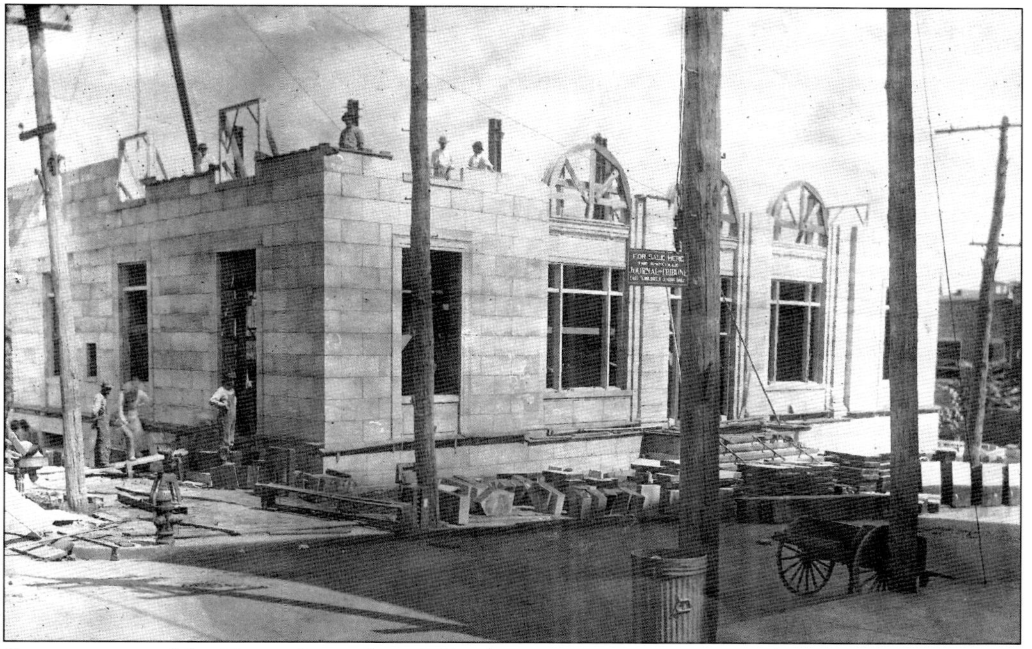

Construction of the Henry Street Post Office began on May 10, 1914, and was completed around May 10, 1915, at a cost of $62,268. The two-story building, with a large basement, was built of Bedford limestone by the George W. Stiles Construction Company of Chicago. The first postmaster to work at this site was John E. Helms. (Courtesy of the Henry Street Post Office.)

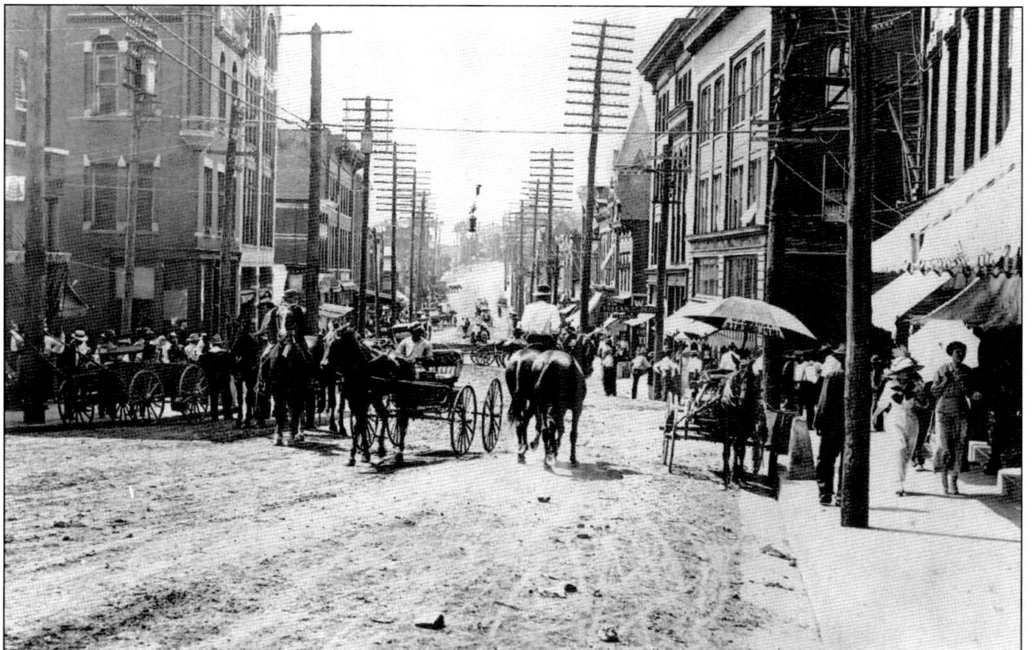

Looking westward, this is how Main Street appeared on a busy Saturday in 1910 near the intersection of Main and Cumberland Streets.

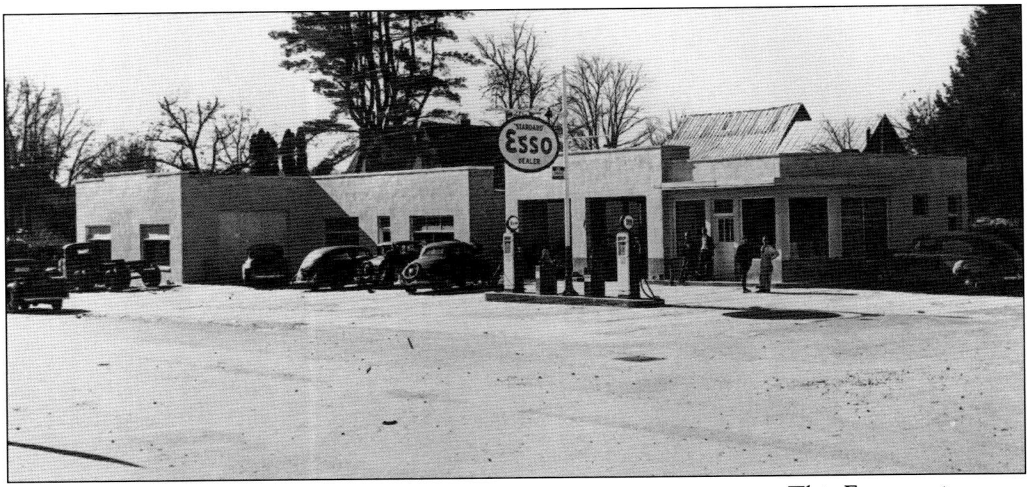

This Esso service station, located on South James Street, was in operation during the 1950s.

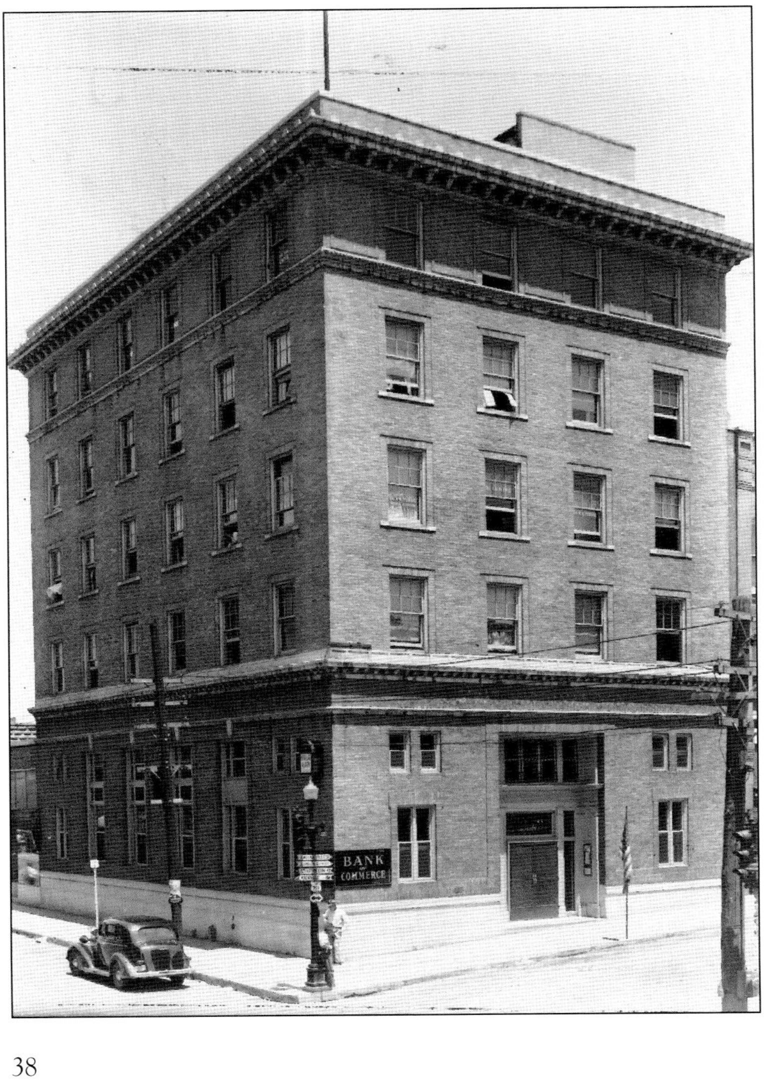

This building, erected around 1920, is located on the northeast corner of Main and Cumberland Streets. It has been home to many offices, including three banking institutions: First National Bank (1920–1933), Bank of Commerce (1936–1986), and Bank of East Tennessee (1986–1991). This building sits on the same site where the McFarland Opera House once stood.

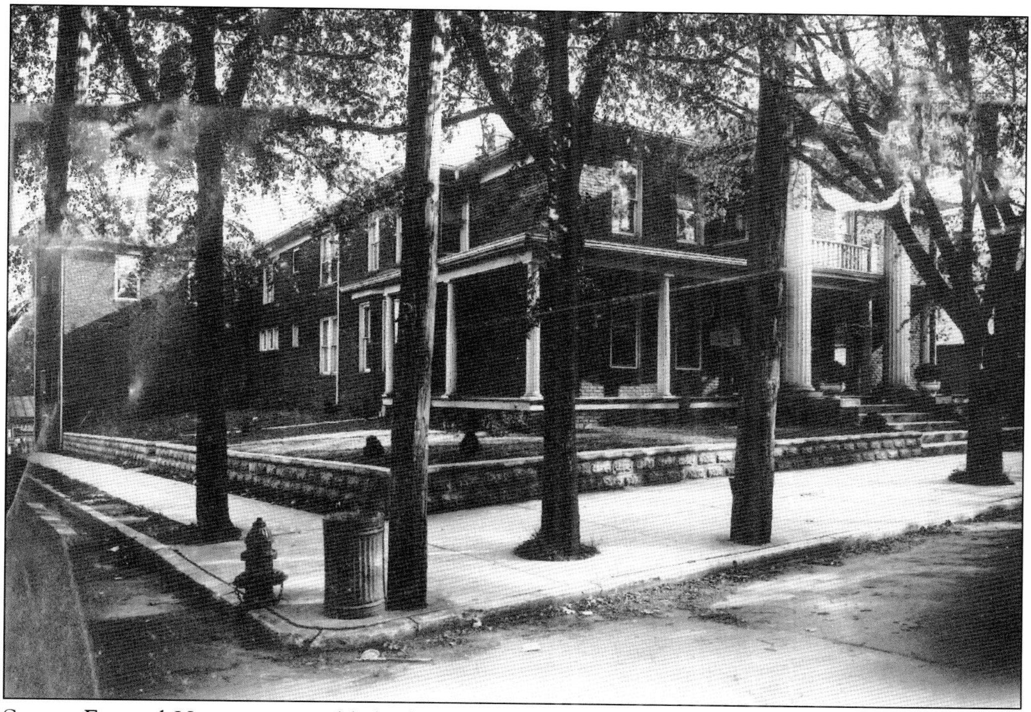

Stetzer Funeral Home was established in 1900 by Martin Joseph "Harry" Stetzer and his wife, Allie. In 1921, they moved from a small frame building on Main Street to their current location at the southwest corner of Main and Hill Streets, in what was known as the Bewley Boarding House. The funeral home remained under the ownership and operation of the Stetzer family until 2007, when grandson Mack Harvey Longmire Jr. sold the family business to J.B. Gulley and Stephen Bales. (Courtesy of Stetzer Funeral Home.)

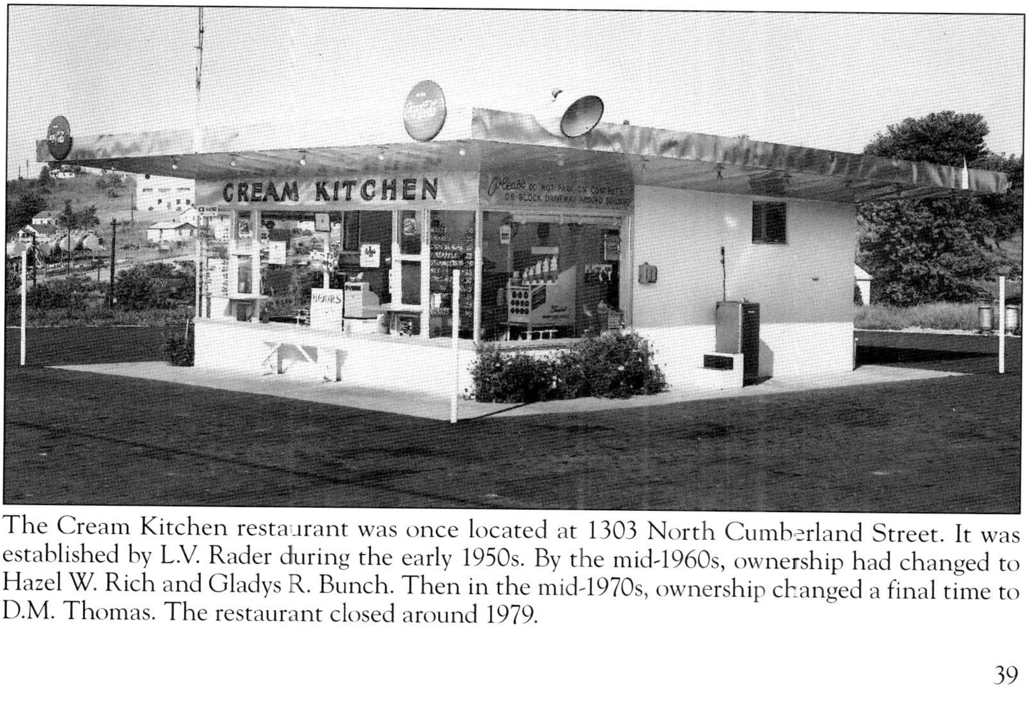

The Cream Kitchen restaurant was once located at 1303 North Cumberland Street. It was established by L.V. Rader during the early 1950s. By the mid-1960s, ownership had changed to Hazel W. Rich and Gladys R. Bunch. Then in the mid-1970s, ownership changed a final time to D.M. Thomas. The restaurant closed around 1979.

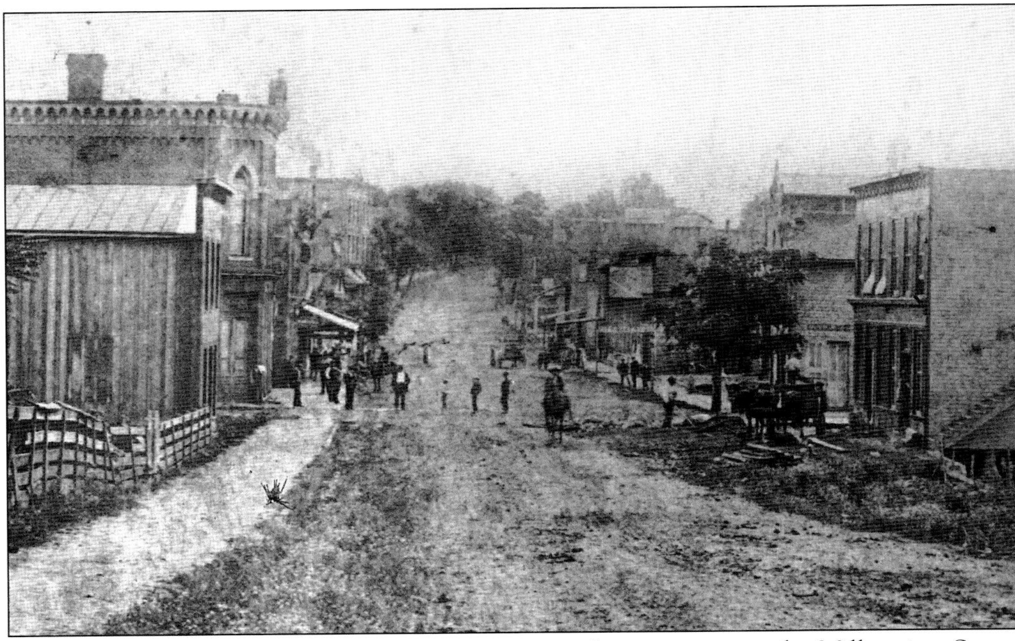

This early photograph of downtown Morristown was taken near present-day Millennium Square looking eastward. Morristown was incorporated in 1855, fifteen years before Hamblen County was formed. As a result, Main Street was the dividing line between Jefferson and Grainger Counties. Property lying south of Main Street was in Jefferson County, and property lying north of Main Street was in Grainger County. The brick building (second left) was home to the Lookout Bank. Established in 1874, it was Morristown's first bank and was located on the northeast corner of Main and Henry Streets.

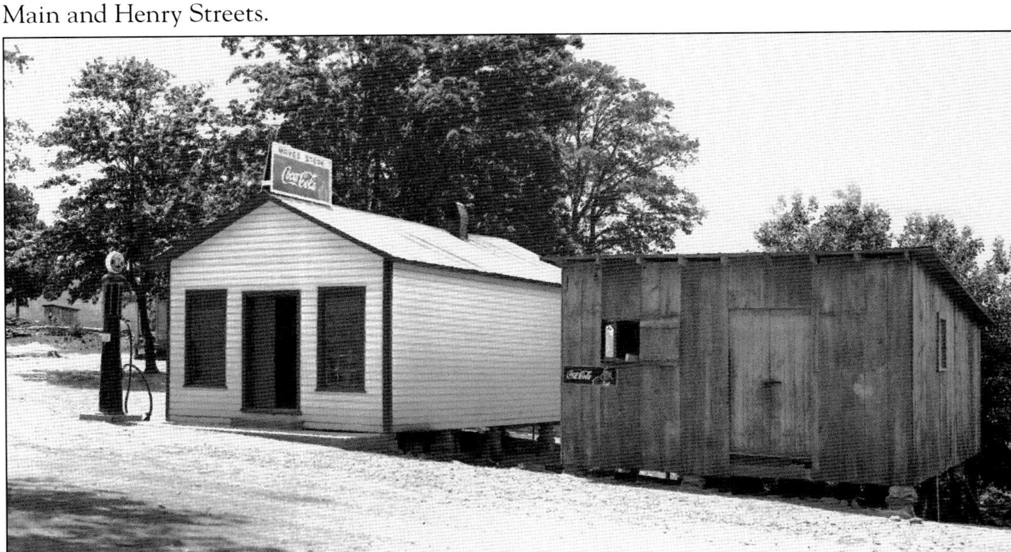

Before the Tennessee Valley Authority bought this property in 1944, it was site of James W. Mayes's store and mill, located in the Kidwell's Ridge community. The Mayes home was located behind the store, and the coal house (left) belonged to Kidwell's Ridge School. (Courtesy of the National Archives.)

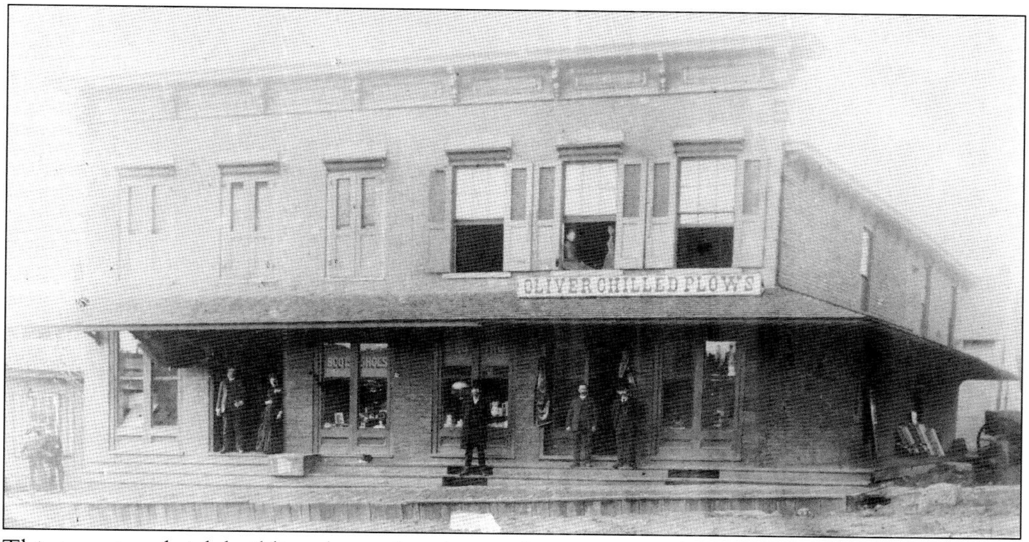

This two-story brick building, located at the northwest corner of Main and Cumberland Streets, was built by Joe Brown. It was first occupied by the Brown and Crowell dry goods store before being succeeded by the general store of Brown and Stubblefield. This photograph of Brown and Stubblefield was taken prior to 1891. By 1902, this building was razed and replaced with a four-story structure for Dosser Brothers, and around 1932, the Parks-Belk Store opened.

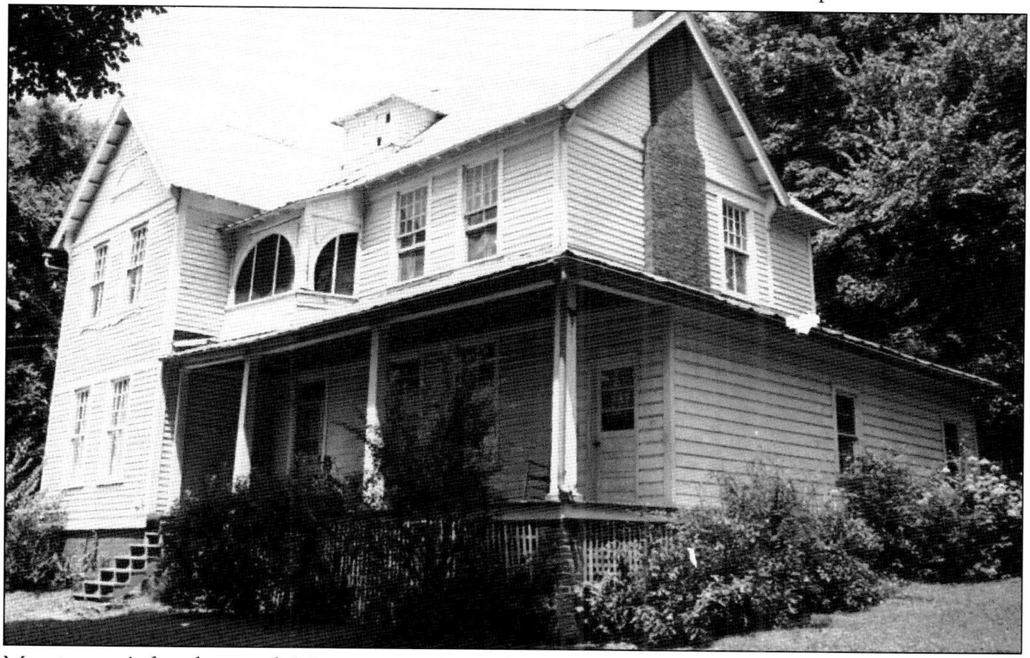

Morristown's first hospital, Morristown General Hospital, opened on May 1, 1908, in the former home of F.H. Gregg on North Cumberland Street. After remodeling, the two-story building had eight beds and an operating room. Dr. Pleasant Littleton Henderson was president, Dr. David Ephraim Shields was vice president, Dr. H.M. Cass was secretary, and Dr. T.L. Smith was treasurer. An investment of over $1 million and 47 years later, the Morristown-Hamblen Hospital opened in its present location on West Fourth North Street on August 18, 1955.

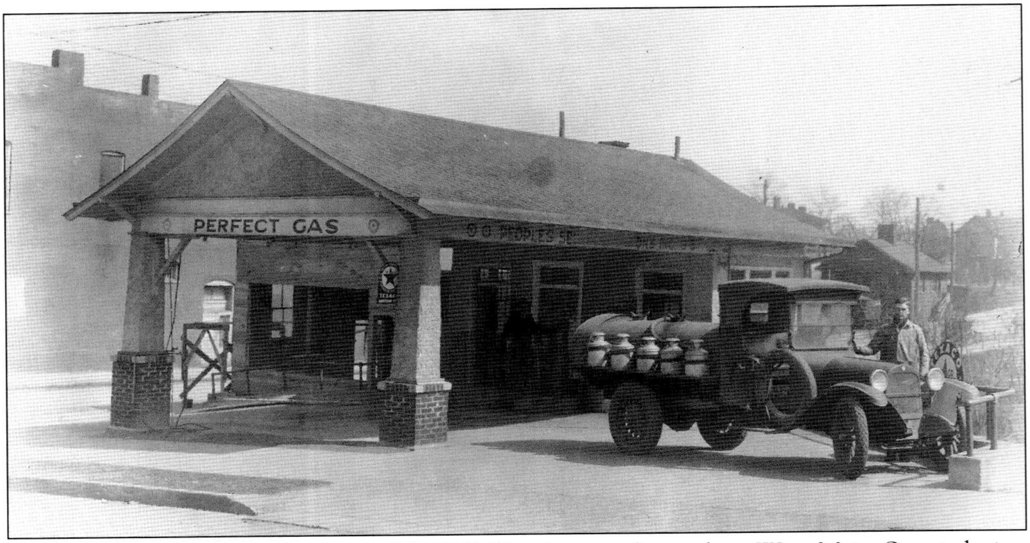

The Peoples Service Station, owned by S.S. Peoples, was located on West Main Street during the early 1920s. This 1923 gas truck was capable of hauling 500 gallons of gasoline in the large center tank and 10 smaller containers of kerosene. The station was later sold to Jack Click and renamed the 31 Tire Station.

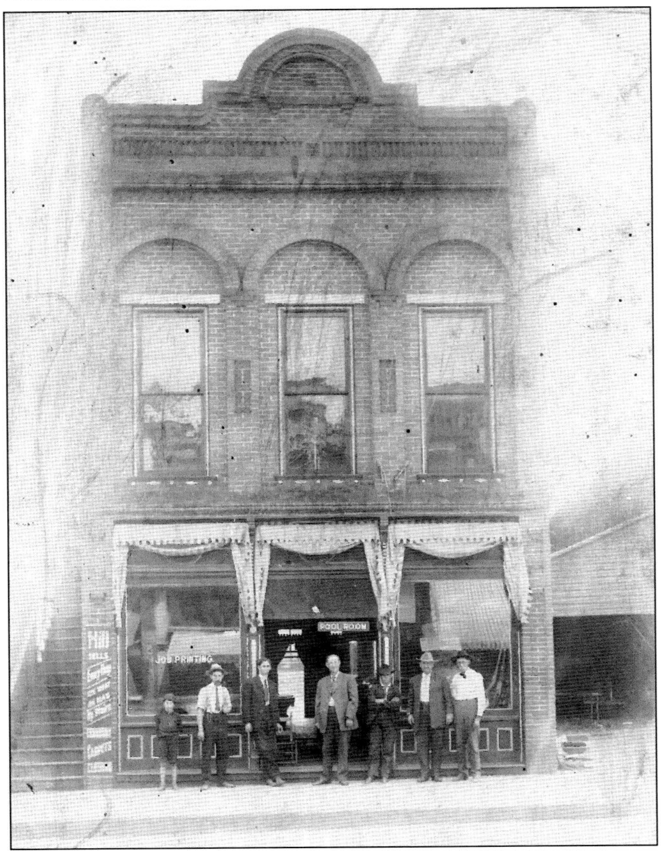

This building, located on the south side of Main Street, was built soon after the Civil War and is still standing today. It is currently home to the Yummy Cakes and More Bakery. Back in 1914, when this photograph was taken, it was home to a poolroom and printing shop. In earlier times, it housed a saloon. The tall man standing in the center is Joe B. Hill, and he worked in the printing shop. Stewart McCrary, left of Hill, worked in the poolroom.

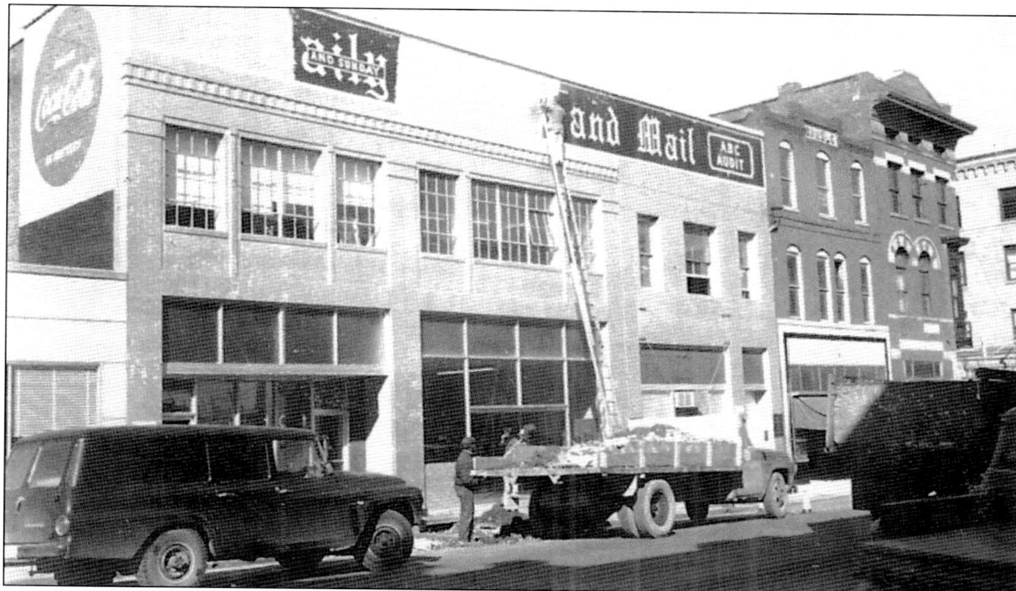

When the *Daily Gazette and Mail* closed its doors on September 30, 1975, after 109 years of continuous operation, it was the oldest firm in Morristown and Hamblen County. Established in 1866 by W.W. Neal, it was the first newspaper published in Morristown after the Civil War. The business was sold in 1867 to Lawrence F. and George E. Speck and then sold again in September 1873 to John Edward Helms. It remained in the Helms family for 102 years. The long-vacant and neglected building was torn down in August 2010 as part of a new downtown renovation project.

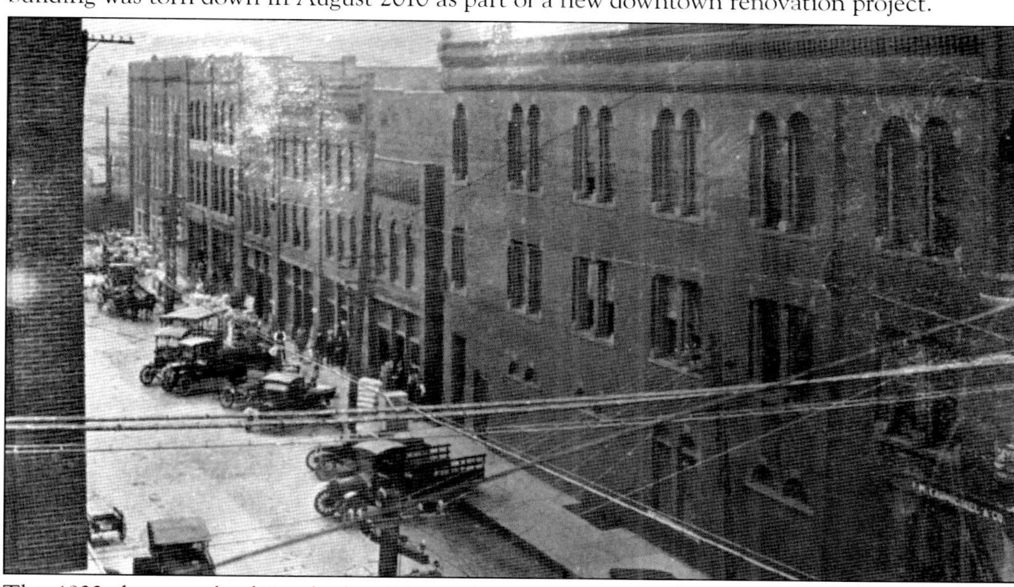

This 1922 photograph of Cumberland Street shows what was then known as Morristown's wholesale district. This photograph was taken from the northeast corner of Main and Cumberland Streets looking south toward the railroad. On August 10, 1964, fire completely destroyed the three-story building right of center, which was then occupied by Evans Book Store. It had been home to Hale Brothers from 1926 until the store moved to East Main Street. With the coming era of chain stores, the wholesale district eventually disappeared from downtown.

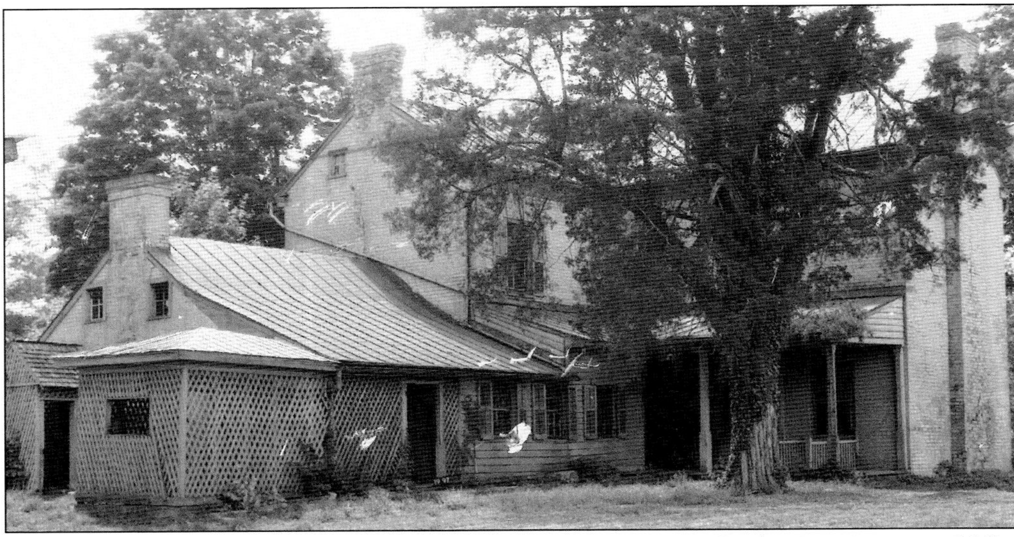

This is a rear view of Greenwood, torn down in 1959 to make room for the East Tennessee Valley Industrial Park on Morris Boulevard. It was home to the Deadrick and Taylor families. Greenwood was built in 1832 by James Deadrick for his young wife, Adeline McDowell Deadrick. Franklin William Taylor purchased the home in 1844, and it remained in the Taylor family until they sold it in 1939. The name "Greenwood" came from the Taylors' planting of some 200 boxwoods on the property. When Franklin W. Taylor died in 1886, he was considered the wealthiest man in Hamblen County. (Courtesy of the Library of Congress.)

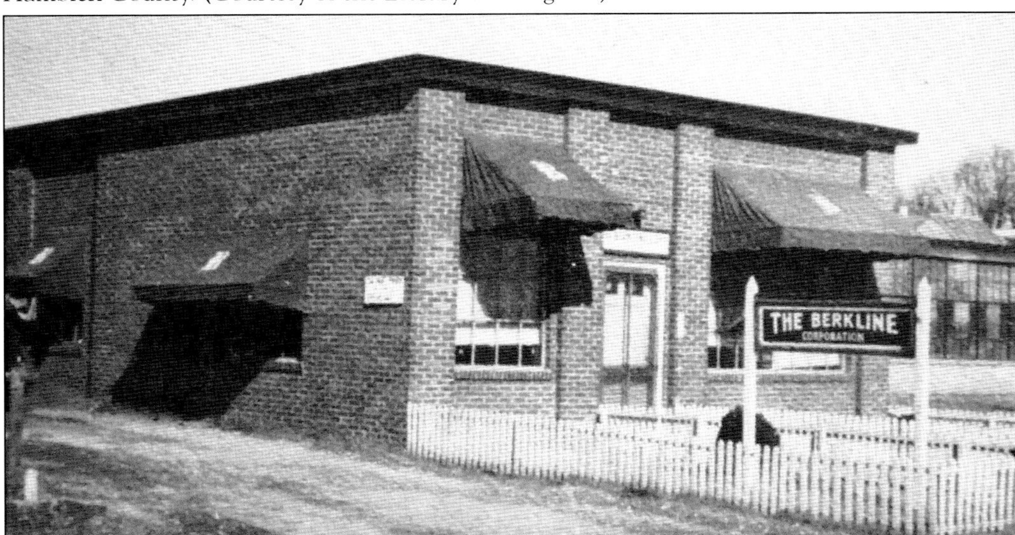

When Jacob Popkin, also known as "Mr. Jack," moved Berkline Corporation to Morristown in 1937, production began in George Brothers Garage with 10,000 square feet of floor space and 18 employees: Clifford Rice, Linnie Felknor, Lester Popkin, Roscoe Haun, Fannie Morelock, Orpha Long, Dana Seals, Lawrence Wampler, "Peck" Burchell, Bessie Monroe, Hal Cross, Leonard Pressley, Henry Southerland, Elbert Weems, James Burchell, James T. Farmer, Clarence Morris, and Roy Pressley. This photograph shows the Berkline Office when it was located on Trade Street in 1947.

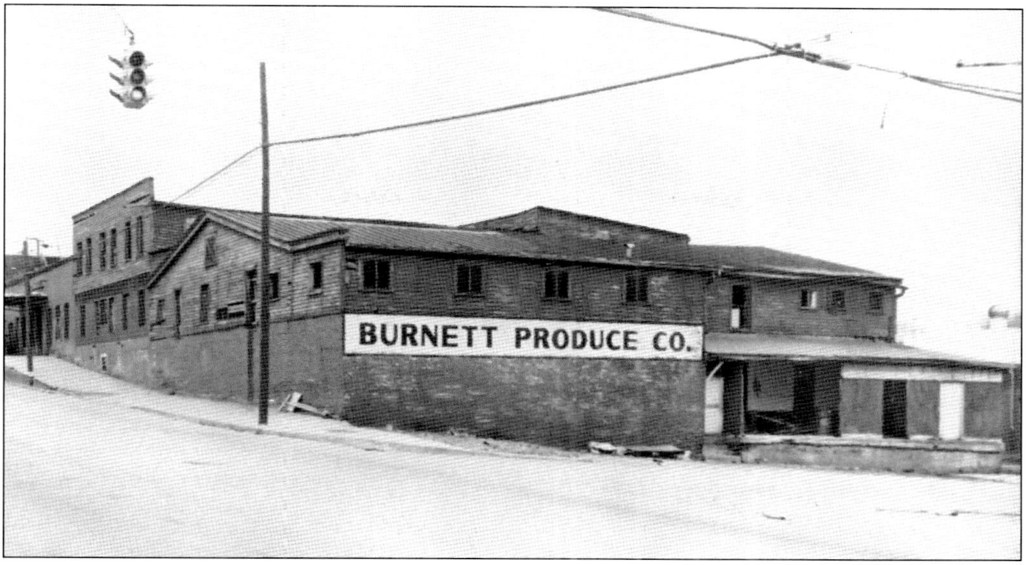

Burnett Produce Company was established in 1948 by Lloyd T. "Pop" Burnett and his sons James W. "Bud" Burnett and Lloyd E. "Tub" Burnett. The company trademarked its products as Pride of the Valley, and in 1997, the chicken processing company was processing 825,000 chickens per week. The family sold the business in 1999 to Koch Poultry Company. This photograph was taken when it was located on the southwest corner of Cumberland Street and Morris Boulevard, then known as Second South Street. (Courtesy of the Hamblen County Archives.)

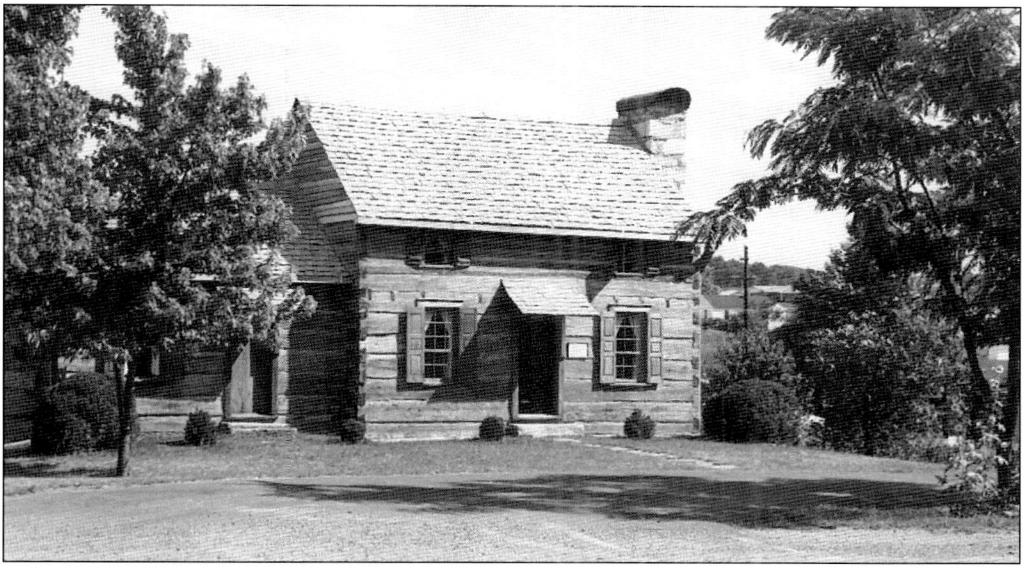

Before becoming a legend, Davy Crockett moved with his parents and eight siblings to Morristown in the late 1700s. His father, John, owned a tavern. The Crockett Tavern Museum is a replica of that tavern and is located near the original site. The museum, located on Morningside Drive, opened to the public in April 1958. Many of the items used to build and furnish the museum are accurate to the time period and are significant to the area. The front door, for instance, came from the Tate Store, where the Charter for Hamblen County was signed in 1870. (Courtesy of Tennessee State Library and Archives.)

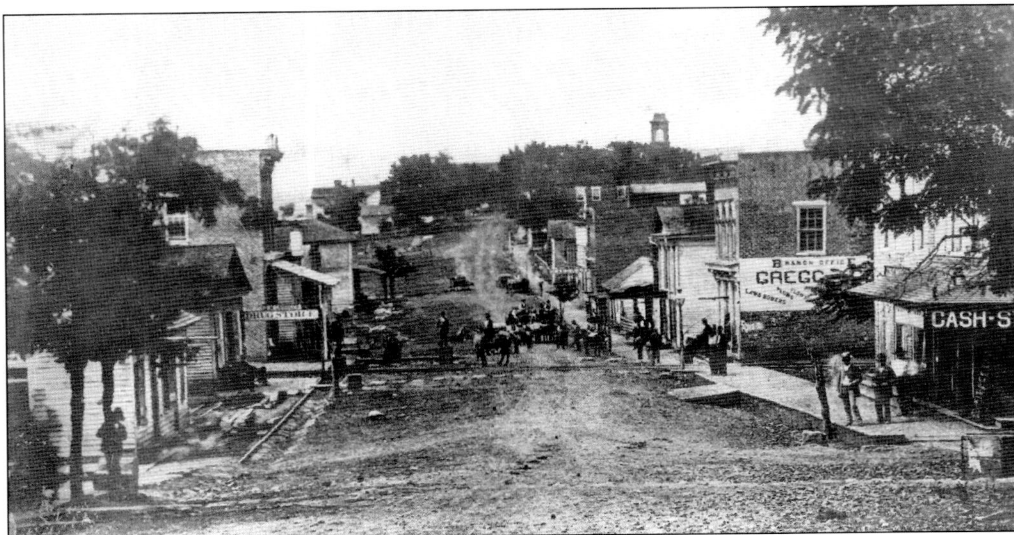

This is Main Street around 1875, standing at Cumberland Street and looking westward. It is comprised mostly of wooden-framed structures. Turkey Creek, originally called Cub Creek, crossed Main Street and was a popular watering hole for horses (center). A bridge was not built until 1892. The second building on left is the drugstore of Dr. Michael Carriger. He was Morristown's first physician. It is believed two of the oldest buildings on Main Street are pictured here and still standing today: the two-story brick building second from right and the three-story brick building third from left. In the distance (far right), peering over the tree tops, is the steeple of the First Baptist Church built in 1871.

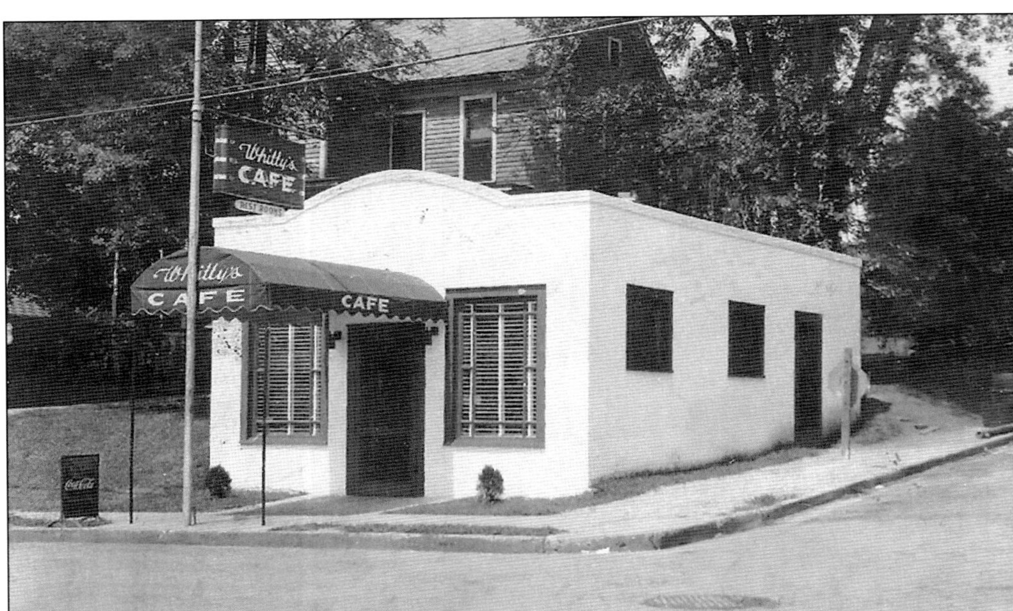

Whitty's Café, owned by George and Bertha Whittington, was located at the northwest corner of Main and James Streets during the late 1940s and 1950s. (Courtesy of David Whittington.)

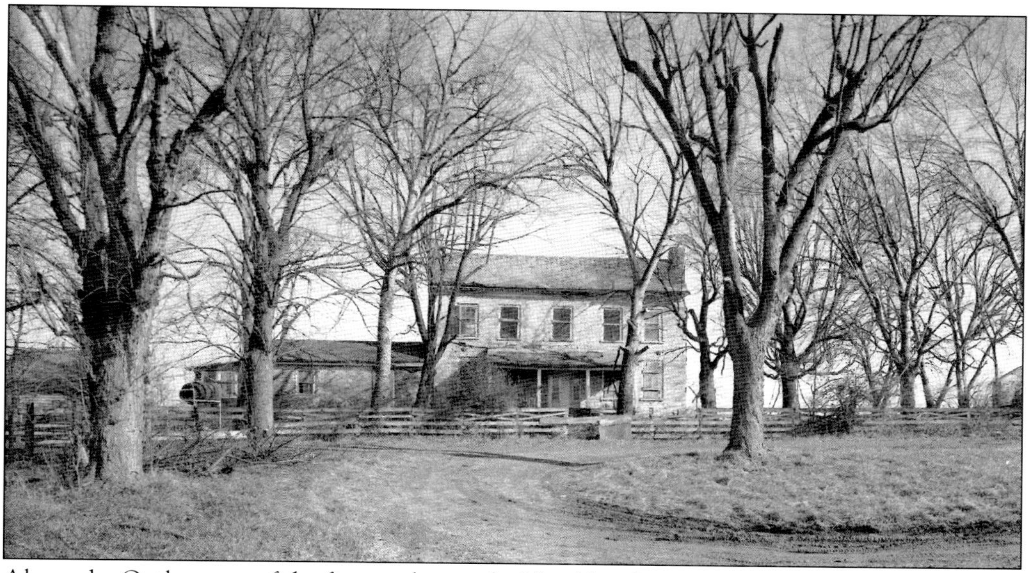

Alexander Outlaw, one of the first settlers to the Hamblen County area, built this home, known as Rural Mount, in 1799 as a wedding gift for his daughter, Penelope, and son-in-law, Joseph Hamilton. It was built of limestone and sits on a ridge in southern Hamblen County overlooking the Nolichucky River. Both Outlaw and Hamilton were actively involved in the founding of the state of Franklin and the state of Tennessee. In 2011, the East Tennessee Preservation Alliance placed Rural Mount on its list of endangered historical sites.

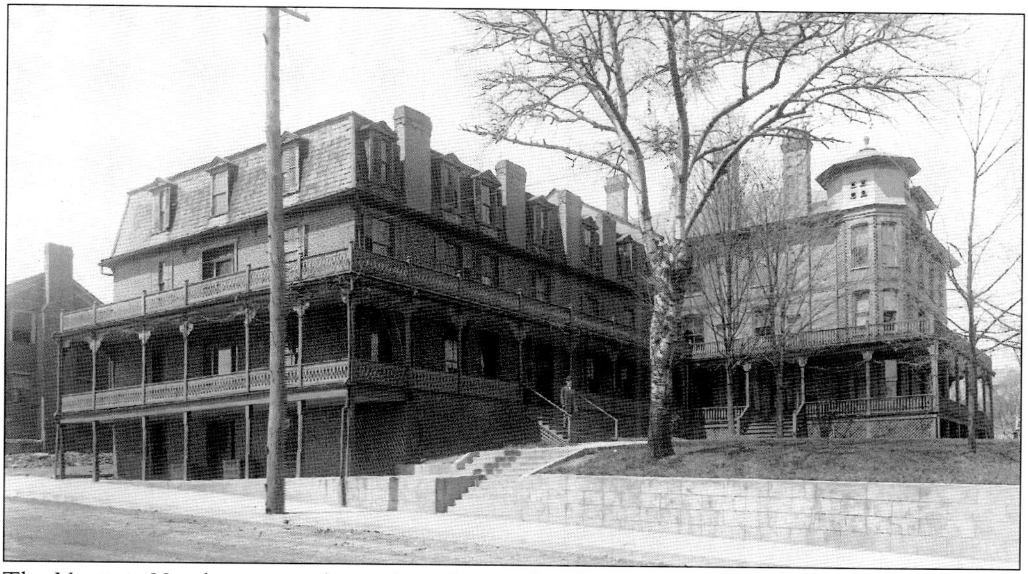

The Virginia Hotel was once located on the north side of Main Street near the intersection of Mill Street, about where Millennium Square office building is today. When built before the Civil War by John F. "Jack" Noe, the hotel was in Grainger County, because Hamblen County had not yet been established. John S. Crump bought the hotel around 1885, and in March 1899, it was enlarged and completely remodeled. The Virginia Hotel became one of the most popular and best known hotels in East Tennessee. Unfortunately, fire destroyed the hotel in 1911. (Courtesy of C.M. McClung Historical Collection.)

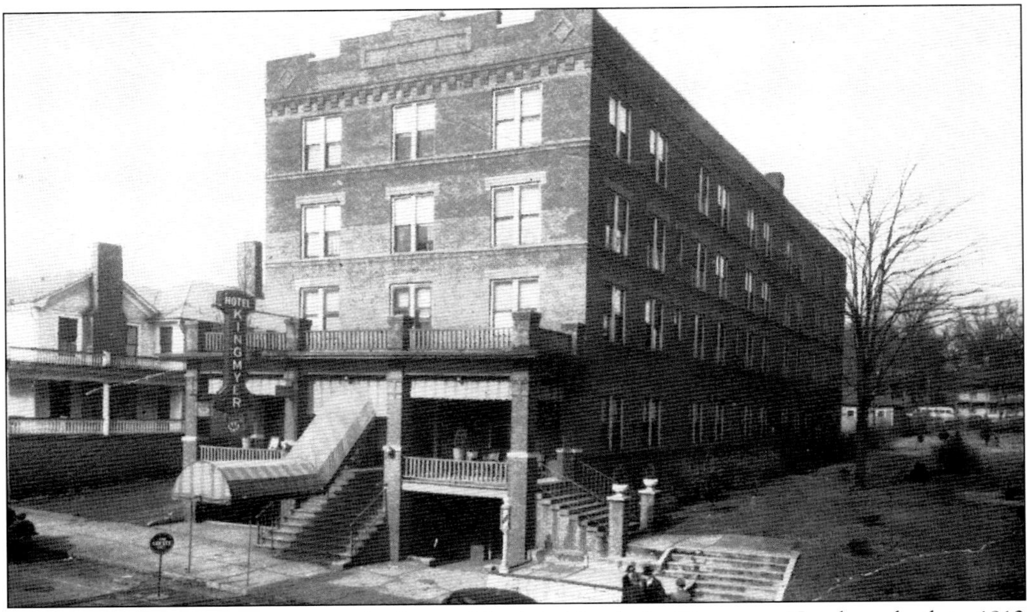

Once located on the same site as the former Virginia Hotel, the Kingmyer Hotel was built in 1913 by the Mitchell brothers, and it was called the Mitchell Hotel. When William Sylvester Myers became owner, the name was changed to Kingmyer Hotel. In later years, the Kingmyer Motor Inn was added to the rear, which faced First North Street. The hotel was sold at auction in 1997, and it was demolished in 2000. The site is now home to the Millennium Square office complex. (Courtesy of Tennessee State Library and Archives.)

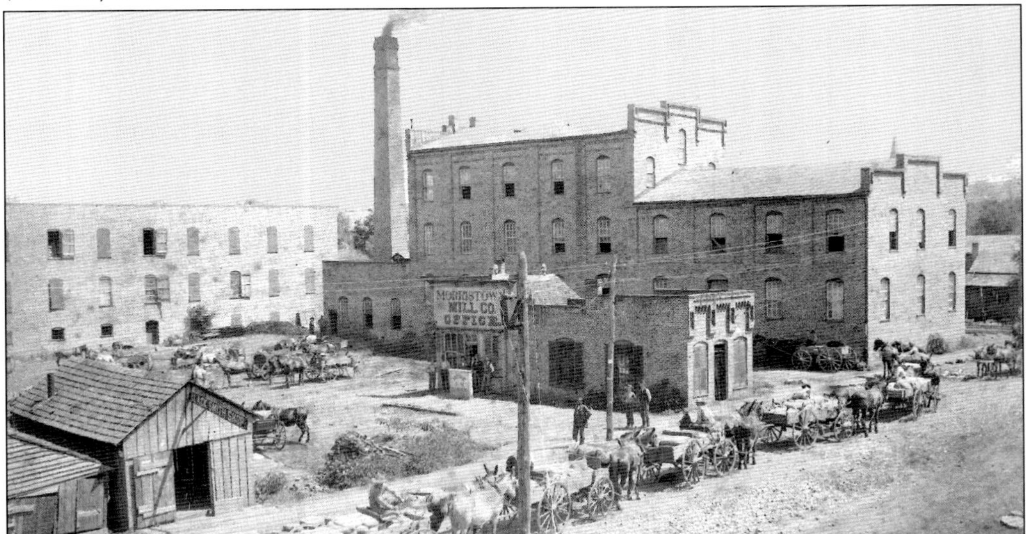

In 1889, farmers lined up to bring grain to the Morristown Mill Company, located on the northeast corner of Cumberland Street and the railroad. This mill, erected in 1888 under the direction of Charles Dabney Merritt, manufactured high-grade roller flour and was touted as being the best equipped and finest mill in East Tennessee. This property changed hands many times before being partly demolished in 1992 due to structural problems and a need for parking space at the Little Dutch Restaurant.

This photograph, taken on March 12, 1965, shows the demolition of Henry Street properties on the south side of Main Street. Morristown's Urban Renewal Program during the 1960s led to the destruction of many buildings and homes throughout town. The buildings in this photograph were replaced by a parking lot. (Courtesy of Hamblen County Archives.)

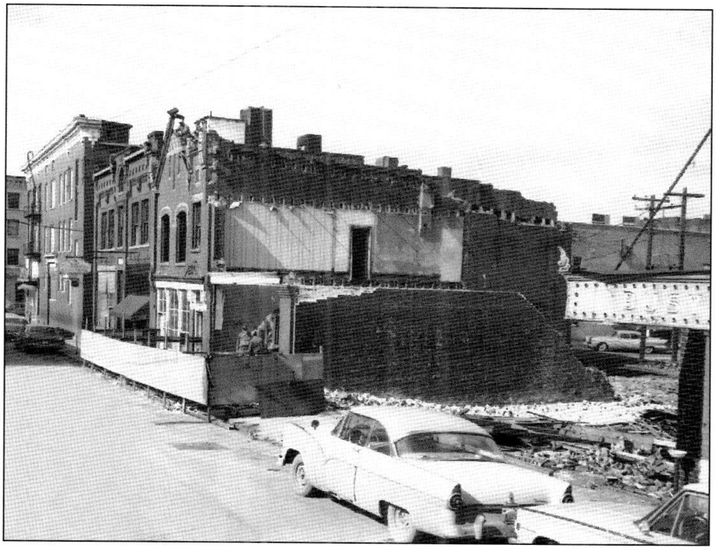

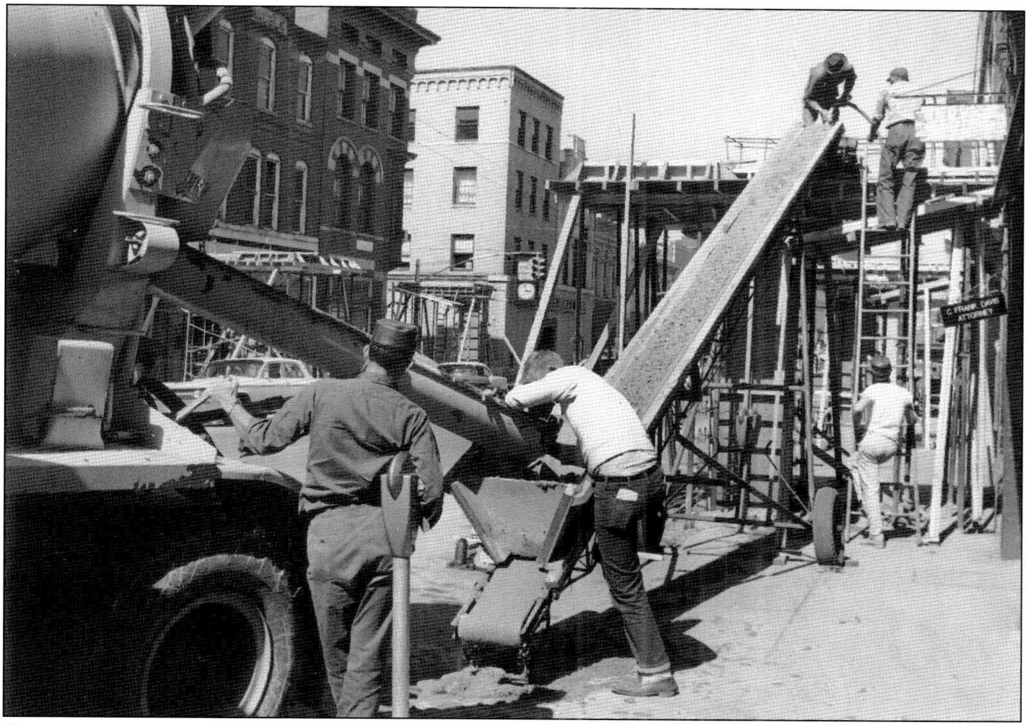

Downtown construction of the overhead sidewalks began in September 1963 as part of a $5 million urban renewal project. The inspiration and idea for the sidewalks came from Chester, England, where elevated sidewalks were first established during the 13th century. Architect Hubert Bebb adapted the unique sidewalk design to fit Morristown, and they became the first elevated sidewalks in America. As a result, Morristown received worldwide publicity. The three-day grand opening celebration and dedication, held from May 4 to May 6, 1967, included a parade, car show, and performances by Tex Ritter, Porter Wagoner, and Dolly Parton. This photograph shows the construction crew forming one of the support columns. (Courtesy of Hamblen County Archives.)

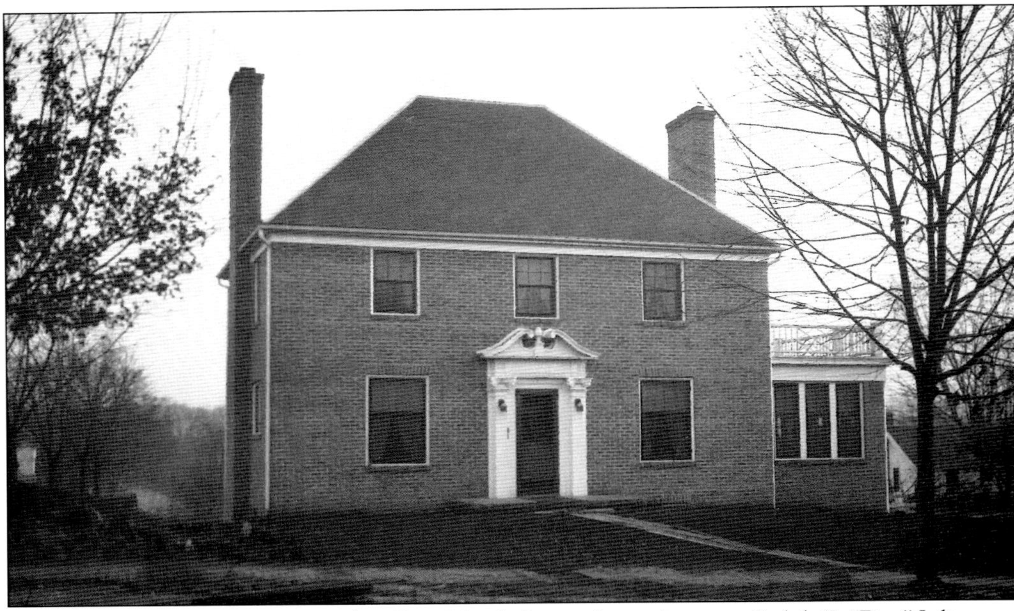

In 1925, this building was erected on First North Street. It was home to Ralph E. "Doc" Julian and family. For a time he was co-owner, along with Marion Roberts, of the Roberts and Turner drugstore, located on Main Street. The home is still standing today. (Courtesy of James Haywood Julian.)

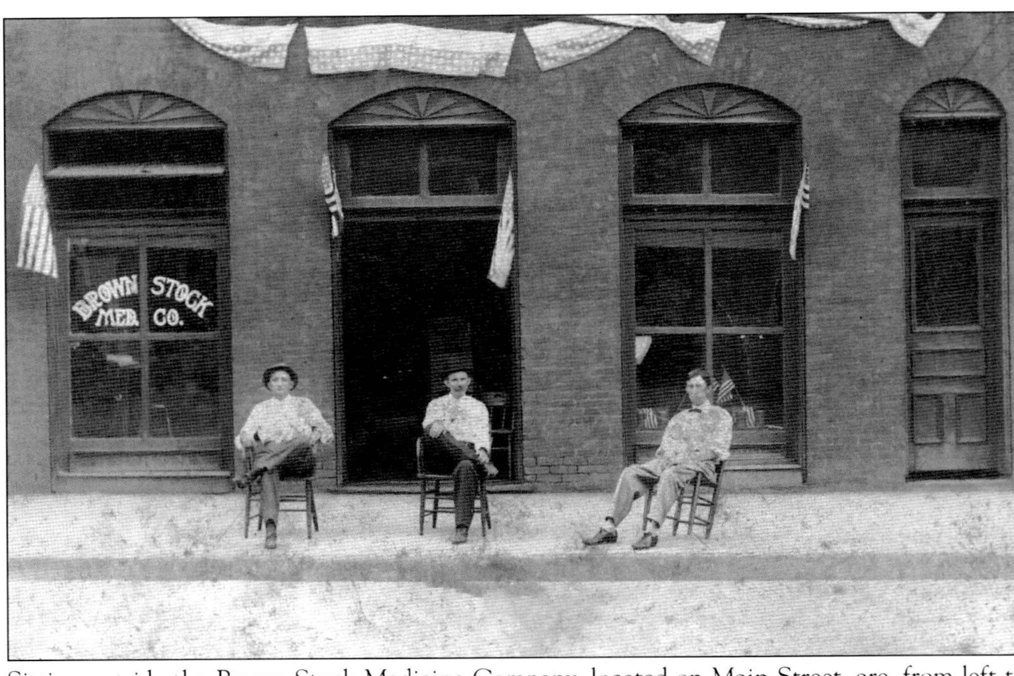

Sitting outside the Brown Stock Medicine Company, located on Main Street, are, from left to right, Perry C. Walker (1883–1950), William S. Brown (1842–1915), and Onnie L. Wall Sr. By the 1920 census, Perry Walker was the manager.

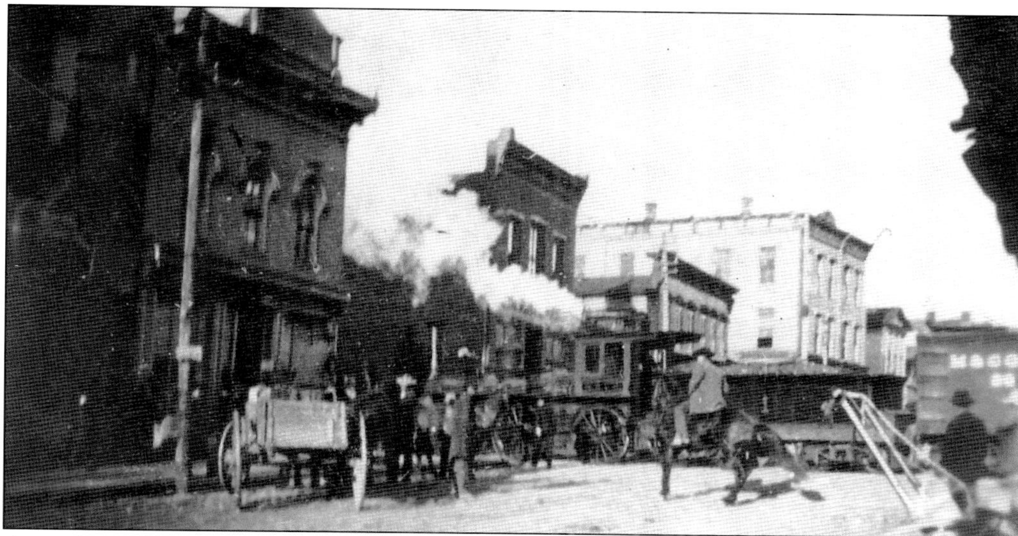

As evidenced by this early-1890s photograph, trains crossing through downtown on Main Street used to be a familiar sight. The railroad crossing was located just a few buildings west of Cumberland Street. In 1855, the first rail was laid in Morristown. The three-story white building beyond the train is the McFarland building on the northwest corner of Main and Cumberland Streets, which housed the McFarland Opera House.

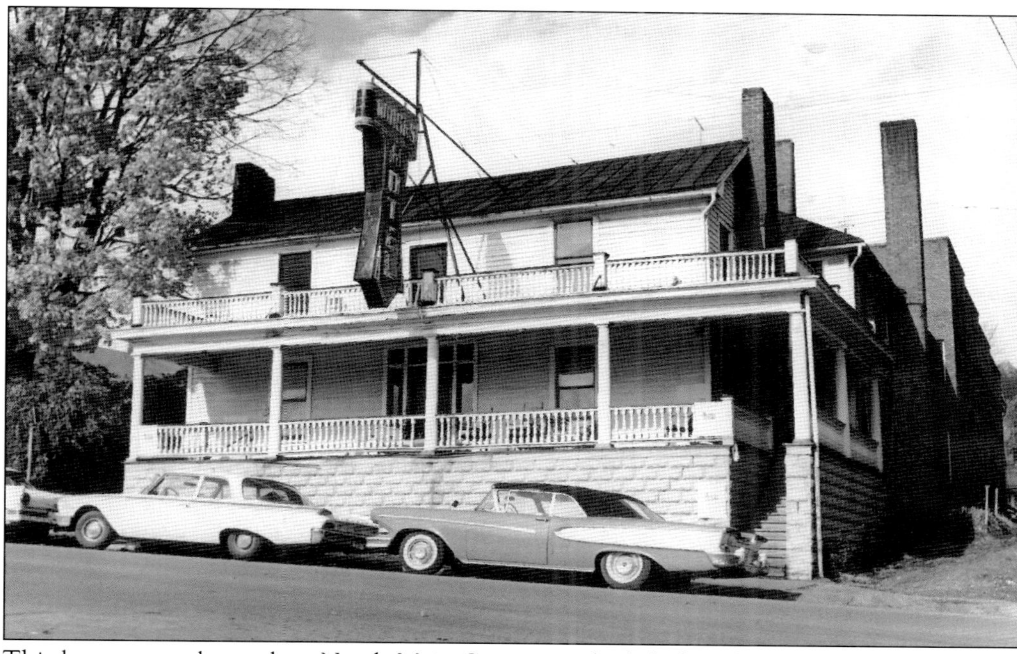

This home, once located on North Main Street, was built before the Civil War by Lt. Noah Felps Read. He would later die in prison during the war, and his family was left to cope with the 1882 smallpox epidemic. The disease started in the Read home and quickly spread throughout the area, killing over 300 people. It nearly wiped out the entire Read family. Jacob Iulus Hodges purchased the home in the early 1900s, and it became known as the Hodges Hotel. It was razed in the 1960s.

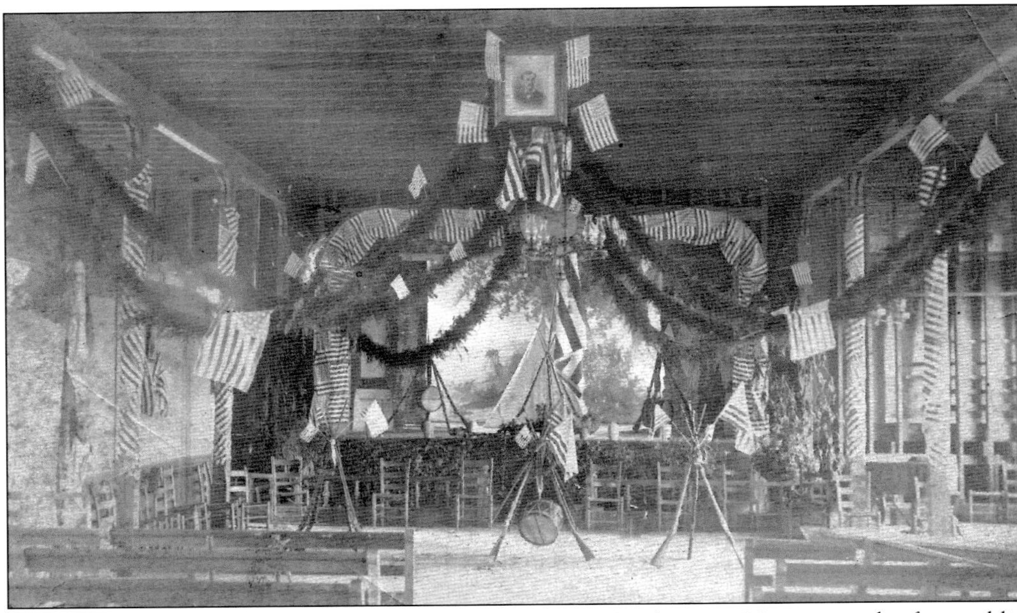

With the exception of churches and schools, the McFarland Opera House was the first public auditorium in Morristown. It was located on the third floor of a brick building constructed around 1883 by William McFarland on the northeast corner of Main and Cumberland Streets. Including all city school commencement ceremonies, it served all local and visiting productions until Read's Opera House came into existence in 1908. This interior photograph of the McFarland Opera House was taken in October 1885, when it was decorated for a military wedding reception. The McFarland building was demolished in 1916.

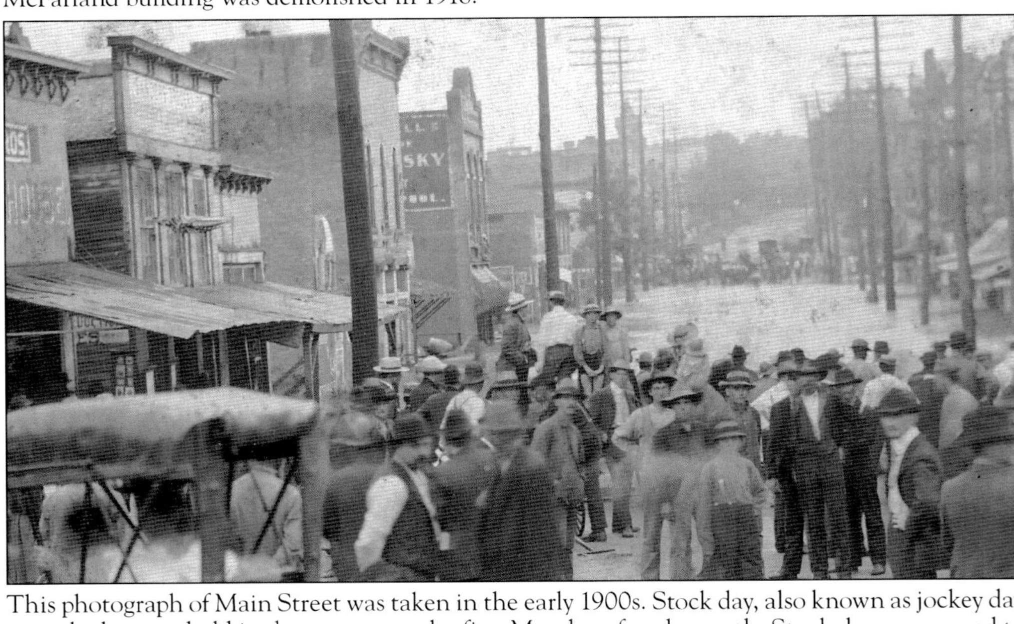

This photograph of Main Street was taken in the early 1900s. Stock day, also known as jockey day or mule day, was held in downtown on the first Monday of each month. Stock day was moved to North Cumberland Street when the stock barn was built around the 1920s. This tradition of buying, selling, and trading livestock and produce continues today and is now called First Monday.

Four

Cessna, Ford, and All Aboard

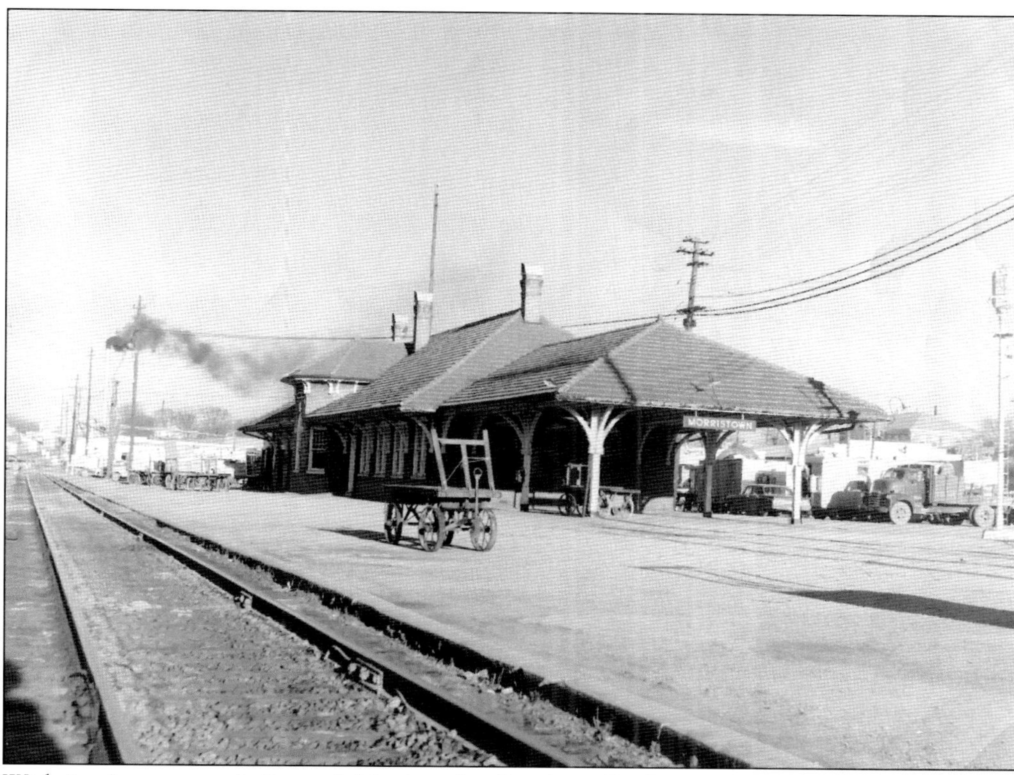

With its signature red-tile roof shingles, this Southern Railway station was constructed from around 1911 and replaced the older railroad station, built in 1887. This station was used by many travelers during its day but was razed in the 1970s as part of the county's urban renewal program. Part of the pavilion still stands at Gluck Park at the corner of Sulphur Springs Road and Rosedale Avenue.

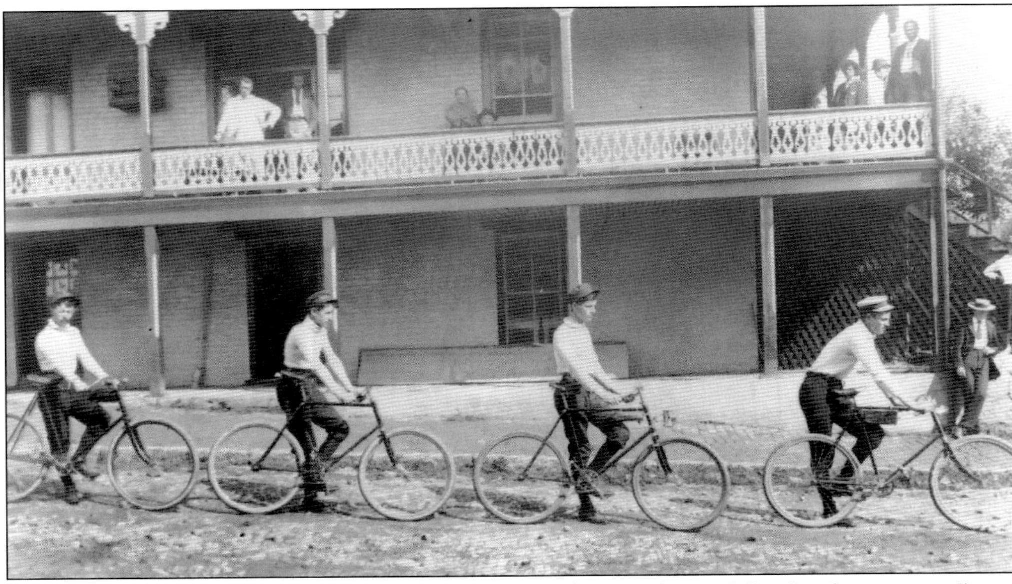

Pictured in front of Virginia Hotel on July 1, 1895, the members of this "cycling quartet" were departing for a month long journey. The members are, from left to right, Ed Holmes, Max Glenn, Albert Carriger, and W.C. Carriger. While in Bristol the following Saturday, more than 1,000 people witnessed the feature attraction—a two-mile race between W.C. Carriger and Cy W. Pendleton of Bristol, which Carriger won in 5 minutes and 40 seconds. The cycling quartet arrived in New York City on August 1 and returned home by train due to the poor road conditions.

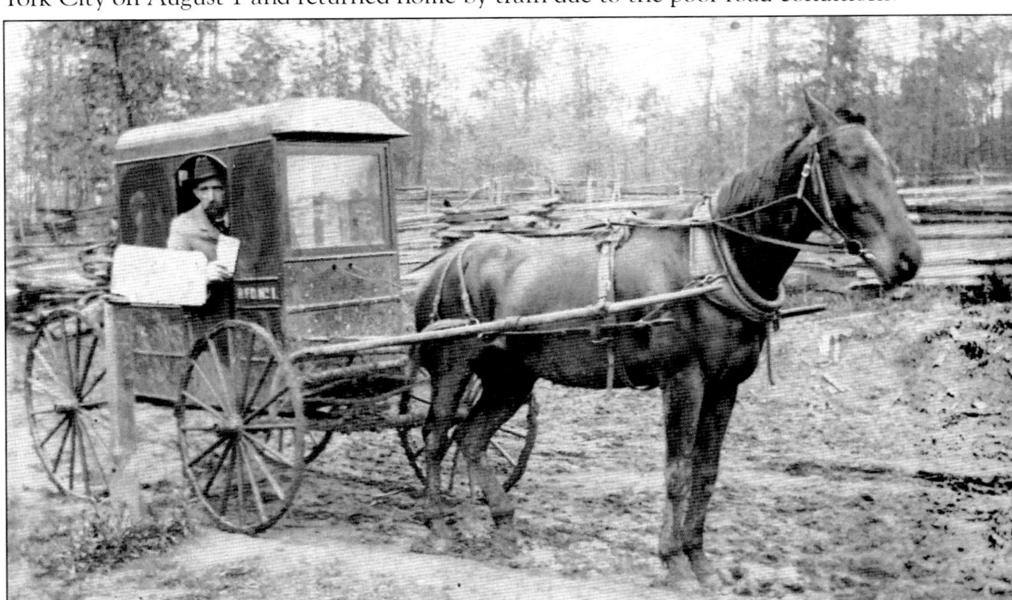

Hamblen County was the first county in East Tennessee where the rural mail carriers used covered mail vehicles like the one shown above in which to deliver the mail. The photograph shows Charles Robertson in his covered buggy, which he designed and had built by Witt Wagon Company, local manufacturers. Most carriers had to deliver mail horseback because of the rough conditions of rural roads.

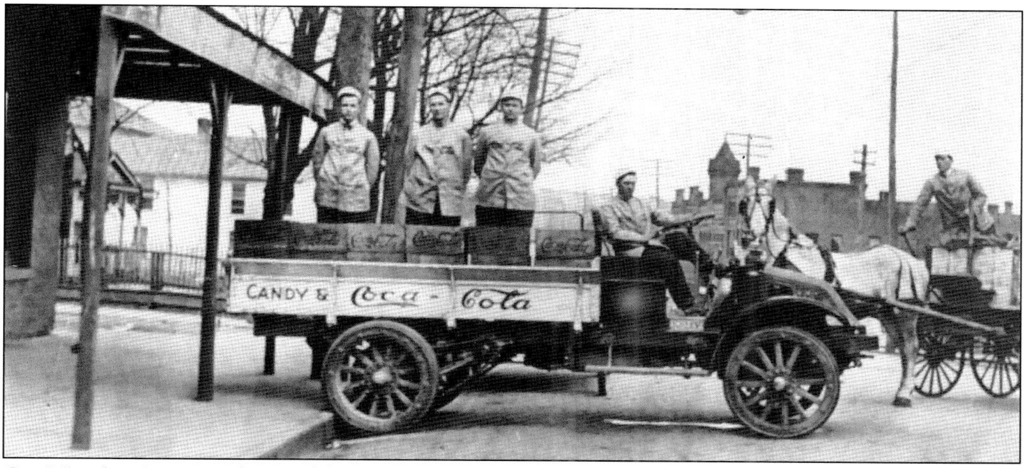

On March 12, 1913, the Roddy Bottling Company, with proprietor brothers J.W. and Aida A. Paxton, opened the first Coke plant in Morristown, located on corner of Hamilton Avenue and West Main Street. A horse-drawn wagon brought the first bottling equipment from Knoxville in 1913. This photograph from 1914 shows, from left to right, Hubert Smith, Gene Smith, Ross Davis, Aida A. Paxton (truck driver) and J.W. Paxton (standing on wagon). In the summer of 1914, they were already making plans to enlarge the plant due to the production of 2,400 bottles daily that could not meet demand.

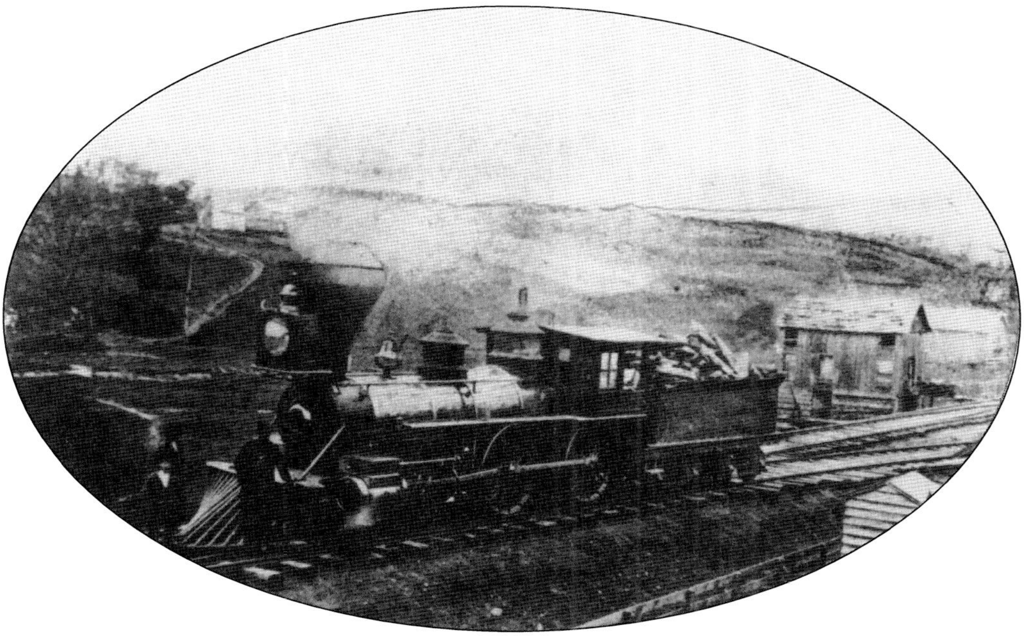

Old Governor Senter, sometimes called *Old Buncombe*, was the first wood-burning engine to carry passengers over the Buncombe Railroad from Morristown to Paint Rock, then to the North Carolina terminal. The engineer, T.D. Craig of Morristown, is pictured at the First North Street crossing on May 20, 1871. The well-worn path leading up the hill from Luttrell Spring was created from water being carried for students at the Morristown Male Academy on Second North Street. The engine was named for DeWitt Clinton Senter, who following his two terms as governor of Tennessee resided in Morristown.

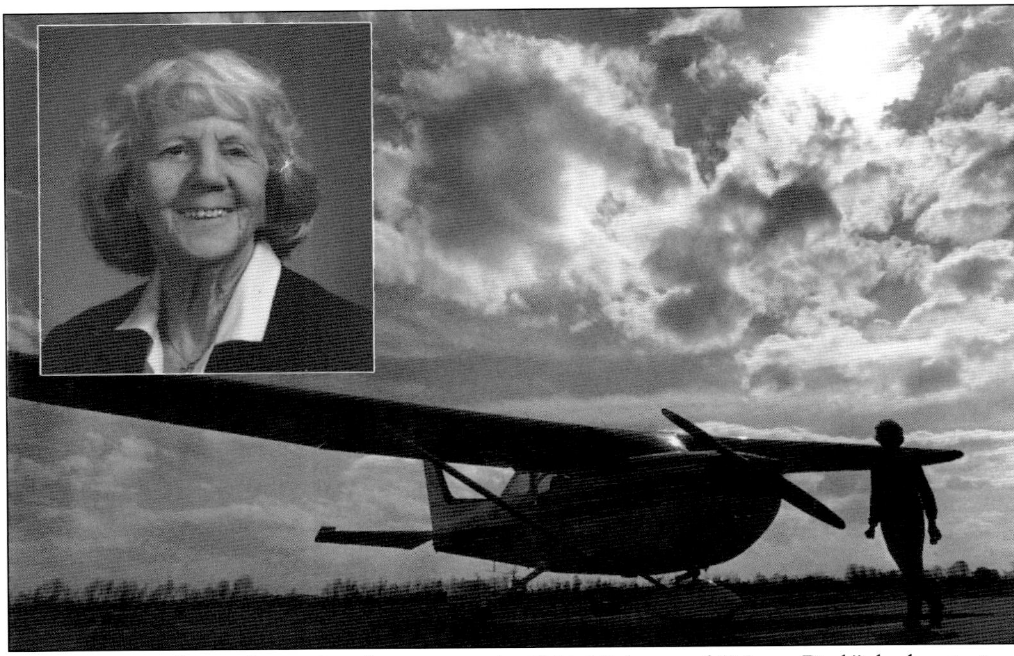

Evelyn Bryan Johnson began her flying career in 1944. Nicknamed "Mama Bird," she has trained more pilots and given more Federal Aviation Administration exams than any other pilot. She has also been named in the Guinness World Records for logging 57,635 hours and for being the female pilot with the most number of flying hours in the world. She was an inductee of the Women in Aviation Pioneers Hall of Fame and the Tennessee and Kentucky aviation halls of fame. She was also awarded a bronze Carnegie Medal for rescuing a helicopter pilot after he crashed. On July 21, 2007, Johnson was inducted into the National Aviation Hall of Fame in Dayton, Ohio, alongside others such as astronaut Sally Ride and adventurer Steve Fossett. Johnson continued to serve as the manager of Moore-Murrell Airport until her death on May 10, 2012. (Courtesy of the late Evelyn Bryan Johnson.)

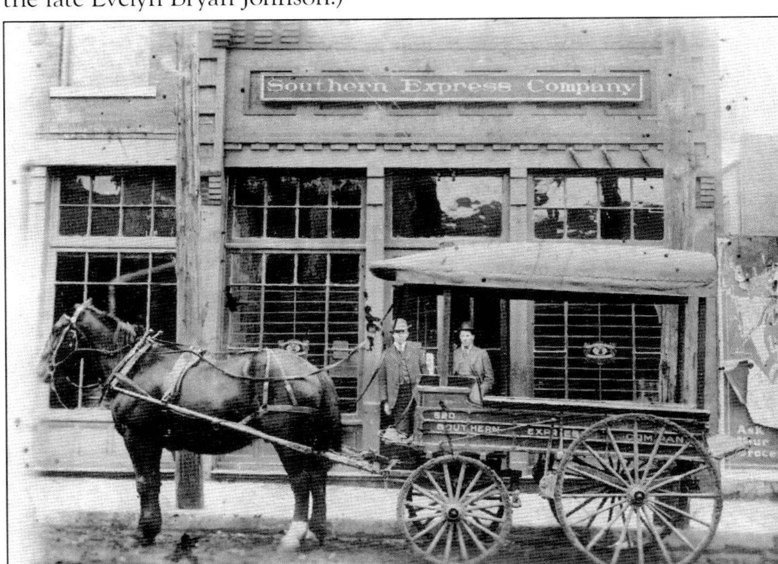

Pictured here is the delivery wagon used by Southern Express Company. The office was located on Henry Street near the railroad and convenient to the Southern Railway Freight Depot. Henry Black (left) was an agent, and Molley Hodge was the assistant. The building on the left is Smith Memorial Company.

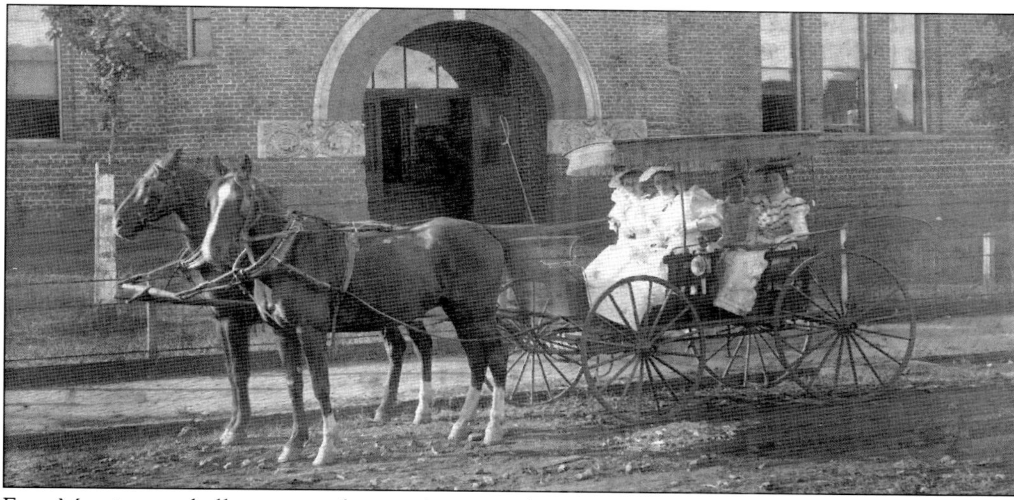

Four Morristown belles are out for an afternoon drive in a two-horse phaeton. This photograph was taken in front of Morristown High School, probably in early 1900s, by Hodges, a local photographer. One of the ladies pictured, in the front passenger seat, is thought to be Lizzie Murphey, who later married Clem Tomlinson of Tate Springs. The others are unidentified. The image shows the original wire fence erected around the school, the brick sidewalk, and that the street had not yet been paved.

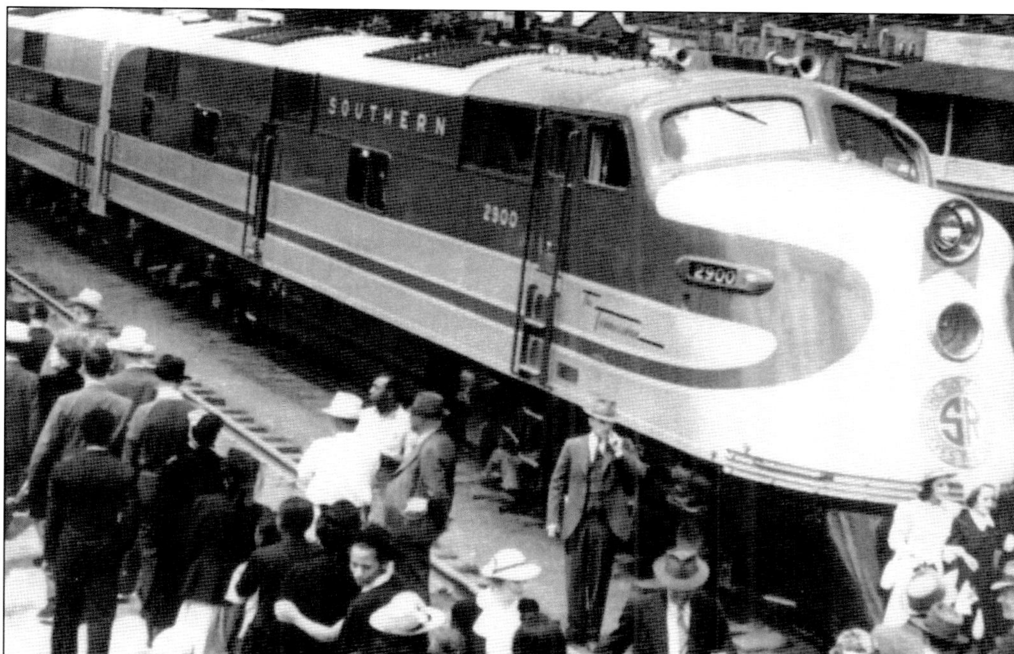

The *Tennessean*, inaugurated on May 17, 1941, was a train jointly operated by the Norfolk & Western Railway and the Southern Railway. This photograph shows people lining up for a tour on the *Tennessean* when it stopped in Morristown in December 1941, just prior to Pearl Harbor. The two men in hats and suits were detectives who traveled with the train. Due to a decline in overall ridership, the *Tennessean* was discontinued on March 30, 1968. (Courtesy of Bill Haskins of the Bulls Gap Railroad Museum.)

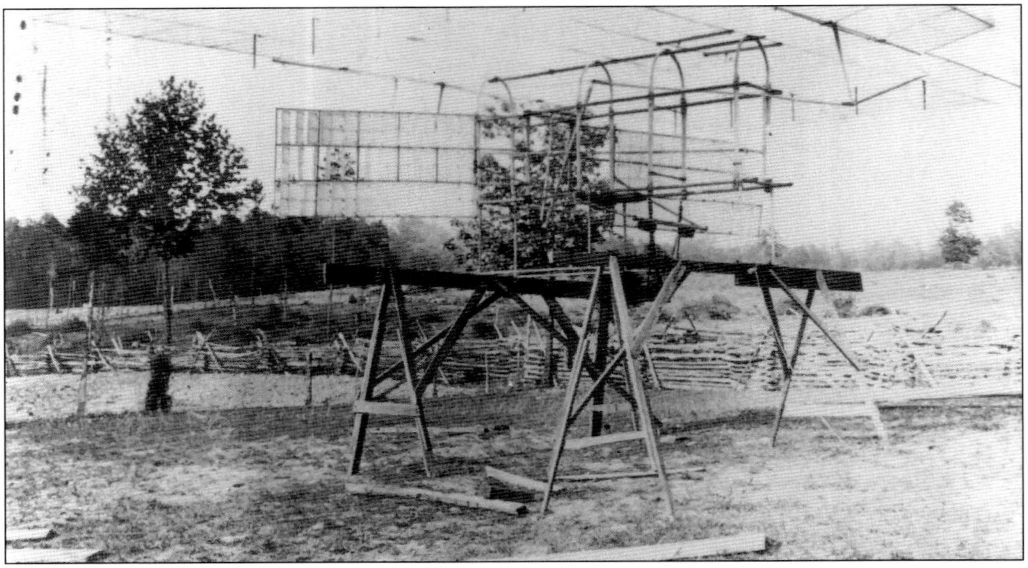

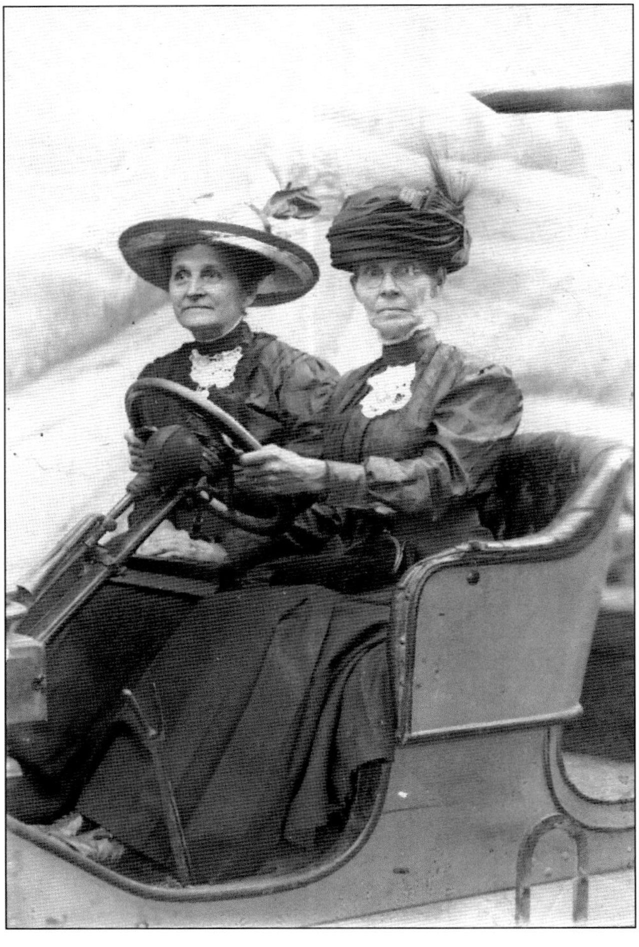

Melville M. Murrell showed an inventive genius at an early age, and with hard work and a fascination with manned flight, he obtained a letter of patent for the American Flying Machine in August 1877. To place this in historical perspective, consider that the Wright brothers were just children and did not accomplish their successful Army test flight until 1908. What remained of Murrell's flying machine was removed in 1964 from an old shed in the Panther Springs community and today is housed in the collection of the Smithsonian Institution in Washington, DC, and on permanent display at the Rose Center.

Two popular Morristown ladies are out for a Sunday spin in an early automobile. Louisa Jane Griffith Parrott (left) was the wife of Methodist Episcopal Church, South, minister John H. Parrott. Hester Anna Trobaugh (right) was the wife of George Marshall Trobaugh, the proprietor of the Trobaugh Farm Implement Store.

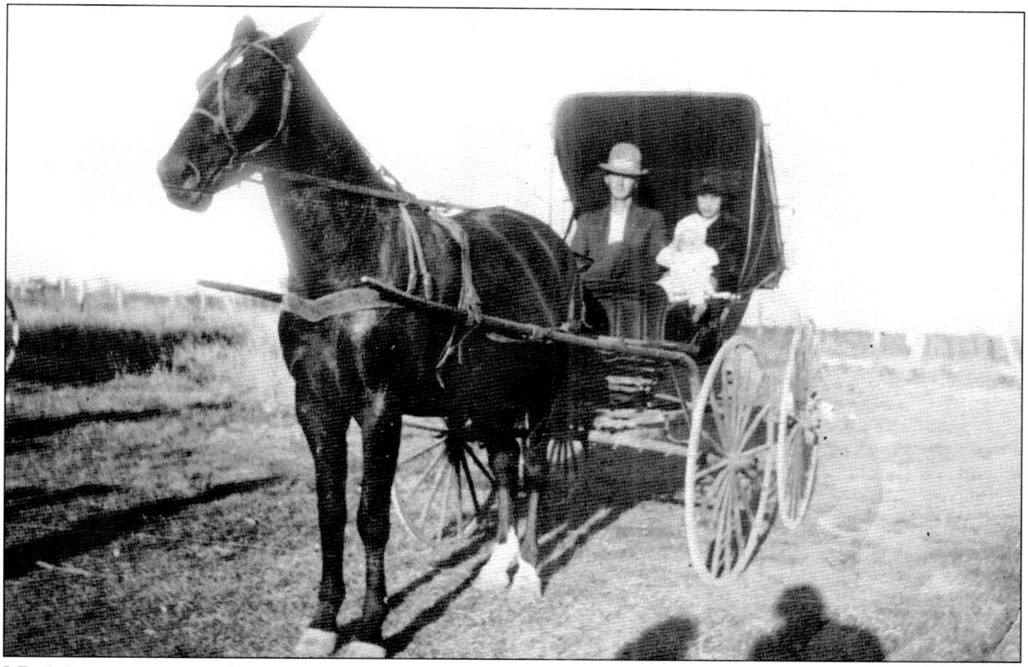

J.B. Mayes is posing for a photograph with his wife, Georgie, and infant daughter, Helen Ruth Mayes, at the family homestead in the Kidwell's Ridge community. This land was later purchased by the Tennessee Valley Authority and flooded in the creation of Cherokee Reservoir.

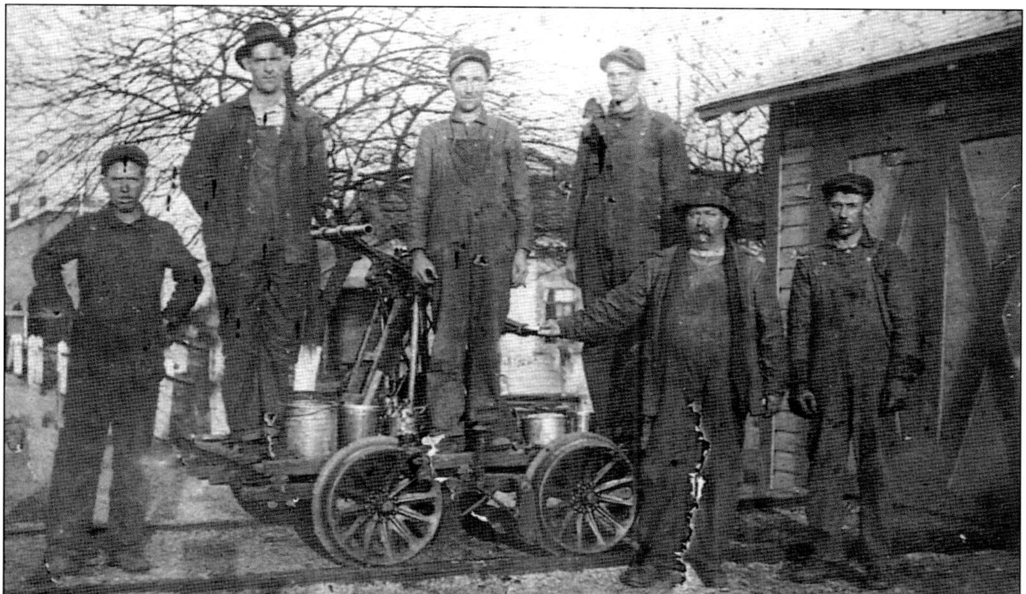

Theodore Hickey (standing on the right), a Native American of the Kituwah tribe, worked for Norfolk Southern Railroad. Theodore married Rebecca Ivy, and they had three children, Annabell, Gereline, and Juanita Hickey. Omer Lane, standing in middle, married Rebecca's sister, Ethel Ivy. (Courtesy of Shelia Carroll Purkey.)

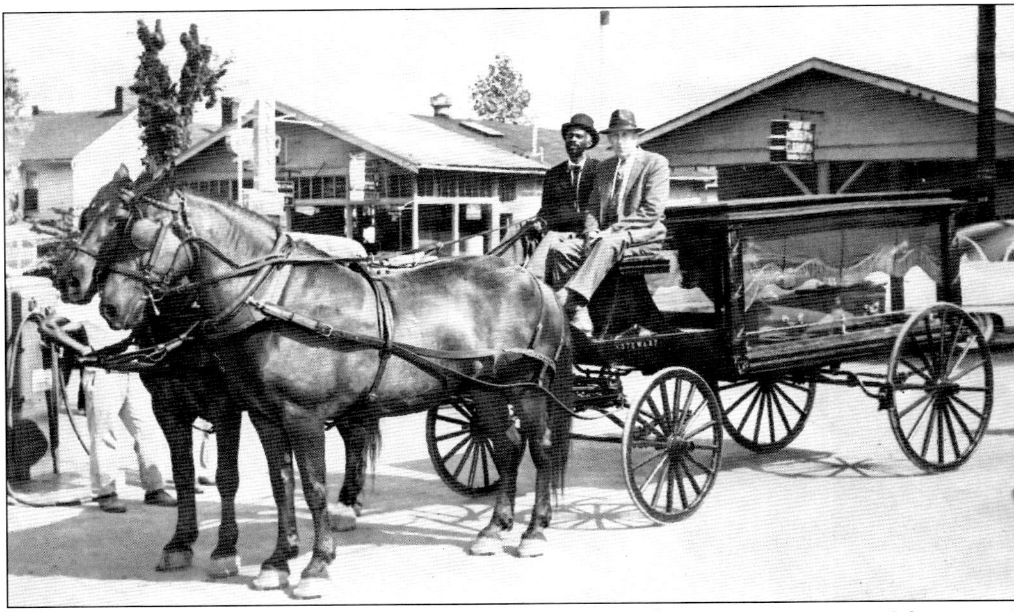

This is the Stewart Funeral Home horse-drawn hearse from Bulls Gap participating in Morristown's centennial celebration in 1955. Charlie Rucker is holding the reins, with Homer Stewart to the right. Stewart owned Stewart Funeral home in Bulls Gap. He had a daughter named Marie Stewart, who married J.B. Gulley, who today owns Westside Funeral Home. This horse-drawn wagon is still in use today by Westside Funeral Home. (Courtesy of Camera Castle, Inc.)

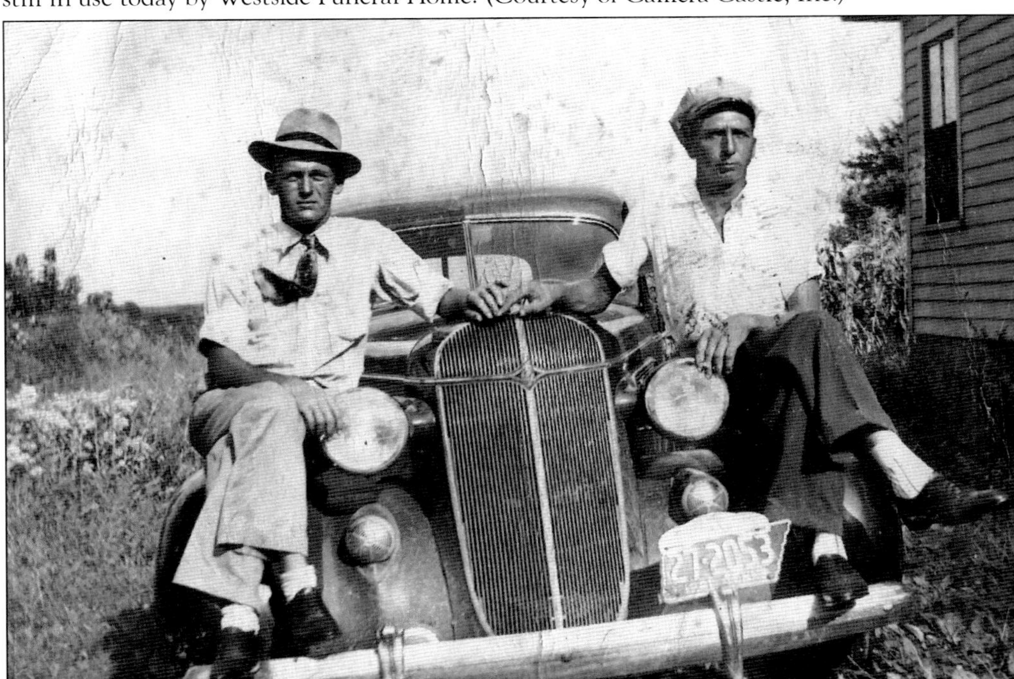

The two men sitting on the car are Henry Coffee on left and Henry Smith. (Courtesy of Billie D. Loveday.)

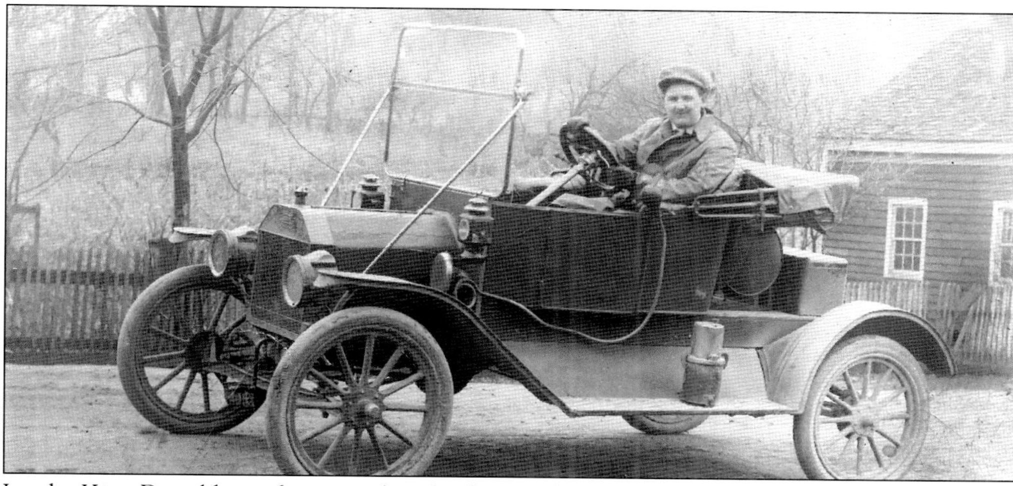

Leader King Donaldson, shown at the wheel, owned one of Morristown's first Ford automobiles. He married Anna Camilla Ponder on January 22, 1908, in Hamblen County. Donaldson was one of the town's most loved citizens. He was elected as mayor from 1937 to 1940, was a charter member of the Morristown Country Club and the Morristown Rotary Club, and served as a deacon for 30 years at the First Presbyterian Church.

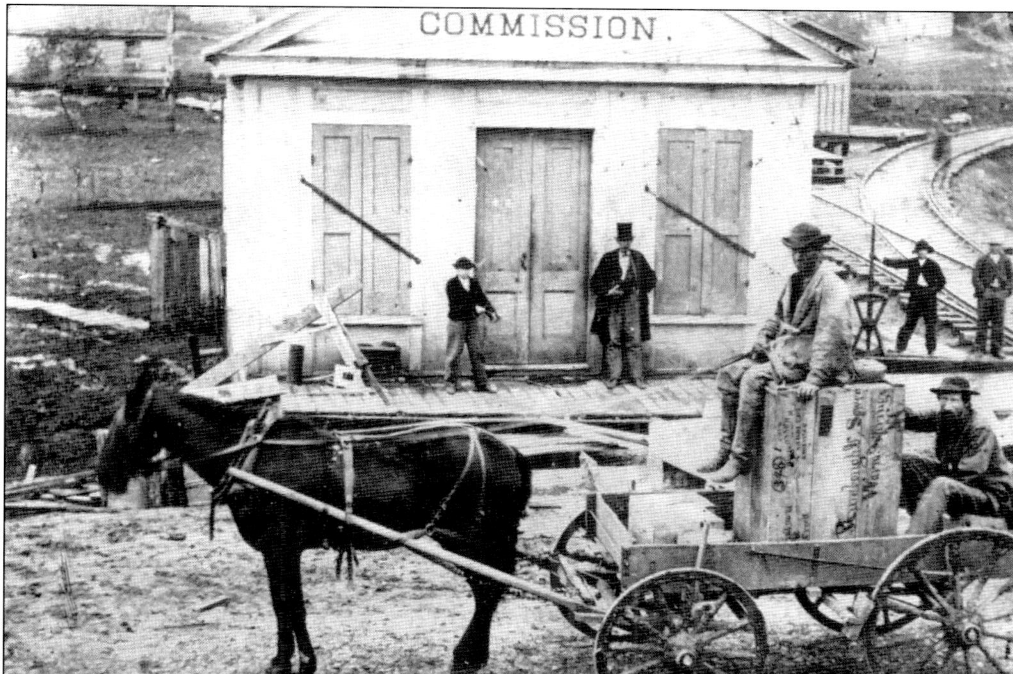

This photograph, dated July 1, 1872, shows the wagon that preformed hauling in Morristown from 1870 to 1883. This wagon was used as the city's first hearse in the burial of the first person in the City Cemetery, that of a little Townsend girl, and was also used during the 1883 smallpox epidemic. Pictured in the wagon are Nat Gourley (left) and R.J. Butts. Standing in front of the commission office building are, from left to right, Charles Lothrop, Coleman Witt (who served as postmaster during the Civil War), S.D. Harris (young man with hand on switch), and Champ Hamblen.

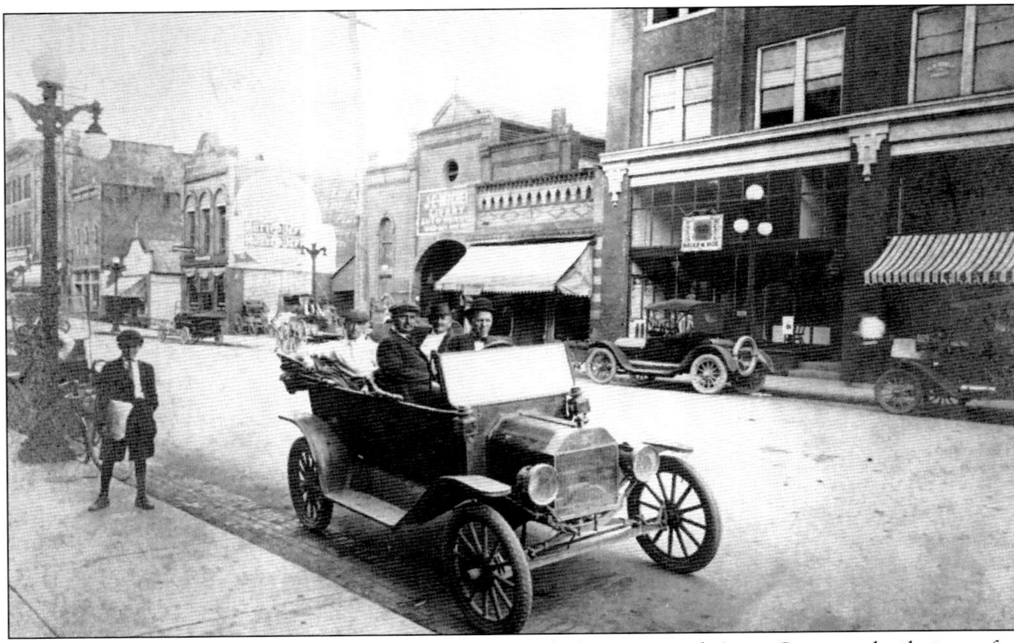

A photograph of Main Street shows the J.E. Mitchel Livery and Auto Service, built just after the Civil War, in the background. Further on the right, the building with the awning is Walkers Barber Shop, and next to it is the Bales & Noe Meat Market, located in the McCanless Building. Driving is George W. Holloway, and seated with him is Ott Riggs, one-time professional baseball player. Sitting in the back seat are Bill Roddy (left) and Sam Sullenbarger.

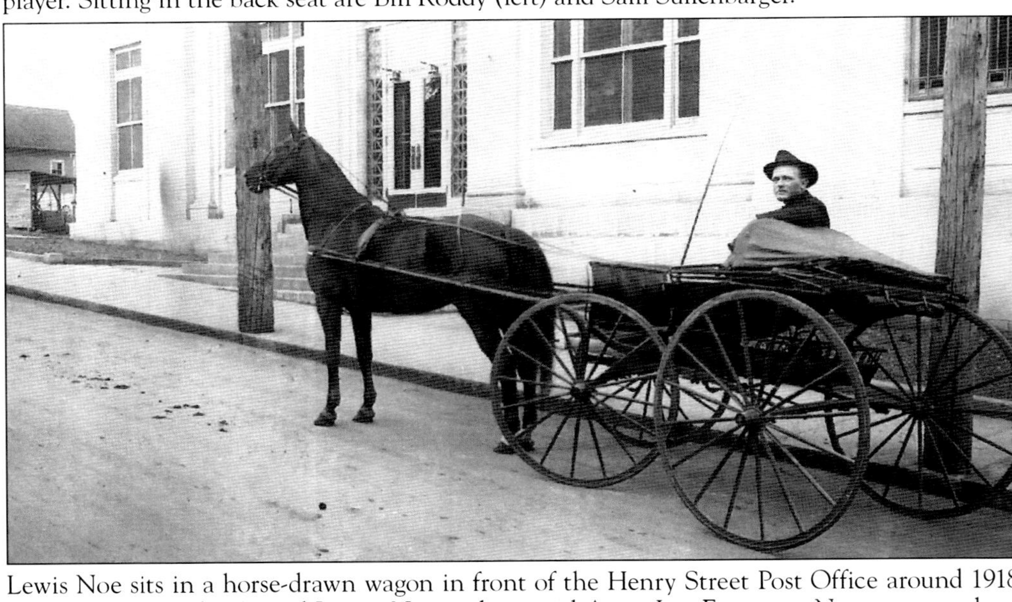

Lewis Noe sits in a horse-drawn wagon in front of the Henry Street Post Office around 1918. He was the son of B.A. and Jennie Noe and married Anna Lee Furguson. Noe was a graduate of the University of Tennessee and served 27 years in the banking industry. An Army veteran of World War I, Noe was also a charter member of Billy Bushhong Post 52 of the American Legion, and he served as county court clerk from 1950 to 1962, when he retired. (Courtesy of Celya Harrell Fields.)

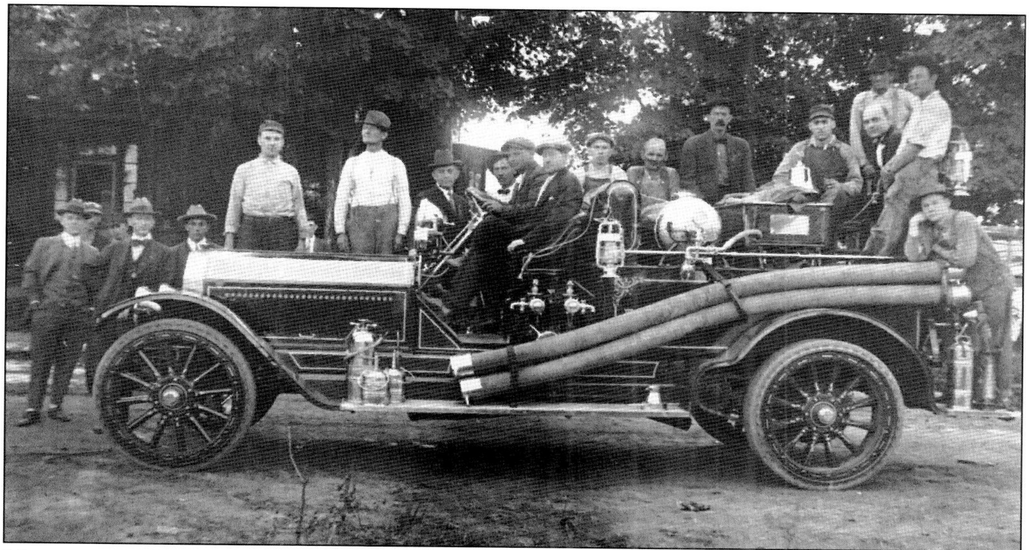

Morristown's first motorized fire truck was purchased while W.B. Whittaker was mayor. Pictured with the truck are, from left to right, Roy Kelley, J.O. Phillips, Bill Blair, Shell Burger, Sam Kelley, W.B. Whittaker, Jim Mathes, Perry Burger (at wheel), J.E. Burke, Austin Fanning, Ross Barnette, Jim Corey, Ellis Carey, Bob Lowe, Sullins Dosser, Oscar Graham, and Bob LaPrade. The truck was acquired from the American LaFrance Fire Engine Company for $9,000 in June 1916. It was retired in the 1950s and was parked for many years at Cherokee Park for children to enjoy. Recently, the Morristown Fire Department has taken efforts in restoring it back to its former glory.

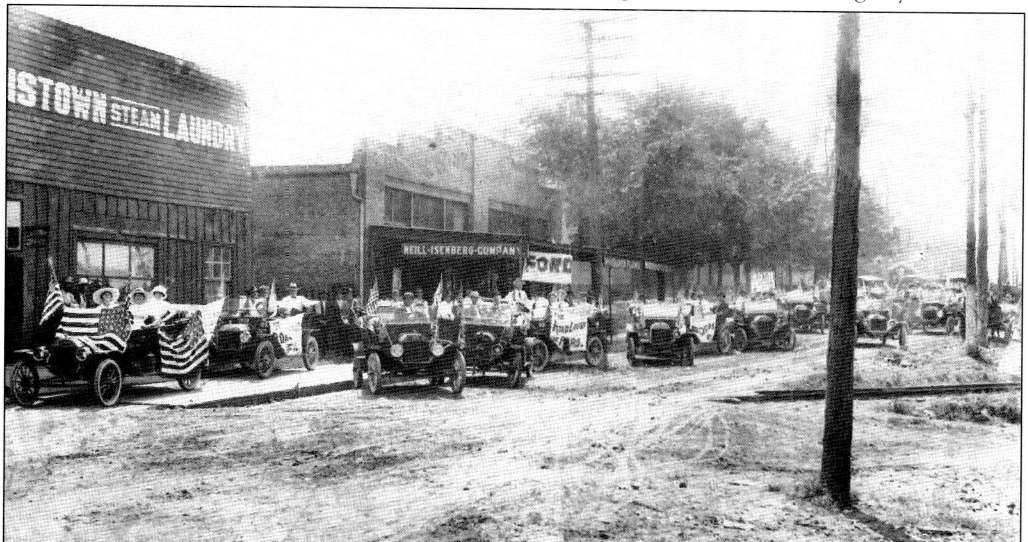

This group of Ford cars lined up in front of Neill-Isenberg Agency are ready to participate in the 1916 Fourth of July Parade. The Model T was ideal for driving on dirty, rough roads. It was reported that in the first seven months of 1914, Neill-Isenberg Agency sold 74 Ford automobiles. Reports of terrible dust on Main and Cumberland Streets were directly linked to increased automobile traffic. Morristown Steam Laundry was then in the building next to the Ford agency, and on the right amid the trees was the home of Judge James George Rose, located on the corner of Cumberland Street and Morris Boulevard.

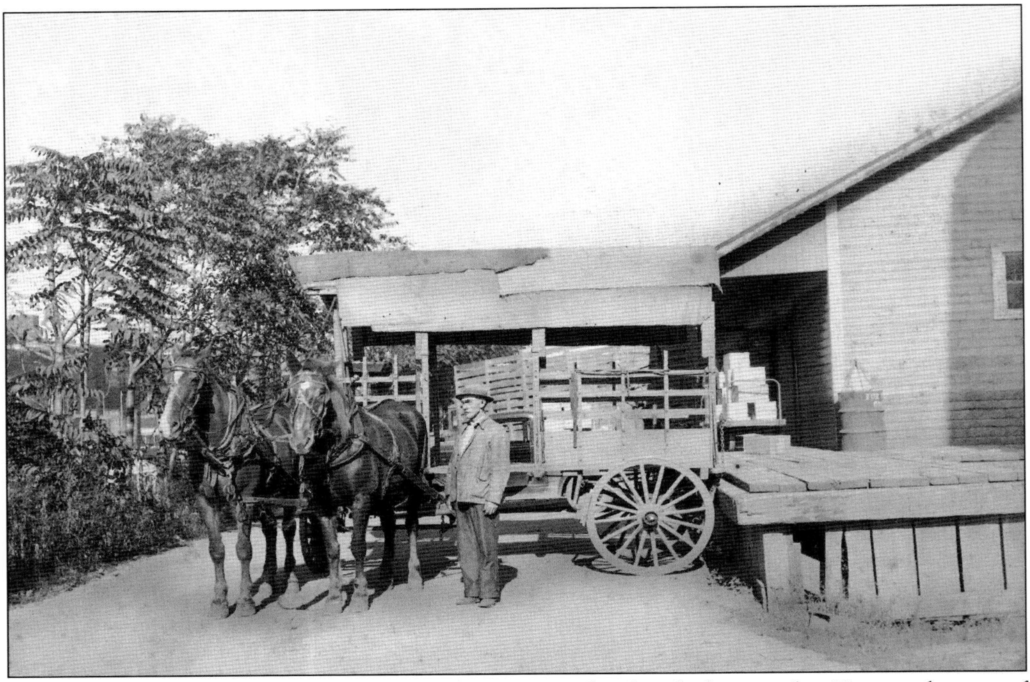

Henry Michael was one of Morristown's draymen in the days before trucks. He was the son of Elijah and Columbia Jane Michael, natives of Virginia who settled in Morristown in 1886. Michael is shown here taking on a load at the Southern Railway freight depot using a team of horses. He worked for 55 years specializing in moving heavy equipment before retiring in 1951.

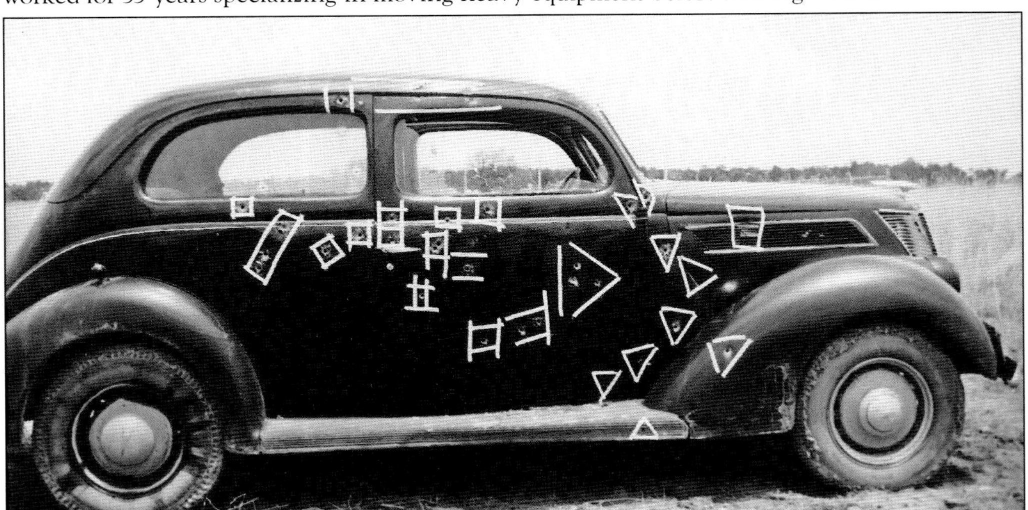

This is the 1937 Ford Sedan that driver William McGinnis and passenger Victor McDaniel were in as they approached American Enka Corporation's union strike roadblock in 1950. There were 47 bullet holes in the right side of the vehicle, and both men were injured. Tennessee governor Gordon Browning dispatched National Guard troops to restore order. Before its end, the strike became national front-page news and subject of congressional hearings held in Morristown led by Hubert Humphrey. (Courtesy of Paul Ollis.)

Five

Singing, Swinging, and Celebrations

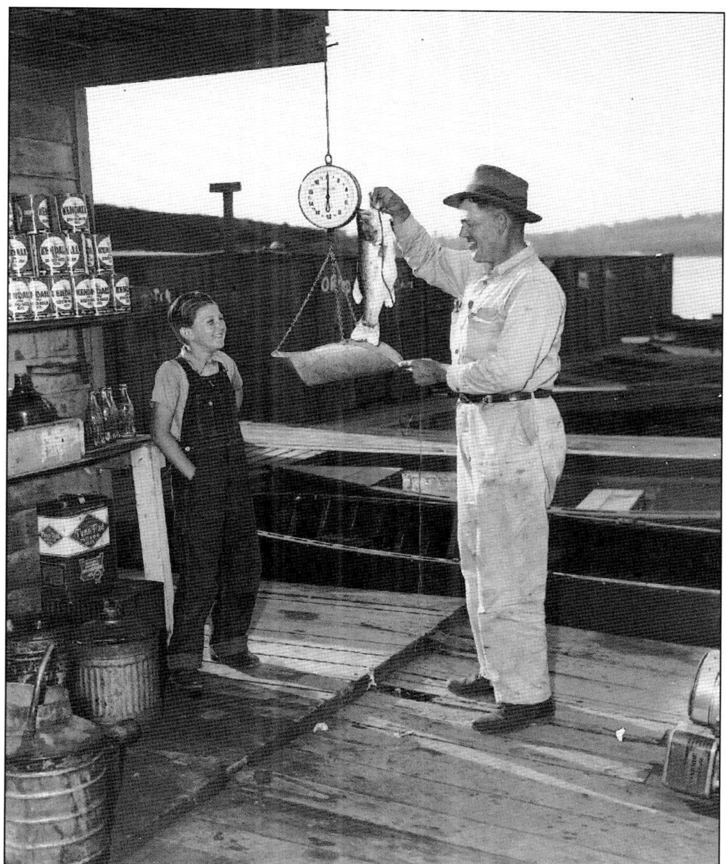

Lee Hipshire and his son are photographed during a Tennessee Valley Authority fish census on Cherokee Lake on May 16, 1946, at the Hamblen Boat Dock. This was an important census monitoring healthy fish populations because Cherokee Lake was such a young body of water. (Courtesy of the Tennessee State Library and Archives.)

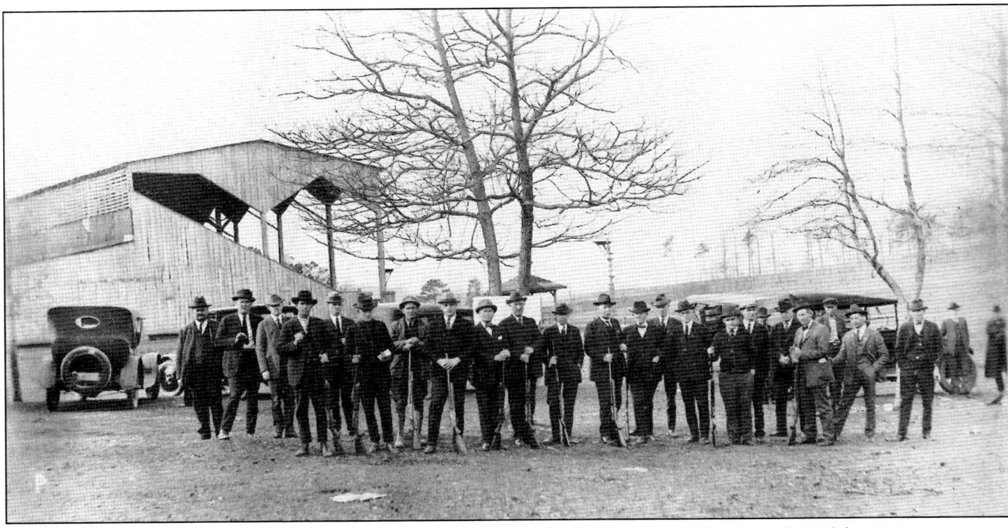

Morristown Gun Club Turkey Shooters, comprised of many well-known local businessmen, are pictured here at the fairgrounds in 1923. The participants are, from left to right, Hardy Dougherty, R.L. Moore, Dr. J.C. Freels, Hubert Shipley, W.J. Donaldson, Bill Peoples, R.H. Miller, Paul Henderson, Schuyler Murphy, Joe Hill, H.F. Mims, D.P. Turner, W.D. Bushong, Floyd Goodson, E.B. Fisher, Algie Peoples, Walter Collins, unidentified, John Carriger, C.D. Trobaugh, John Estes, Nelson Weller, O.K. Capps, George W. Baker, and unidentified.

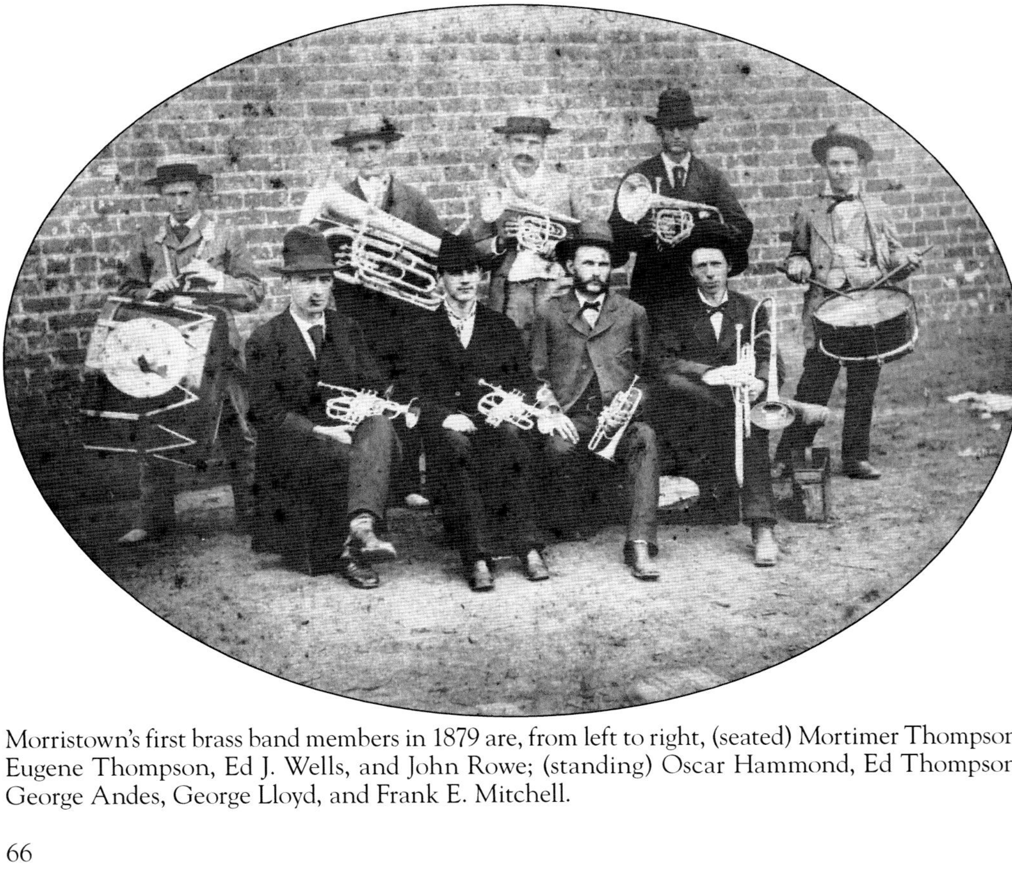

Morristown's first brass band members in 1879 are, from left to right, (seated) Mortimer Thompson, Eugene Thompson, Ed J. Wells, and John Rowe; (standing) Oscar Hammond, Ed Thompson, George Andes, George Lloyd, and Frank E. Mitchell.

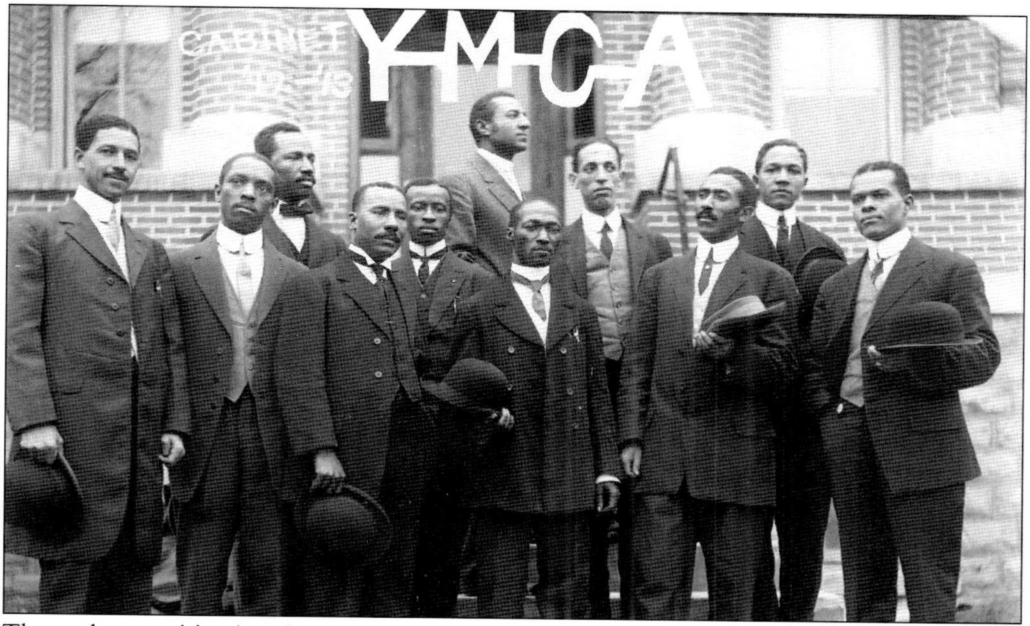

The students and faculty of Morristown College organized chapters of the Young Men's Christian Association (YMCA) to provide support for local and national projects. Shown here is the YMCA cabinet from 1912 to 1913.

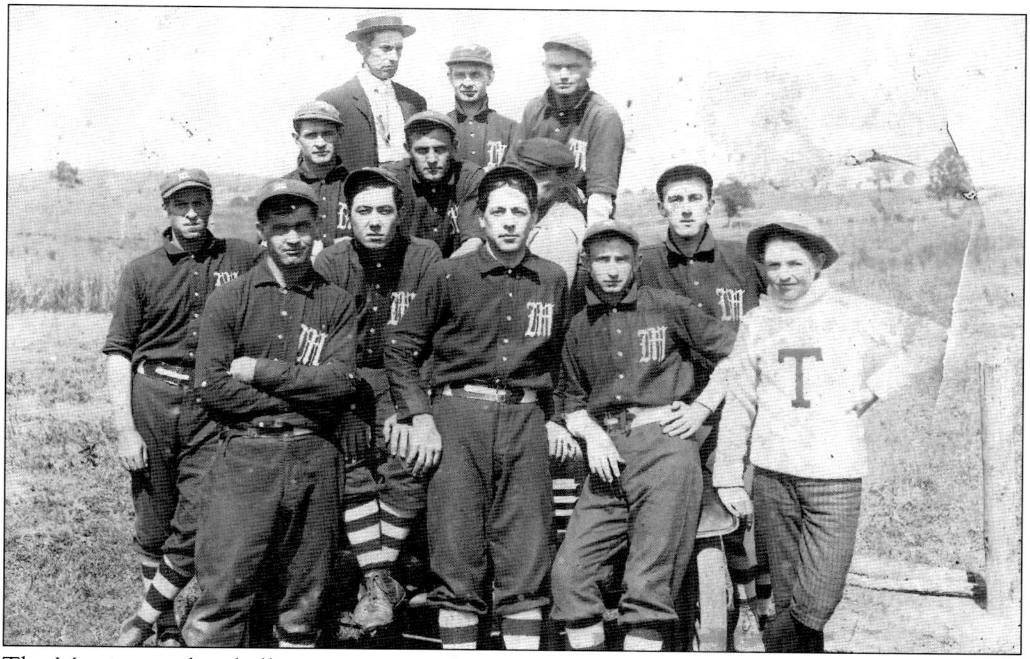

The Morristown baseball team is posing for a photograph around 1907 on Peck Field, now the site of Radio Center. Pictured are, from left to right, (first row) Elmer Webb, Clifford Rhoton, Claude Sanders, and Forest Sanders; (second row) Frank Rhoton, W.J. Donaldson, and Barto Fisher; (third row) War Sanders, "Humpy" McElven, and Sam Welch; (fourth row) E.A. Peck, Curtis Sanders, and Thurrell Sanders.

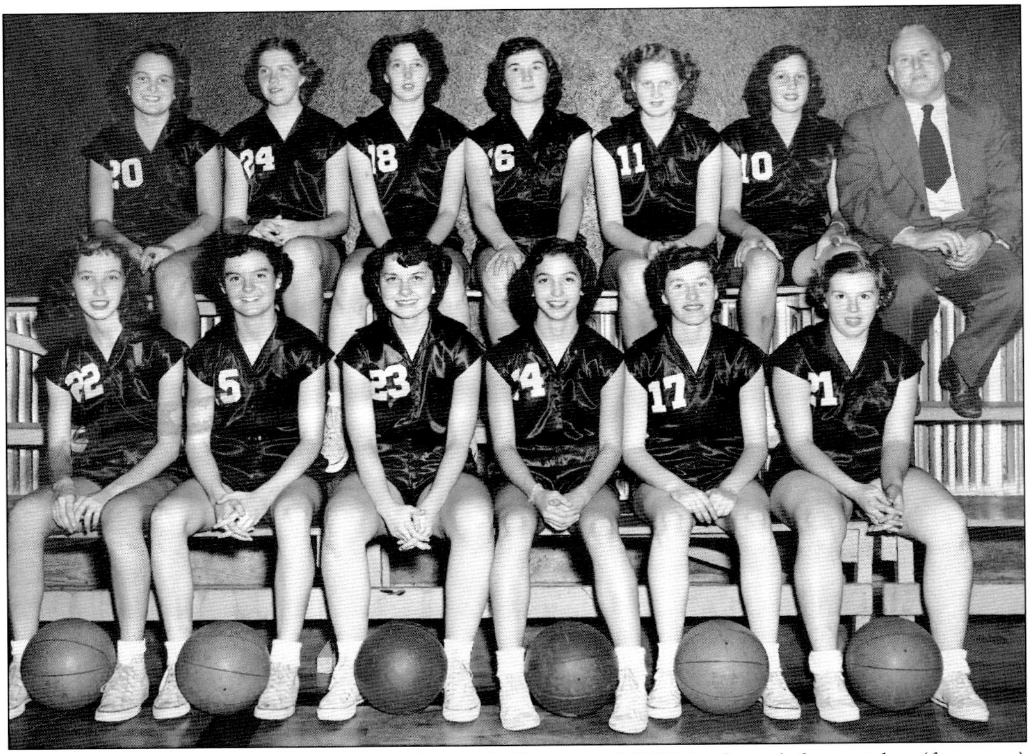

The Morristown High Hurricanettes basketball team of 1950 is, from left to right, (first row) Polly Atchley, Joan Whitley (captain), Betty Jean Buckner, Jennie Rhea Britton, Pat Lovette, and Shirley Smith; (second row) Bobbie Mayes, Betty Lynn Skeen, Hazel Rader, Imogene Duncan, Wanda Western, Shirley Pack, and Petie Siler (coach).

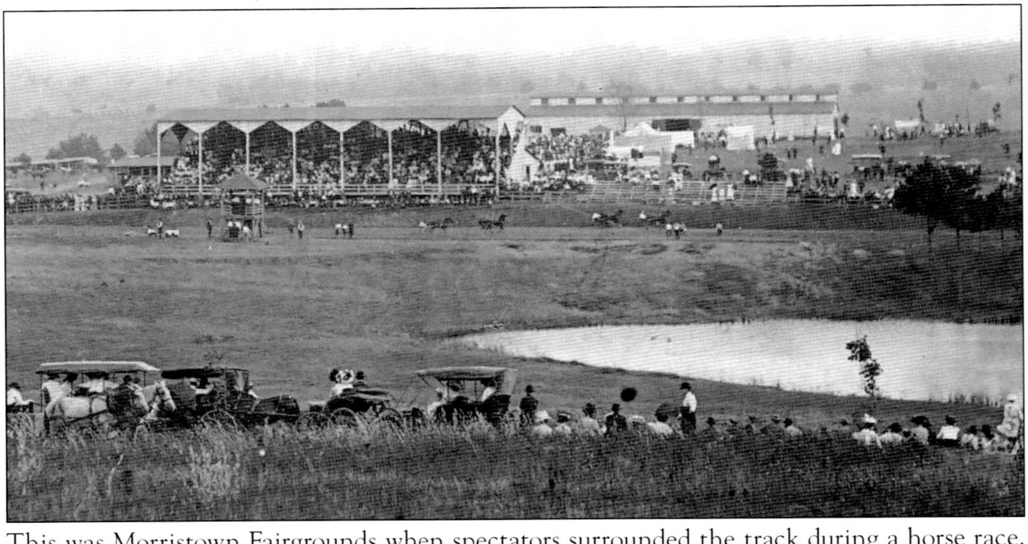

This was Morristown Fairgrounds when spectators surrounded the track during a horse race. Some fans watched in the comfort of the carriages on the hillside, while others looked on from the far-side grandstand near the judge's stand. The location of the fairgrounds was approximately at the corner of East Andrew Johnson Highway and North Haun Drive.

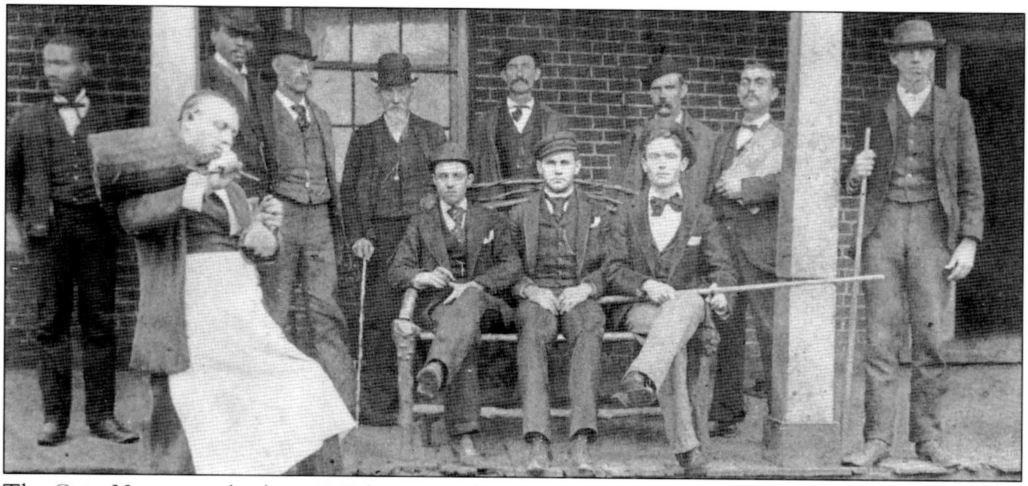

The Cain House was built in 1867 by C.C. Johnson and purchased by Thomas C. Cain in 1875. It stood on the corner of South Henry Street and the Southern Railway. The hotel was the scene of many political gatherings, and its lobby was used for many years as a waiting room for passengers traveling on the East Tennessee, Virginia & Georgia Railroad. The photograph was taken on the front porch of the hotel. The only two people identified in the photograph are Thomas C. Cain, with a white beard and walking stick, and Bill Franklin (far right), who ran the poolroom. Cain was elected and served eight years as Hamblen County Circuit Court clerk. The Cain House was destroyed by a fire on May 8, 1895.

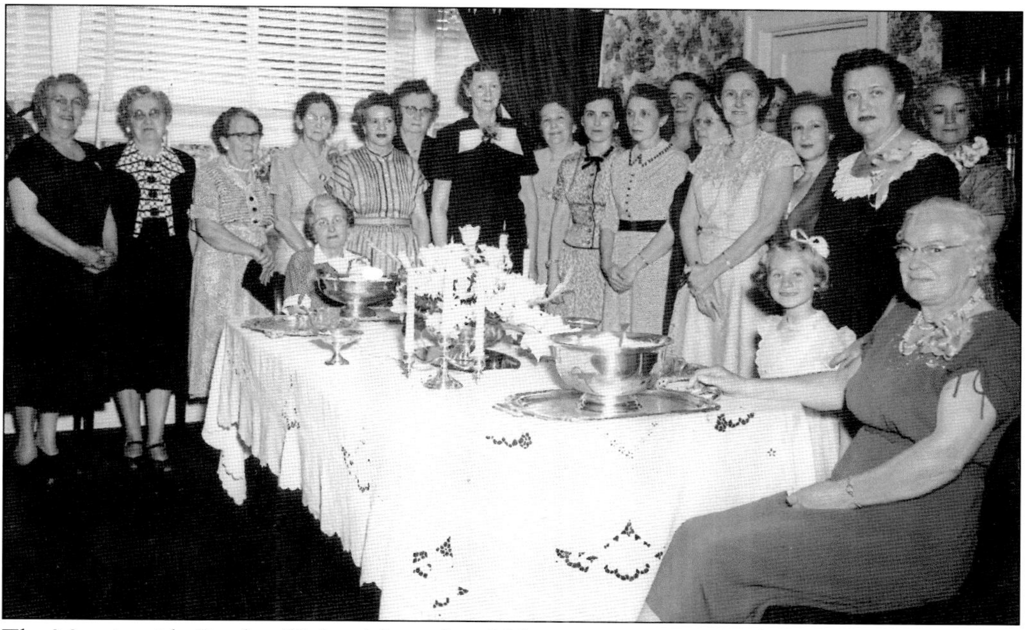

The Morningside Garden Club celebrated its 25th anniversary on April 18, 1955. Members who attended the open house at home of Agnes Hale are, from left to right, (seated) Glenn McCammon and Mae Baker; (standing) Mary Gentry, unidentified, Love Taylor, Margaret Yeary, Mildred Smith, Bessie Fort, Daisy Conner, Clara Emery, Carolyn Marshall, Frankie Byrd, Pauline James, Florence Heffner, Estelle Williams, Mary Ruth Tuttle, Nelle Lowry, Agnes Hale, and Annie Carter. Deborah Tuttle is the young girl.

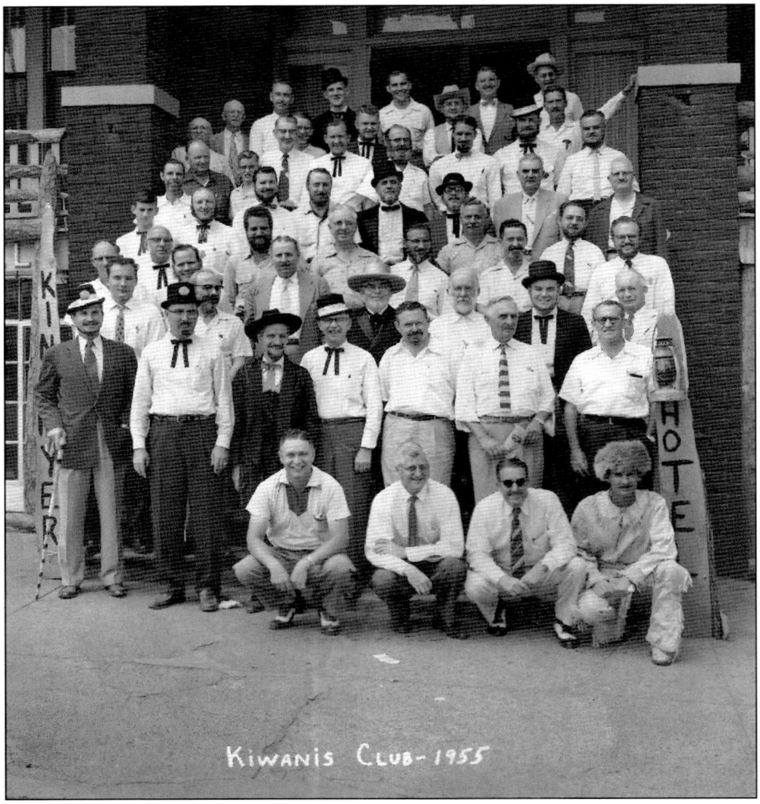

Kiwanis Club members are standing on the steps of the Mitchell Hotel during the 1955 Morristown centennial. The Morristown Kiwanis Club was organized in January 1920, with the main objective being civic betterment and the promotion of social relations. (Courtesy of Steve Litz.)

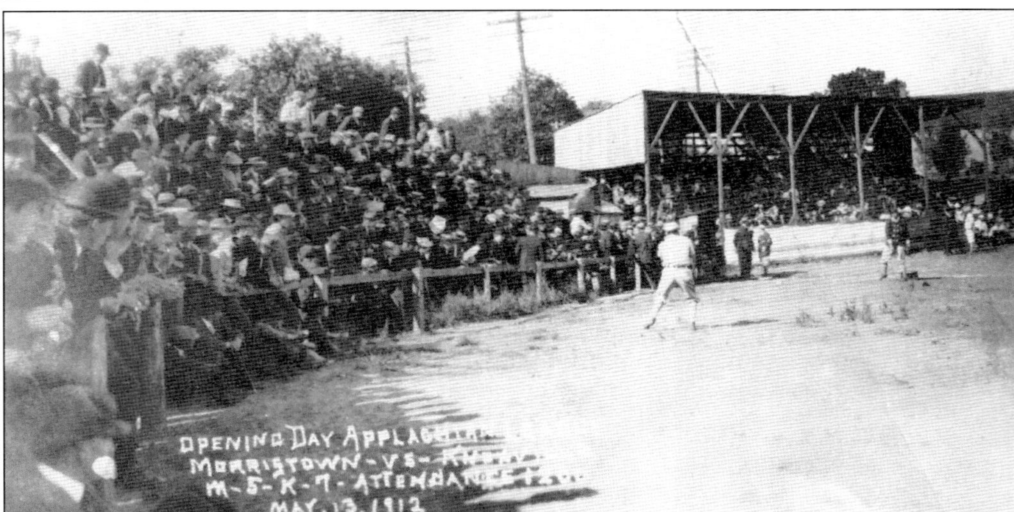

Morristown's professional baseball team was organized around 1910 in the Southeastern League, whose name changed to the Appalachian League a year later. The team had reached its pinnacle when this photograph was taken. On this opening day of the 1912 season at Sherwood Park, over 1,200 fans saw Morristown lose 7-5 to Knoxville. Morristown dropped out of the league after 1913, and the league was disbanded only to be reorganized several years later. Local backers included Jim Burke, Barto Fisher, and George W. Baker, but the team never proved to be a financial success.

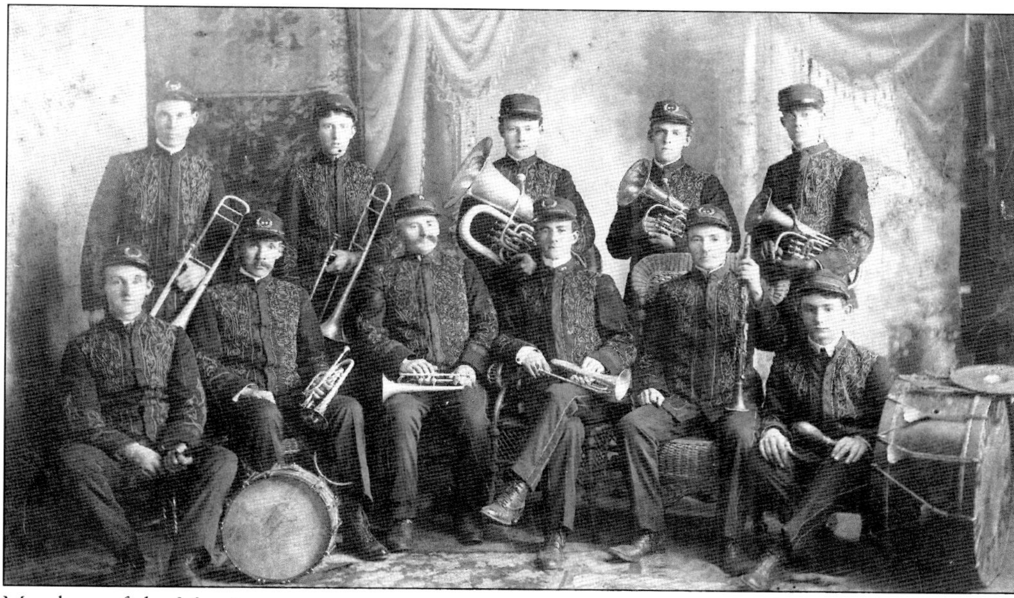

Members of the Morristown Brass Band in the 1900s are, from left to right, (first row) Chart Witt, Coy Willing, Ricky Furman, Charles Wylie, John Wagner, and Hub Witt; (second row) Jim Mathes, Bill Mathes, John Witt, Mort Williams, and Bob Mason.

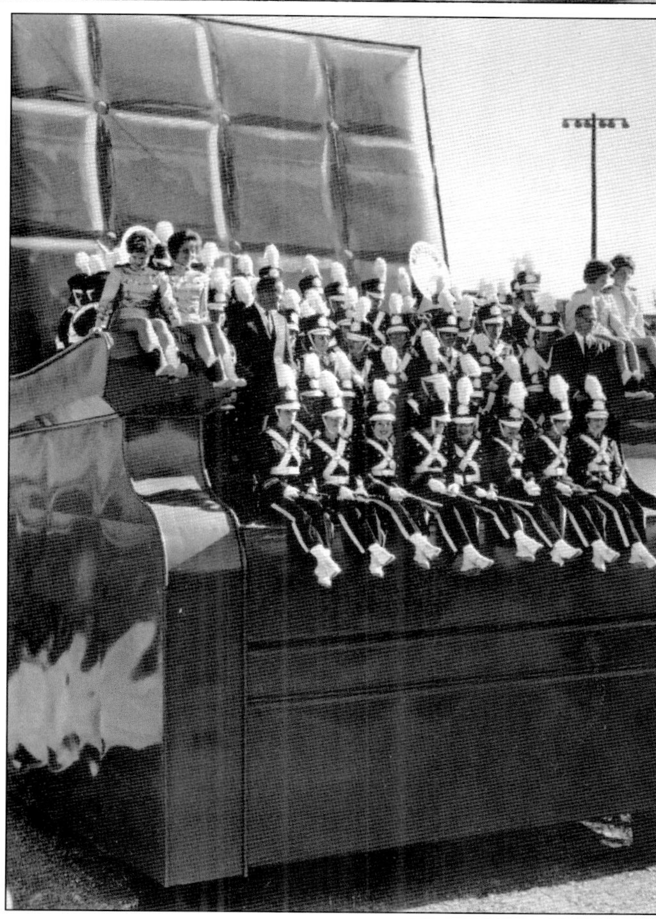

This famous Berkline chair provided seating for the entire membership of the Morristown High School Band at the dedication of the new Berkline office building. The chair, made of sheet metal and painted bright green, for a short time was the world's largest chair measuring, 20 feet tall, and it was located at the intersection of Morris Boulevard and Liberty Hill Road.

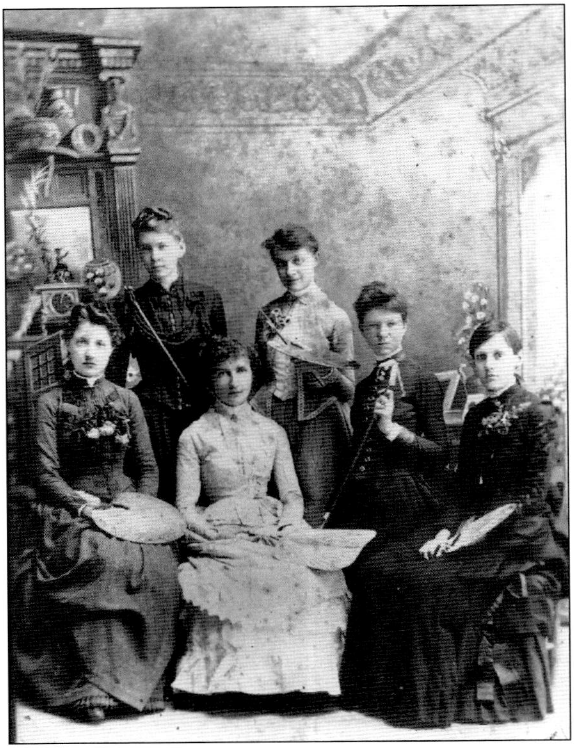

Members of Miss Tipton's art class from around the 1890s are, from left to right, (sitting) Ida VanHuss, Miss Tipton (teacher), Jennie Whiteside, and Cora Davis (local historian); (standing) Nell Harle and Lily Rose.

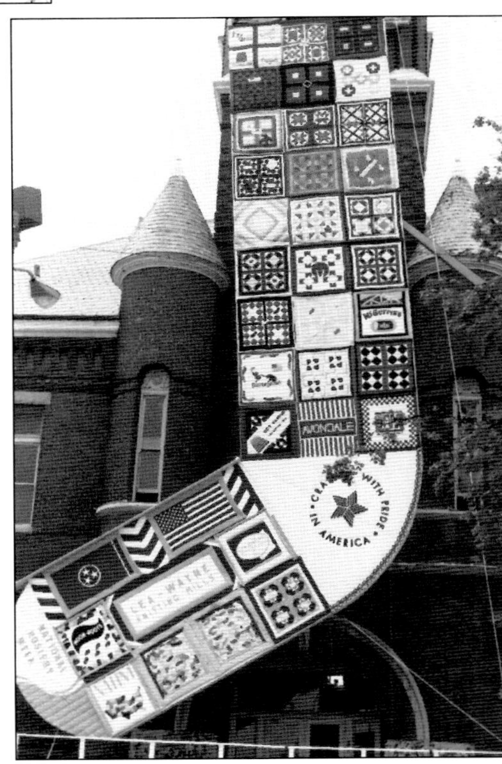

The world's largest sock, sponsored by Lea Wayne Kitting Mills, was presented during the 1987 National Hosiery Week Celebration at the Rose Center. More than 40 Tennessee hosiery mills banded together to help create a sock that was over 65 feet tall and over 12 feet wide. Each mill made a four-foot square, and Lea-Wayne Knitting Mills was responsible for stitching all the pieces together. It was so heavy that it needed the assistance of a crane to raise it for its unveiling.

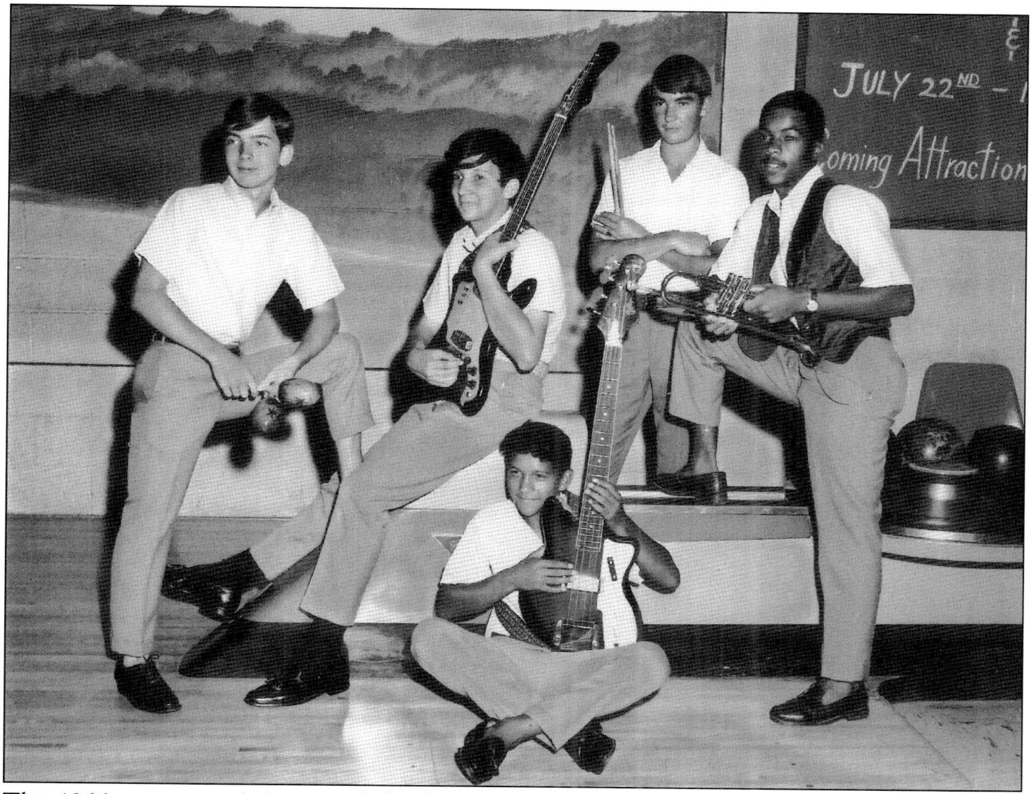

This 1966 promotional photograph for the new Morristown bowling alley featured the Corbatas; members are, from left to right, Randy Goan, B.J. Smith, Joe Senter (sitting) Junior Howell, and Alvin Nichols. They were one of the hottest high school bands in the region, winning several battles of the bands and playing many gatherings in the area. The Corbatas made appearances on the *Cas Walker Farm and Home Hour*, in conjunction with Dolly Parton during the 1967 Downtown Skywalk dedication ceremony, and opening for Janis Joplin at the Tennessee Valley Fair when she sang with Big Brother and the Holding Company. (Courtesy of Joe Senter.)

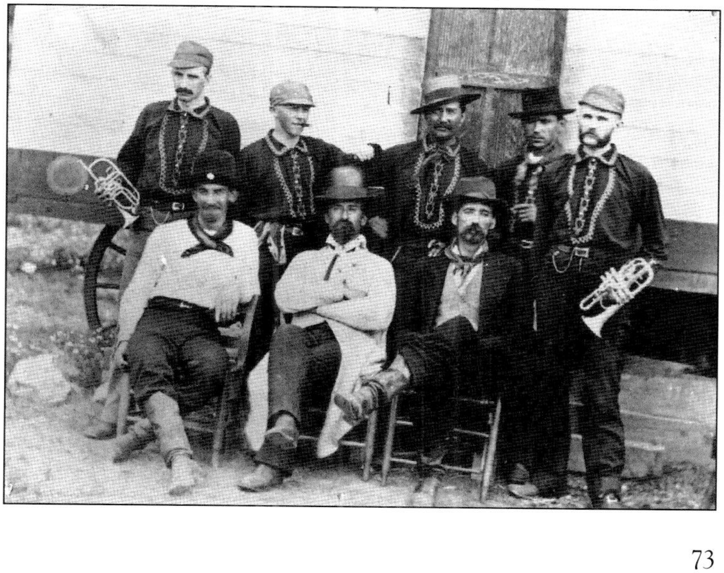

In 1879, the Morristown Beaux prepared for a two-week trip by covered hack to Mount Mitchell, North Carolina. Pictured are, from left to right, (sitting) George R. Stuart, Joe Stubblefield, and Mel Shannon; (standing) George Andes, Oscar Hammond, Nathan Stubblefield, unidentified, and Ed J. Wells. George R. Stuart later became a well-known Methodist minister.

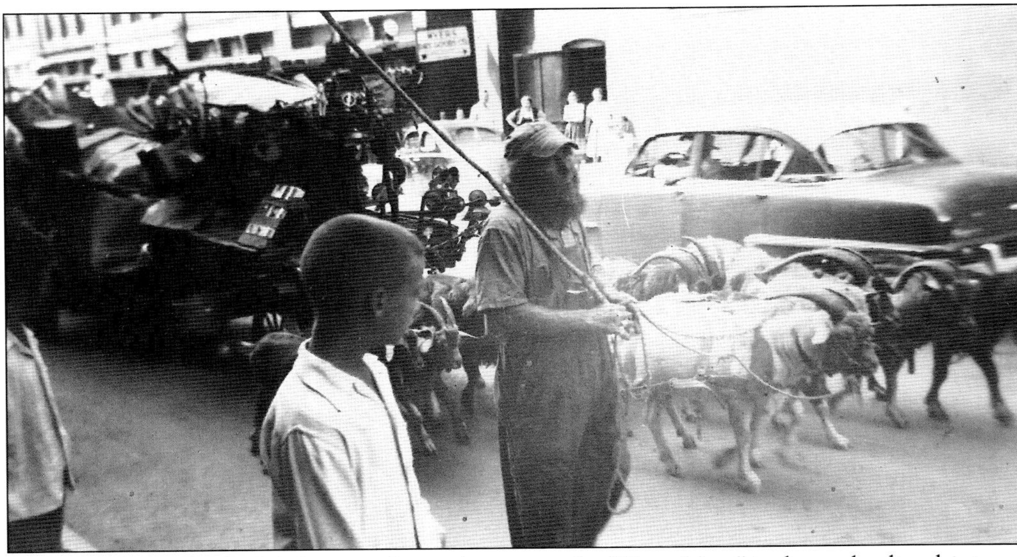

The legendary Charles McCartney, better known as the "Goat Man," is shown leading his team during one of his visits through the area. Charles was a wanderer who spent decades traveling across the country while guiding a massive iron-wheeled wagon led by a team of goats and loaded with pots and pans, pails, bales of hay, and car tags. From 1930 to 1987, legend has it that he walked 100,000 miles, preaching the gospel in 49 states.

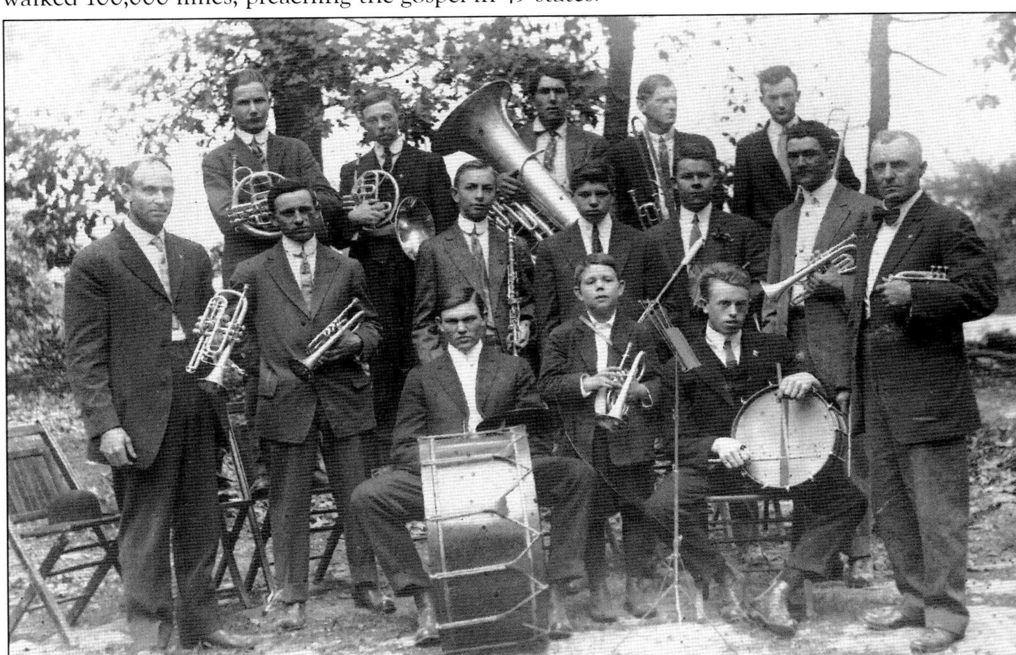

Morristown Brass Band members from around 1912 are photographed as follows, from left to right: (first row) Carl Akers (with brass drum), Curtis Wagner, and Paul Horner; (second row) Mr. Warren, Jim Tyler, Deony Williams, Boots Hisey, Hugh Little, Park Prince, and John Wagner (director); (third row) Eugene Smith, Lee Waddell, Lawrence Dukes, Bert Williams, and Hal A. Noe (Morristown historian).

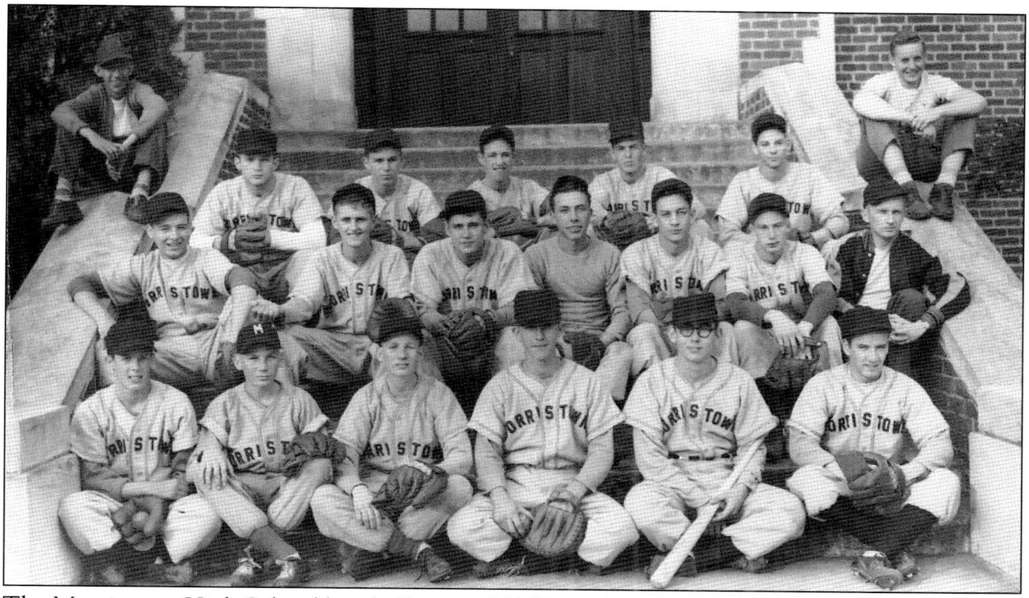

The Morristown High School baseball team of 1950 are, from left to right: (first row) Paul Bruce, Billy Ray, Jerry Ray, Douglas Sykes, Donald Martin, and Floyd Covington; (second row) G.W. Noe, Stancil Ford, Wade Cowan, Harold Rouse, Kenneth Lingerfelt, Wayne Bishop, and coach Bill Keezel; (third row) Marvin Williams (manager), Jack Cunningham, W.C. Martin, Charles Jenkins, Curtis Dalton, Monty Stiles, and Louis Robertson (manager). (Courtesy of Wanda and Ginger Cowan.)

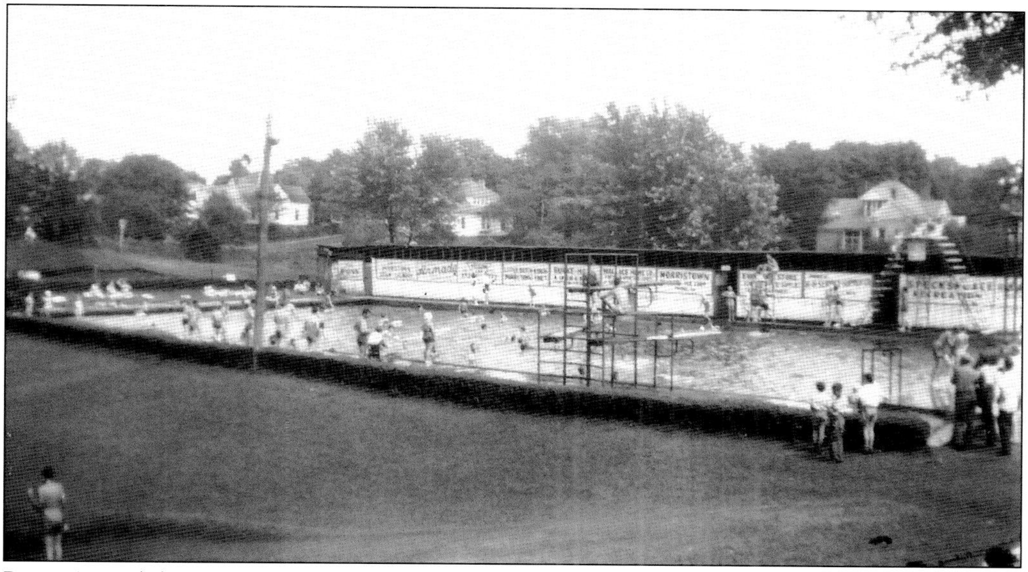

Peneto's Pool, better known as Petie's Pool, was a favorite summertime hangout, and the only community swimming pool in the area for many years. It was owned and operated by famed local coach Petie Siler and his wife, Monnie. A contest was run in the local paper to name the community pool. The winner was a woman who wrote two letters from the names of three prominent community members: Petie Siler, Neil B. Mim, and Robert Tony Hill. "Pe" is for Petie Siler, "Ne" for Neil B. Mims, and "To" for Robert Tony Hill.

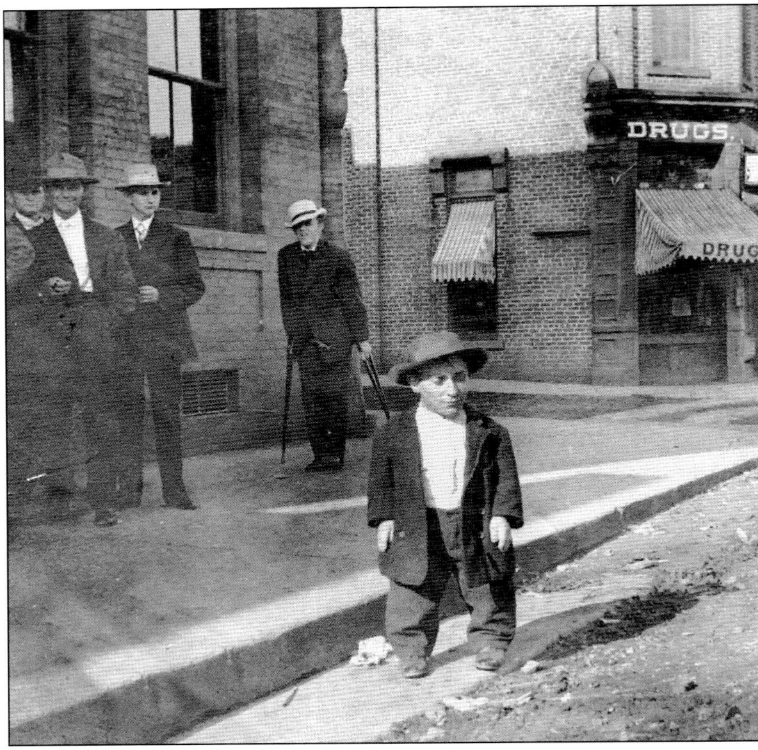

Claud Mallicote, a pint-sized personality originally from Grainger County, came to Morristown around 1912 and joined the sideshow of the John Robinson Circus. He remained with the circus for many years and posed for this photograph in front of the Merchants Bank on the corner of Main and Henry Streets with the Drugs sign from the Corner Drug Store in the background.

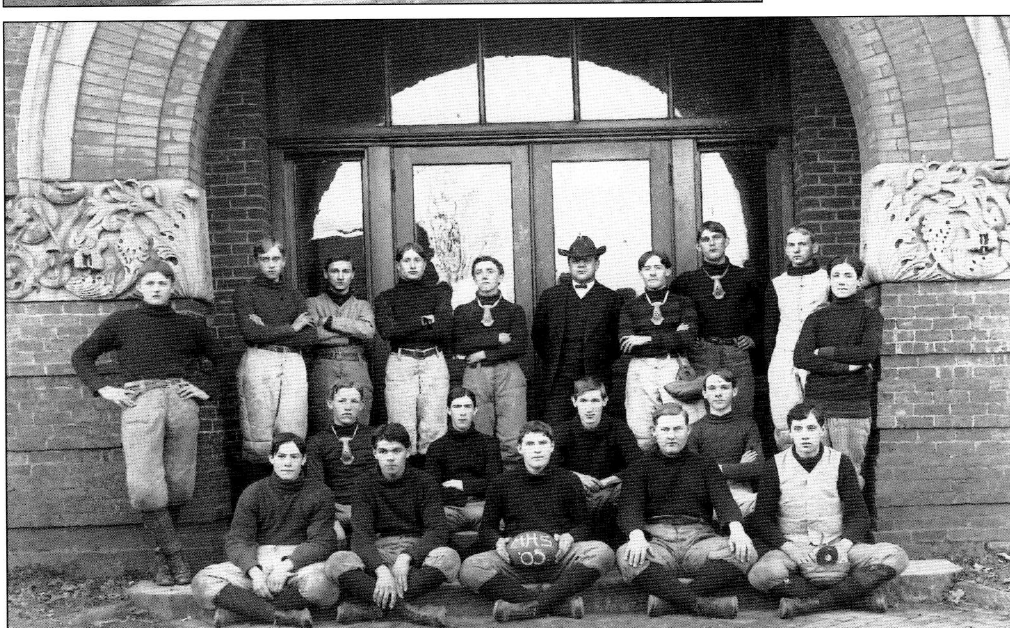

The Morristown High School football team members of 1905 are, from left to right, (seated) Reives Rice, Marvin Lotspeich, Paul Converse, ? Allen, Bob Bettis, John Rhea, Phil Morelock, James Lotspeich, and Dick Richardson; (standing) Austin Smith, Oscar Rucker, Dave Noe, unidentified, Claude Rogers, Professor Heatwold, Jim Burke, Ed Myers, ? Rhea, and Bill John Donaldson.

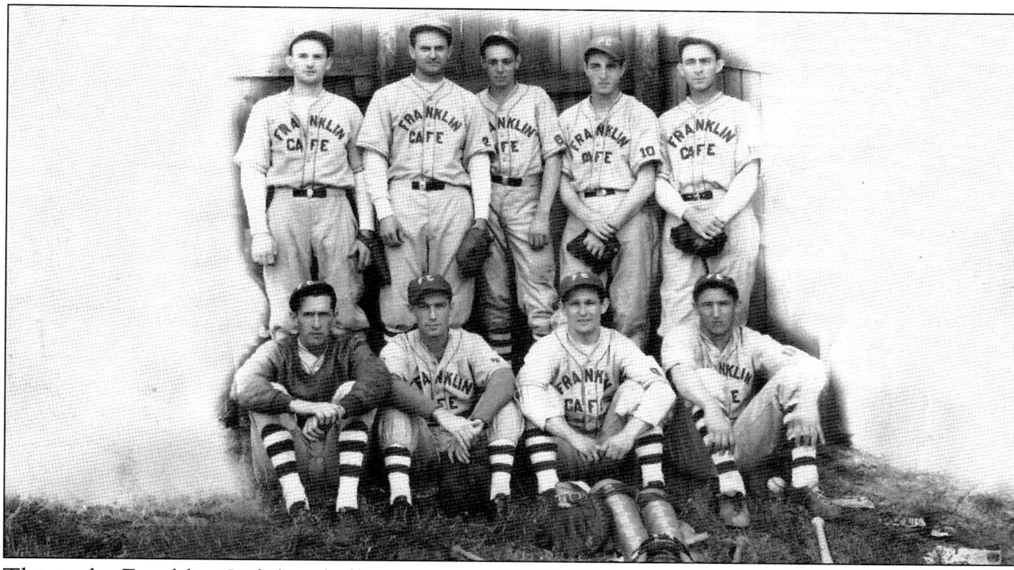

This is the Franklin Café baseball team around 1938. This was part of the four-team Morristown City Baseball League consisting of Berkline Corporation, managed by Lewis Parker; Little Dutch, managed by C. Frank Davis; and the Coca-Cola plant, managed by Dale Amos. The only person identified in the photograph is Franklin Café manager Ethern Turner, first row second from the left. It was common practice, as it is today, for teams to be sponsored by local businesses. (Courtesy of Harve Turner.)

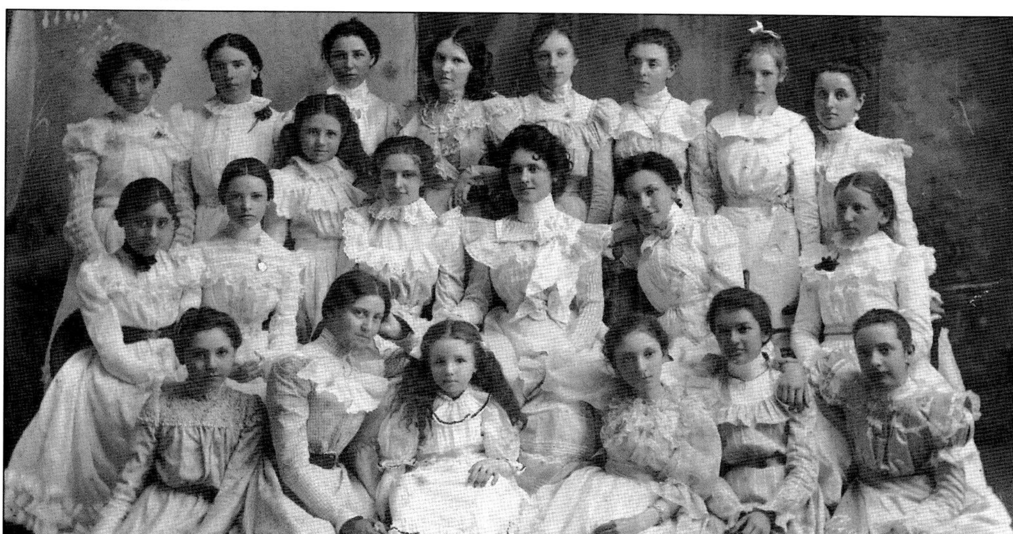

Students from Katherine King Davis's music class posed for this May 5, 1900, photograph. Katherine Davis studied piano at the Cincinnati Conservatory of Music and became the first organist at All Saints' Episcopal Church. Her students are, from left to right, (first row) Mary Brown, Effie Goodson, Pauline Mathes, Mamie Donaldson, Nell Wilkinson, and Willie M. Lilly; (second row) Nele Jarnagin, Daisy Hasson, Pearl Mathes, Mattie Davis, Katherine King Davis, Ethel Murphey, and Josephine Bell; (third row) Nannie Kimbrough, Susan Bell, Mattie Groves, Bess Shields, Carrie Craft, Rose Long, Meta Goodson, and Eliza Scruggs.

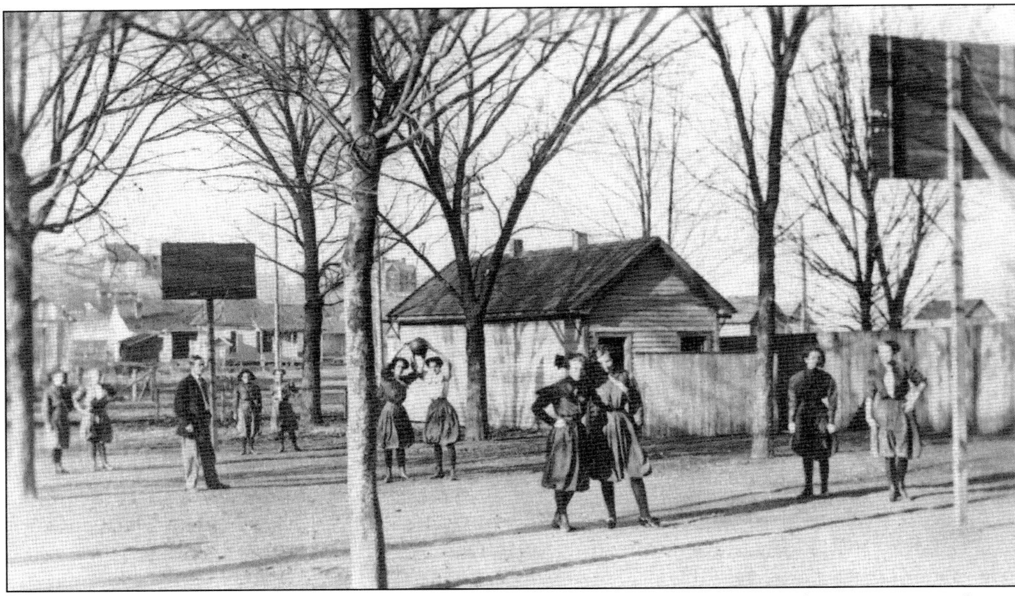

Pictured here is a basketball game at Morristown High School in 1909. The two teams shown playing outdoors near the rear of the school are, from left to right, Penelope Lotspeich, Lillie Myers, Feamster Taylor (referee), Annie Legg, Ellen Taylor, Salina McFarland, Katherine Taylor, J. Grant, Margaret Deadrick, Ema Jones, and Fay Grigsby. Boys were not permitted to stay around to watch the girls play, with the penalty being a visit to the professor's office.

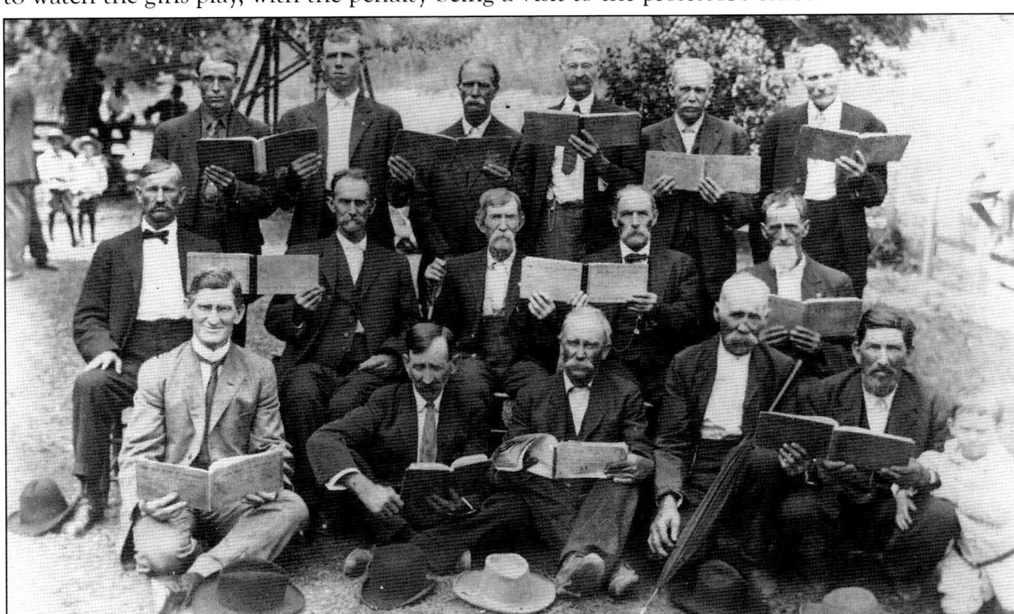

Hamblen Old Harp Singers met at Sulphur Springs Campground in the early 1900s. The members pictured, are left to right (first row) John Loop, Mr. Haun, Ned Mefford, Senter Smith, and Porter Nolan; (second row) W.P. Meacham, John Catron, Houston Williams, Mr. Dalton, and Will Rightsell; (third row) Charles Mefford, Marion Croxdale, John Simmons, Mr. Proctor, John Mefford, and Millard Hodge.

Six

A Bird's-Eye View

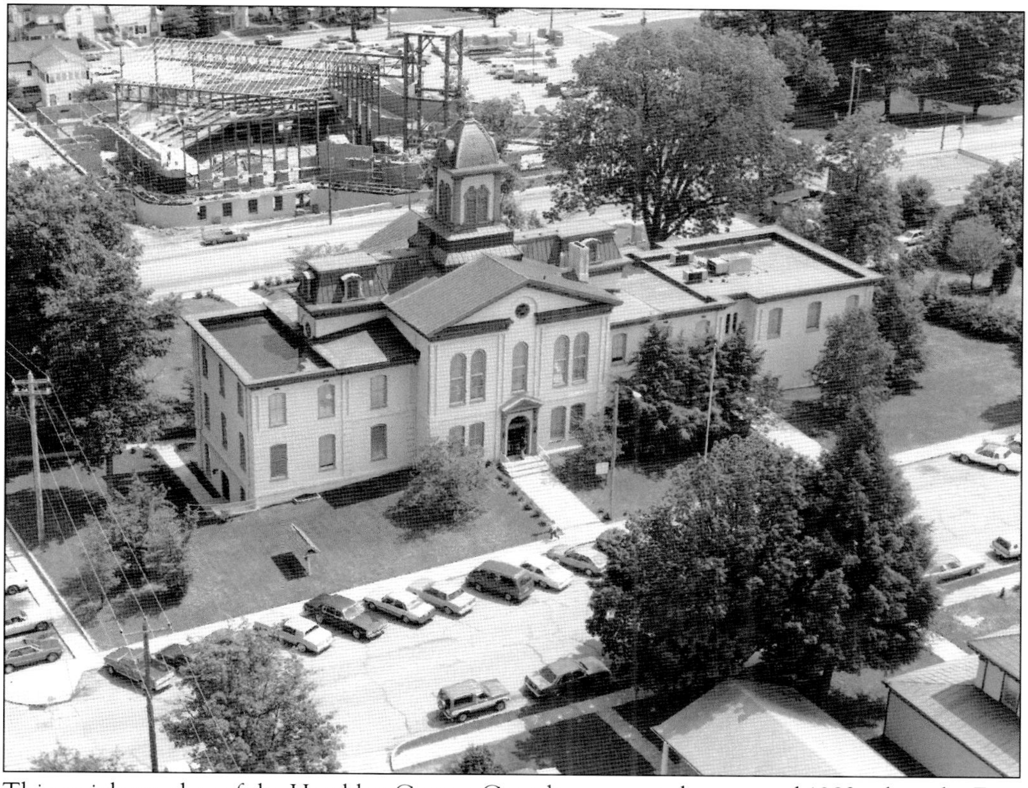

This aerial snapshot of the Hamblen County Courthouse was taken around 1983, when the First Baptist Church was in the process of building a 1,400-seat worship center. The courthouse, designed by famed architect Alexander Campbell Bruce, was completed in 1874 at a total cost of $21,750. The builders were George W. Folsom and John Murphy. This photograph shows the wings that were added in the early 1950s. Not shown is the 1999 three-story office building addition. The courthouse is listed in the National Register of Historic Places. (Courtesy of Eddie R. Davis.)

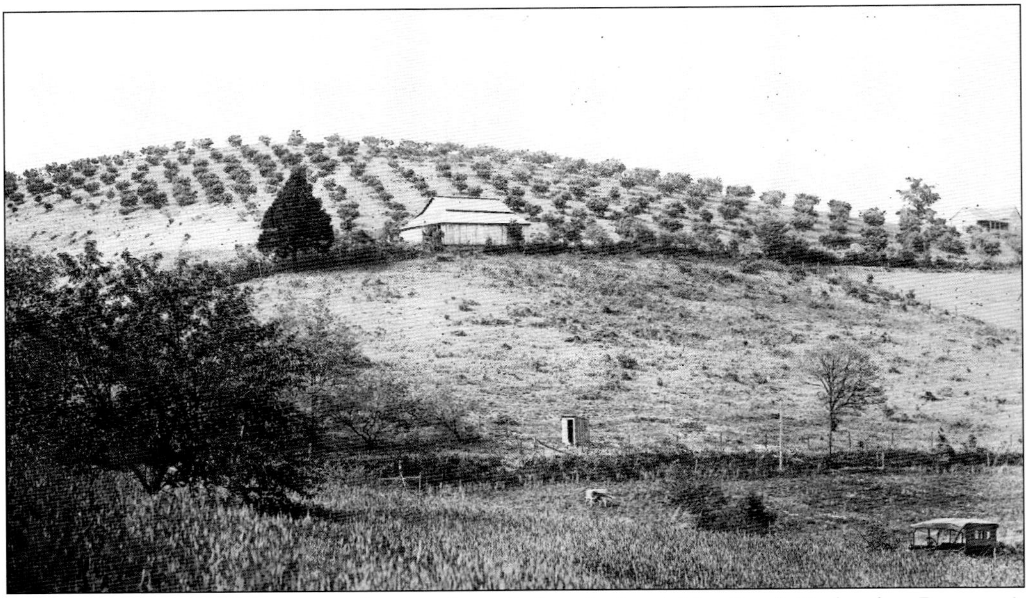

For many generations, Morristown families depended on the Lewis Noe Peach Orchard on Boatman's Mountain in northern Hamblen County. The orchard was later windswept and destroyed. A 57-acre estate and a large gated housing development in the area bear the name "Windswept."

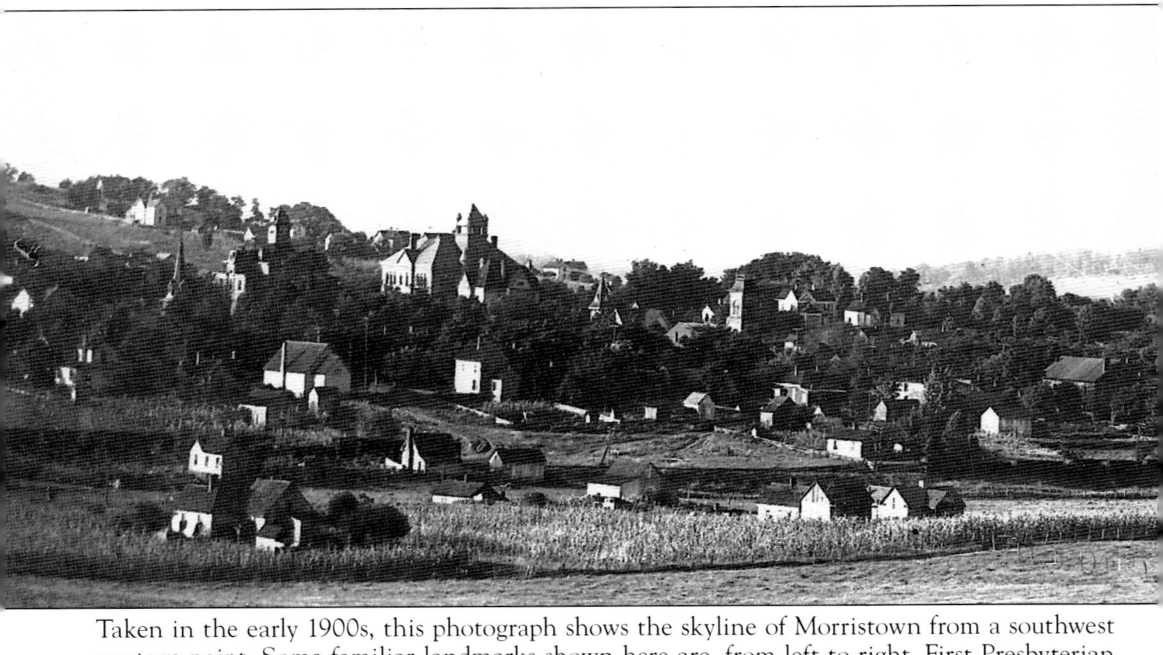

Taken in the early 1900s, this photograph shows the skyline of Morristown from a southwest vantage point. Some familiar landmarks shown here are, from left to right, First Presbyterian Church, built in 1870; Hamblen County Courthouse, built in 1874; Rose School, later called the Rose Center; Centenary Methodist Church, built in 1886; First Baptist Church, built in 1871;

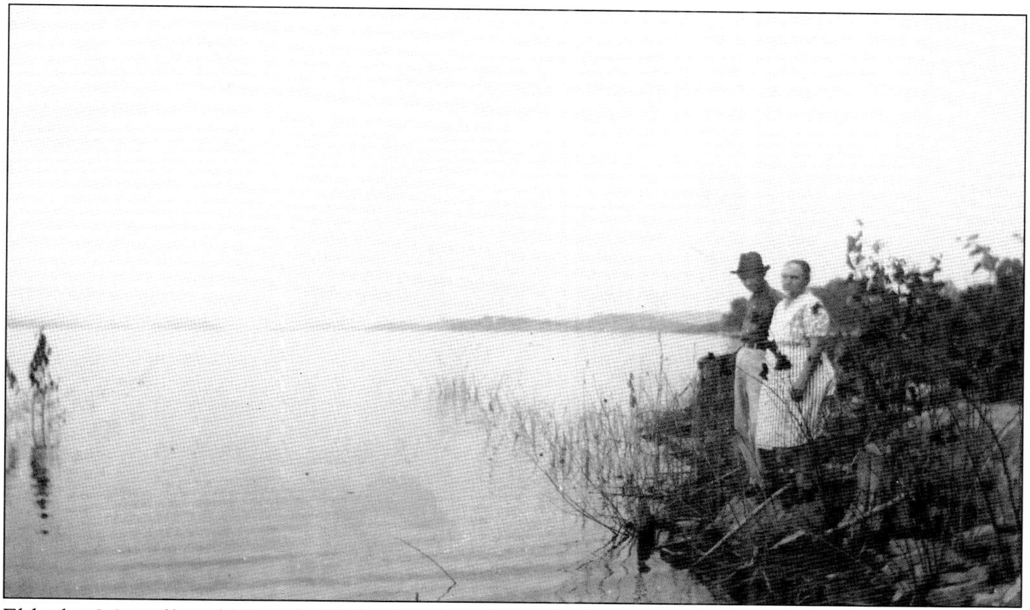

Eldridge Murrell and his wife, Della, lived in the Kidwell's Ridge community. They are seen here watching the water of the Holston River flood their property with the forming of the Cherokee Dam in the 1940s. This scene was repeated hundreds of times as 875 families had to be relocated during this period. (Courtesy of Billie D. Loveday.)

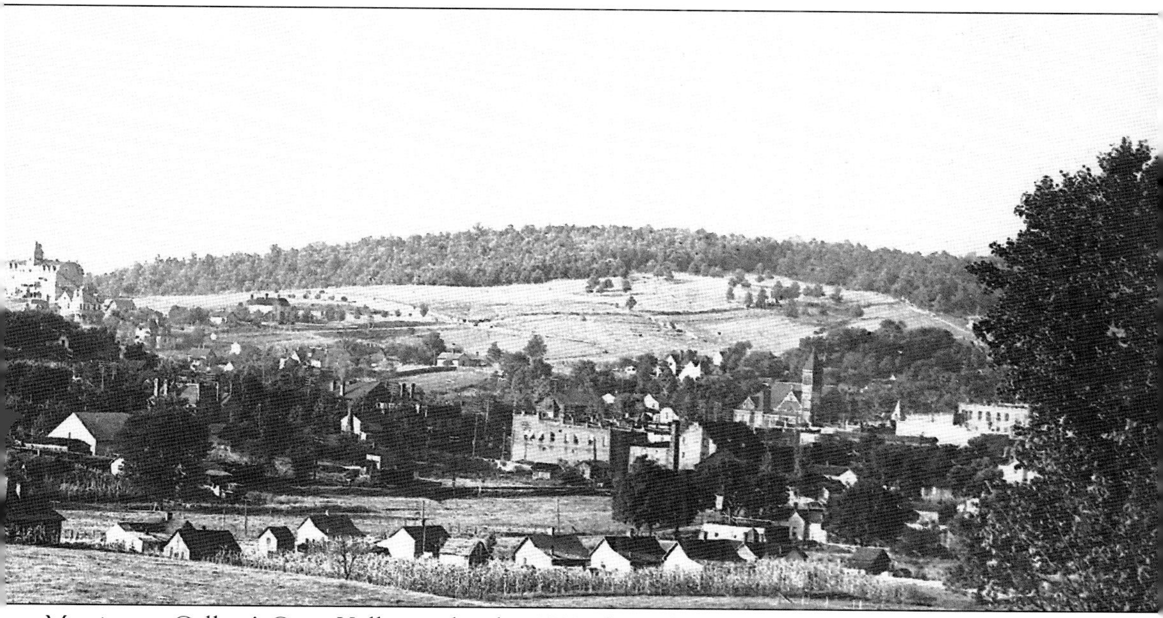

Morristown College's Crary Hall, completed in 1898 after eight years of construction and destroyed by fire in January 1921; the Big House, home to Morristown College founder Judson S. Hill; City Cemetery; and First United Methodist Church, built in 1902.

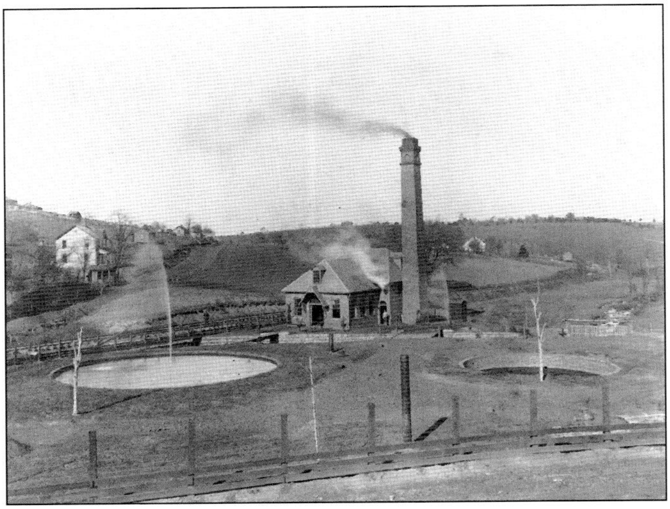

Completed in 1896, this was Morristown's first public water utility. Coal was used to generate the power required to pump water up to an open reservoir from Bethel Springs. In 1901, five years after the water utility was formed, the electric utility was established. The road (left) is today's Cherokee Drive.

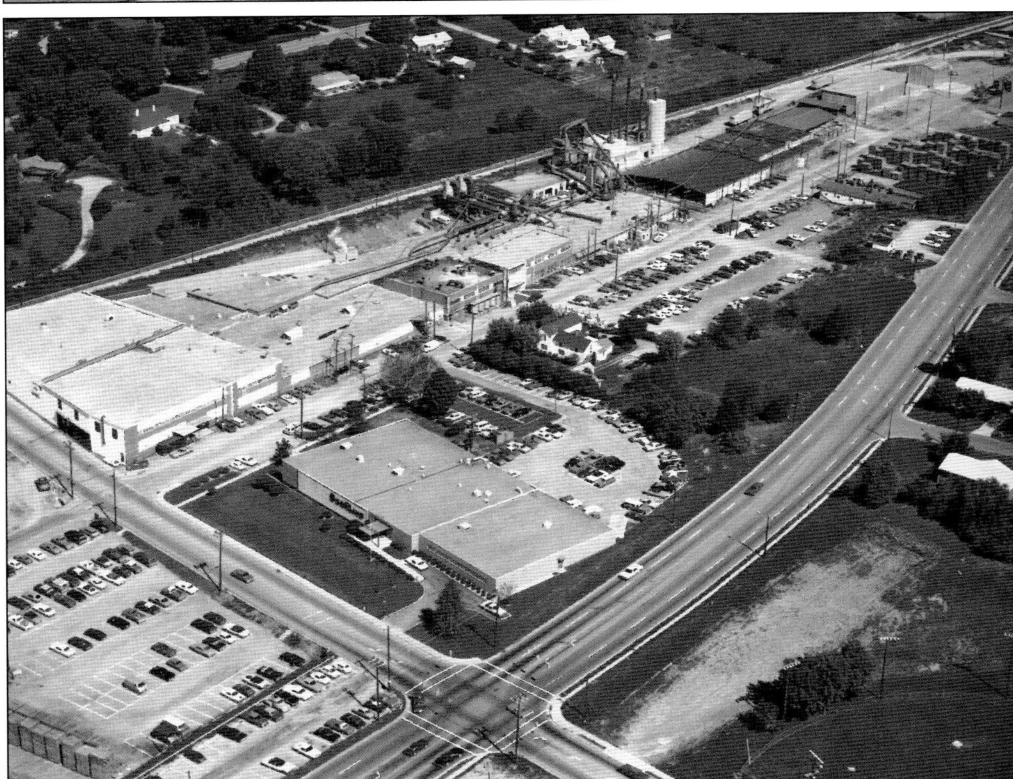

Berkline Corporation, which closed in 2011, was a prosperous institution in Morristown for 74 years. Jacob Popkin founded the company, which originally started in Springfield, Massachusetts, in 1928. With 10,000 square feet of space and 18 employees, Popkin expanded operations to Morristown in 1937. All of manufacturing moved to Morristown in 1941, when the Massachusetts plant closed. By 1966, the company had acquired an office building and two additional plants for an approximate total of 385,000 square feet of workspace. Throughout its life, the company faced several ownership changes.

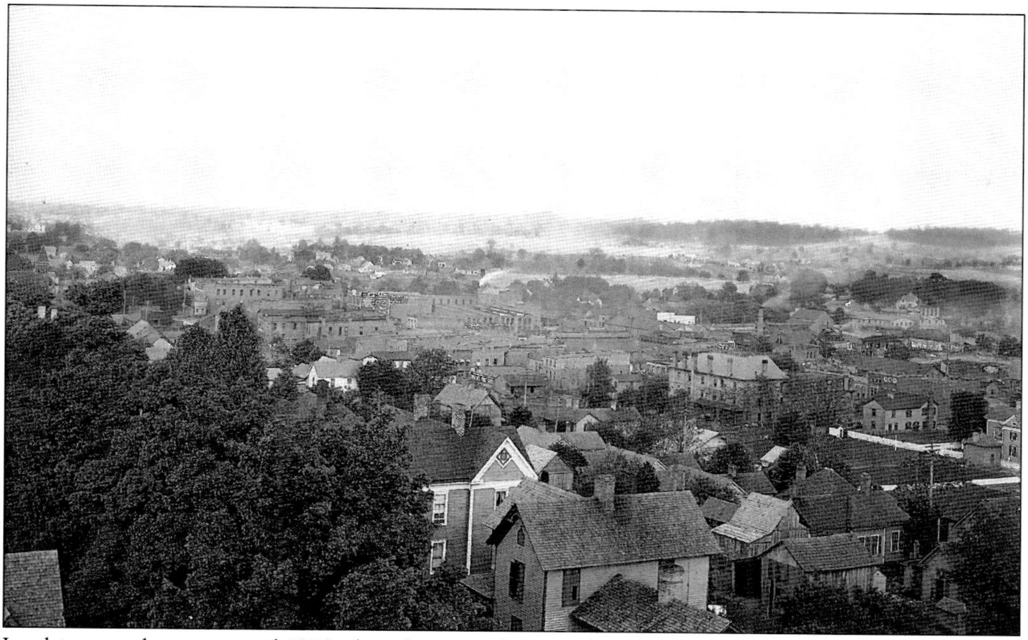

Looking southeast around 1893, this photograph was taken from the cupola of Rose School, now the Rose Center. The rear of the three-story Virginia Hotel can be seen in the right center. It was located on the site of today's Millennium Square. The building to the right of the hotel was the Read Home, which later became the Hodges Hotel. The home on the right, near the photograph's edge, was the home of William S. Myers and is now the site of Wilmyer Court.

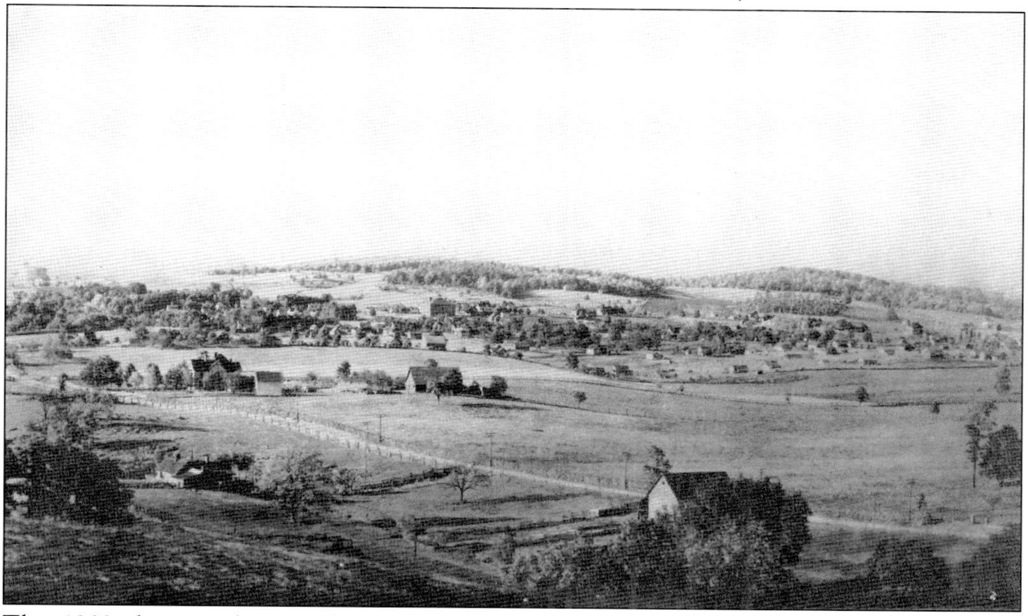

This 1902 photograph was taken of Morristown from the southern part of town, near Cold Springs. The Roberts School, completed in 1901 on East First North Street, can be seen in the top center. In the far left corner is Morristown College's Crary Hall. The two-story home of the Forgey family is located at left center.

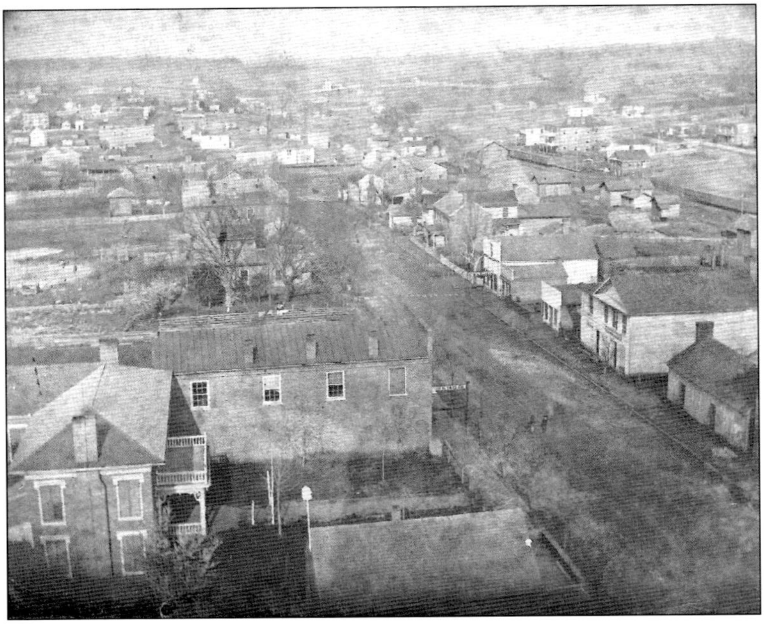

One year prior to Hamblen County being formed, T.H. Lindsey took this photograph from the tower of the newly built First Baptist Church in 1871, looking eastward toward downtown. During this period, the majority of businesses were located on West Main Street between Jackson and Mill Streets.

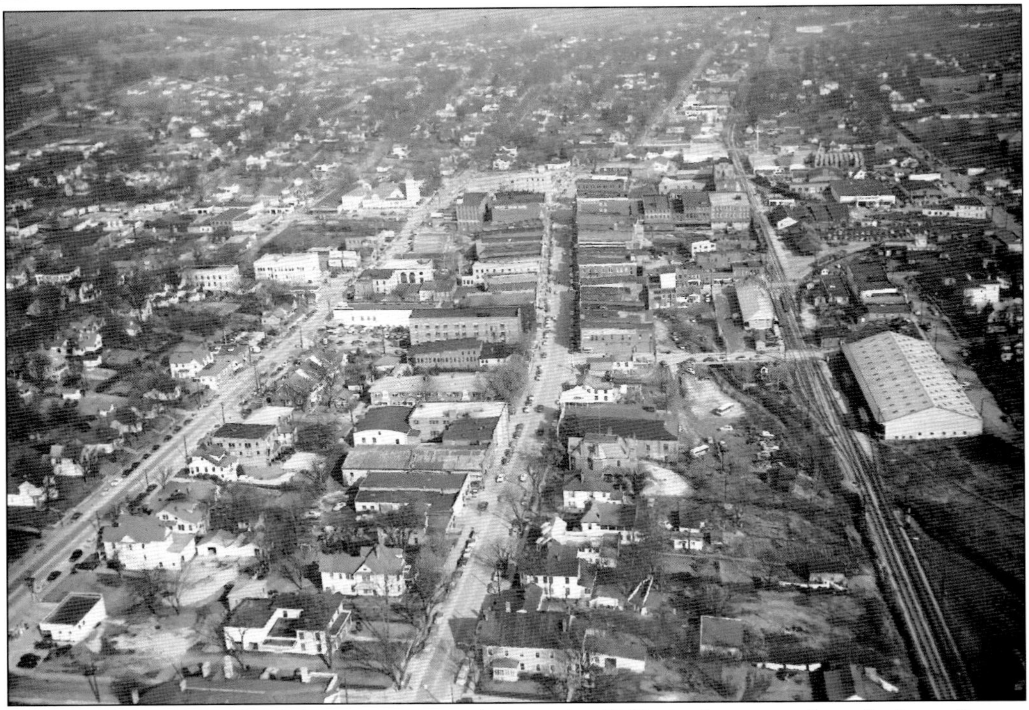

This aerial photograph of downtown was taken in the 1950s looking east from Jackson Street. The vantage point is higher and more southerly than the photograph above, but it shows the same area along Main Street (center) and the railroad (right) only 70 years later. Most of the 1871 homes and businesses were gone, with one exception—the two-story brick home of Maj. John Murphy. In the 1950s, this home was being used as Brooks Mortuary, and today it is home to Mayes Family Services. (Courtesy of Jeffrey Allen Hurd.)

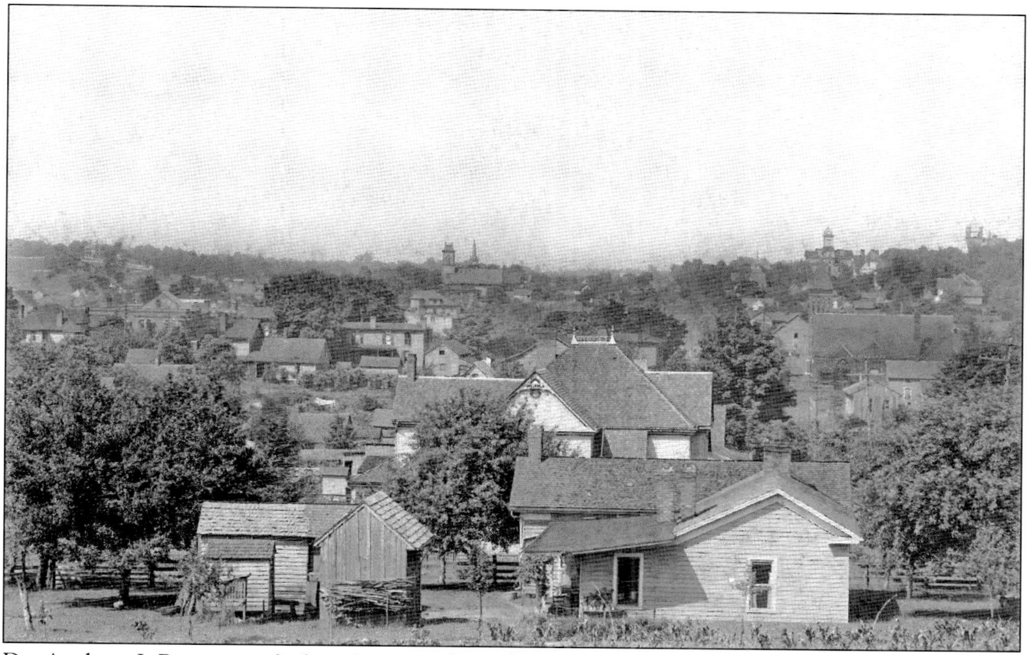

Dr. Andrew J. Bruner took this photograph in the early 1900s. Looking west, it appears to have been taken from the window of the Roberts School, located on East First North Street. In the distance (upper right), the cupola of Rose School, now the Rose Center, can be seen. To the left is the Hamblen County Courthouse, and farther left are the steeples of the First Presbyterian Church and the First Baptist Church. The First Methodist Episcopal Church, South, now First United Methodist, can be seen just below the courthouse.

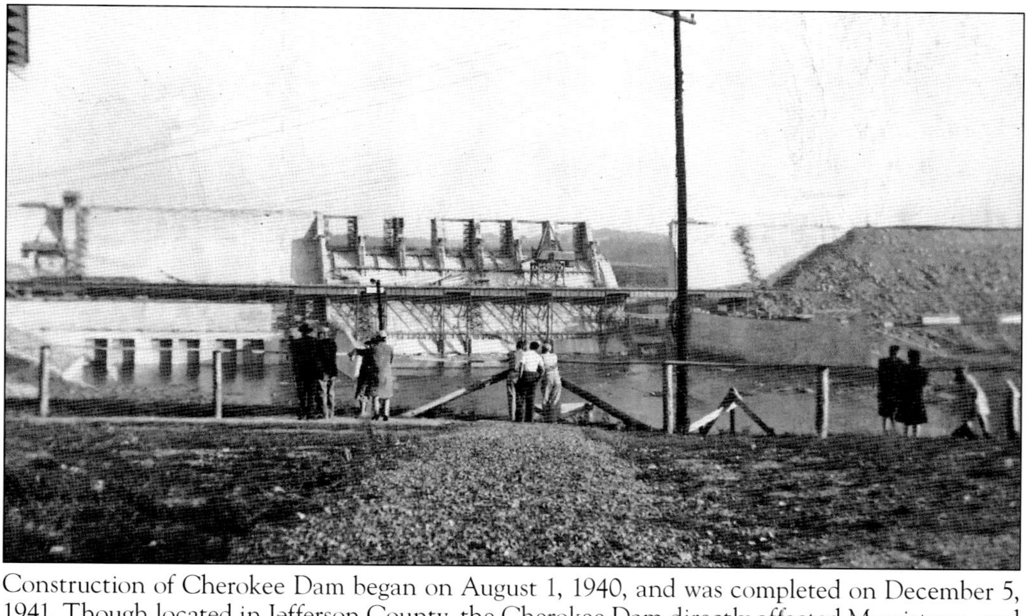

Construction of Cherokee Dam began on August 1, 1940, and was completed on December 5, 1941. Though located in Jefferson County, the Cherokee Dam directly affected Morristown and Hamblen County. Among those watching the progress of the dam's construction are Walter Smith, Henry Smith, and Horace Mayes. (Courtesy of Billie D. Loveday.)

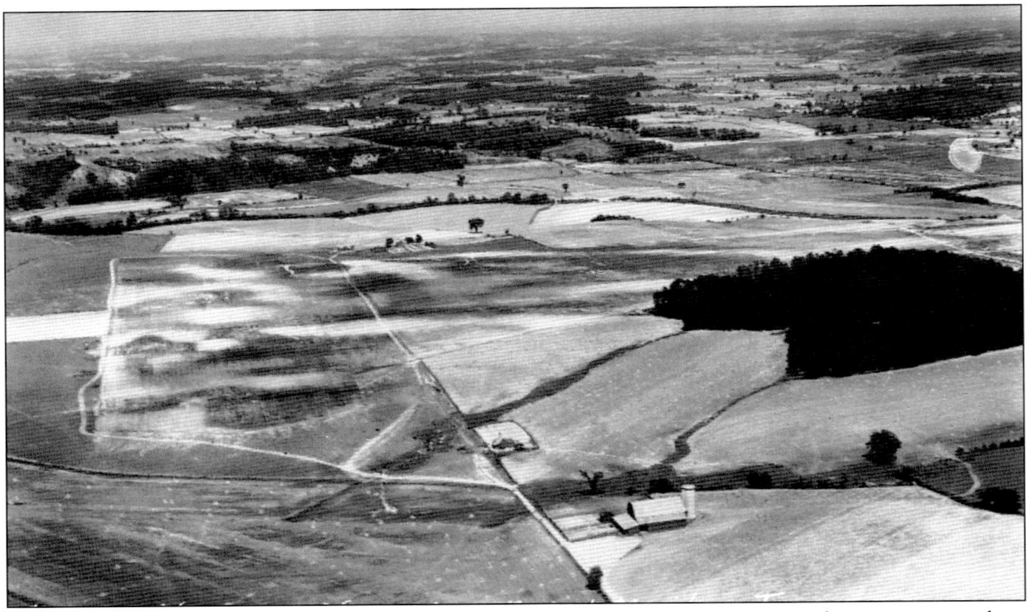

This aerial photograph showing the Moore-Murrell Airport and the surrounding area was taken in 1936. Named Murrell Field in honor of Rev. Melville M. Murrell, the airport was officially dedicated on September 7, 1953. With approximately 3,000 people in attendance, it was one of the largest crowds to gather in Hamblen County and the largest ever to greet an airport dedication in Tennessee. (Courtesy of Tennessee State Library and Archives.)

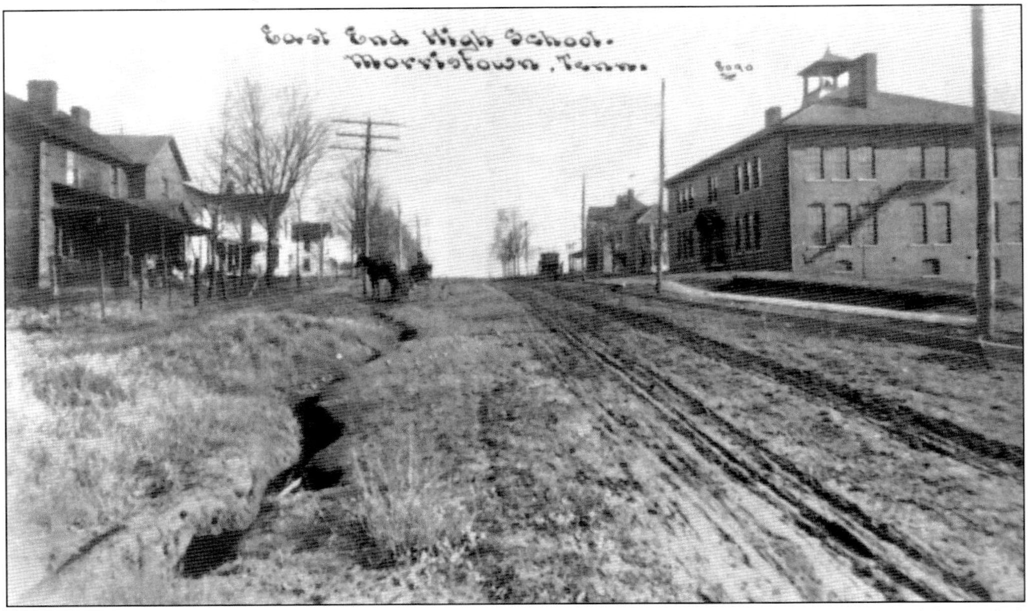

This photograph of East First North Street was taken shortly after the East End School (at right) was erected in 1901. In honor of Marion Roberts, the school's name was changed in 1910 to the Roberts School. James Franklin Goodson, the founder of JFG Coffee Company, lived in the house just beyond the Roberts School (second from right). Both of these buildings are still standing today. East First North Street, however, is much nicer today than it was in the early 1900s.

Seven

Hometown Heroes

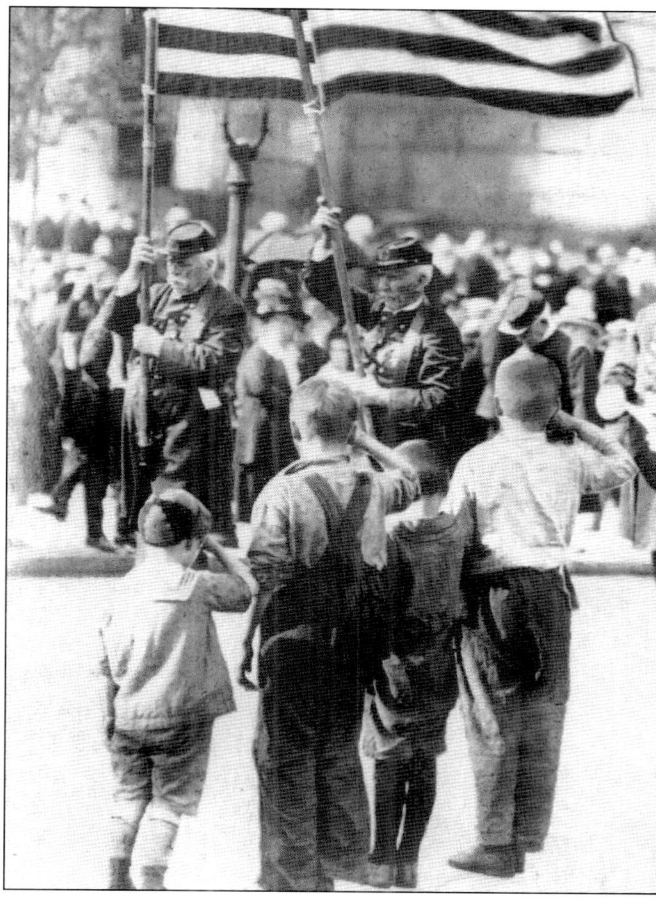

These veterans marched in Morristown's annual Memorial Day Parade while wearing Civil War uniforms and carrying US flags. The boys saluting them are, from left to right, unidentified, Jimmy Mayes, Tip Mayes, and J.C. Mayes. (Courtesy of Billie D. Loveday.)

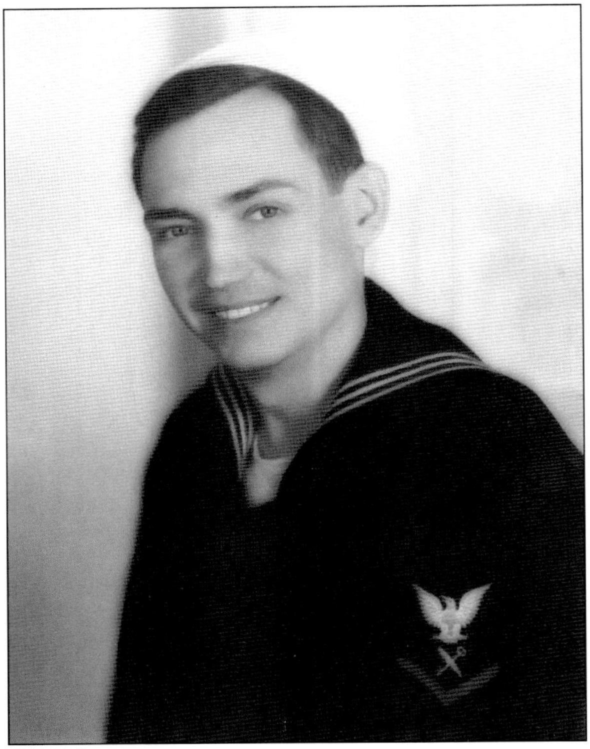

Morris Emerson Livingston was born on November 25, 1917, to Thomas L. and Lucy M. Livingston. He served his career in the US Navy, where he was awarded medals such as: National Defense Service, American Campaign, Asiatic-Pacific Campaign, World War II Victory and Navy Occupation, and Good Conduct. Livingston passed away on June 4, 1965, in Chatham County, Georgia, and was laid to rest in the Livingston family cemetery. (Courtesy of Doris Livingston Stump.)

Edward "Eddie" Haywood Julian enlisted as a Navy apprentice seaman on December 8, 1942. After attending aviation school and becoming an aviation radioman, he served 15 months in Torpedo Squadron 9. Julian, bottom row, fourth from left, is posing with other members of the VT9 squadron. (Courtesy of James Haywood Julian.)

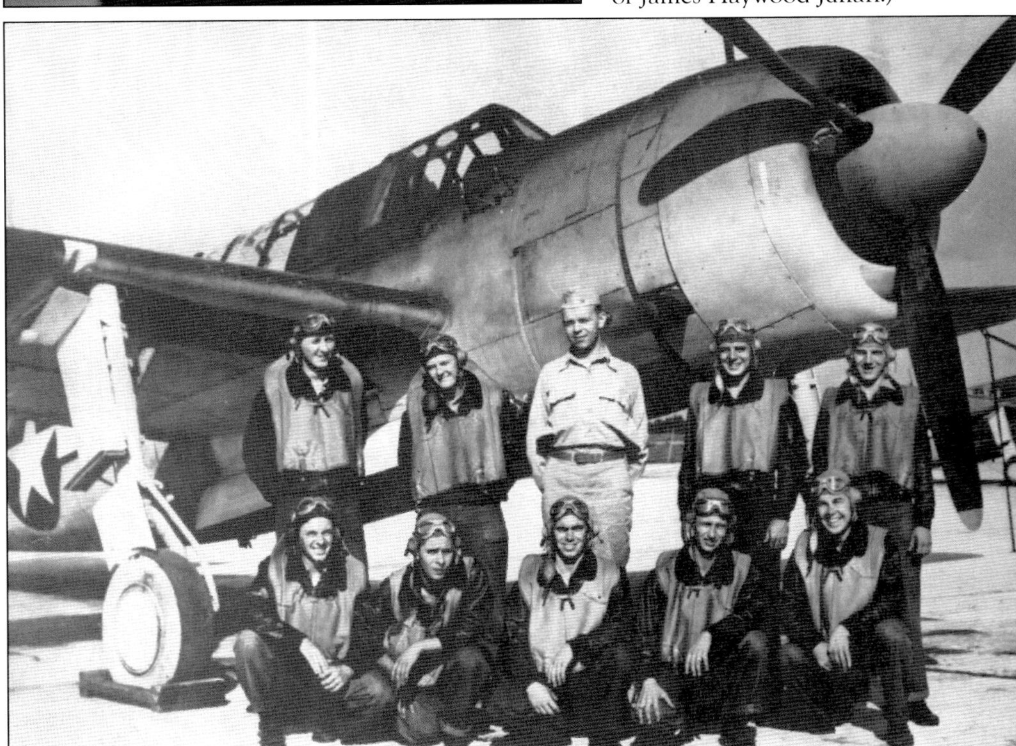

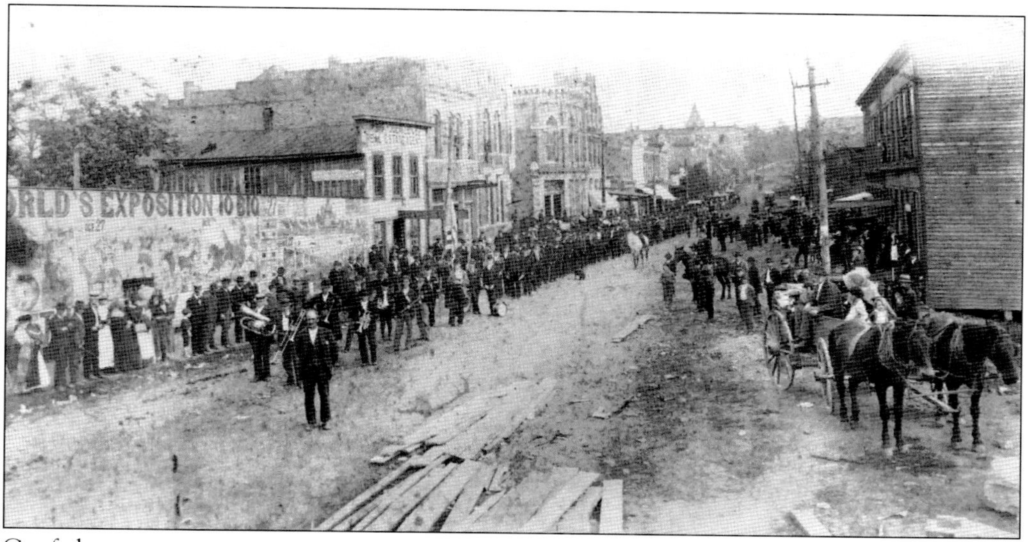

Confederate veterans participated in a parade on Main Street on October 19, 1889, and were led by J.C. Hodges. The W.B. Tate Camp, UCV, was organized in Morristown on August 24, 1894, with 35 charter members. Morristown furnished three companies to the Confederate army. The two-story frame building (left) later became site of the *Daily Gazette* building, with both Merchants Bank and Lookout Bank buildings on the corner of Main and Henry Streets.

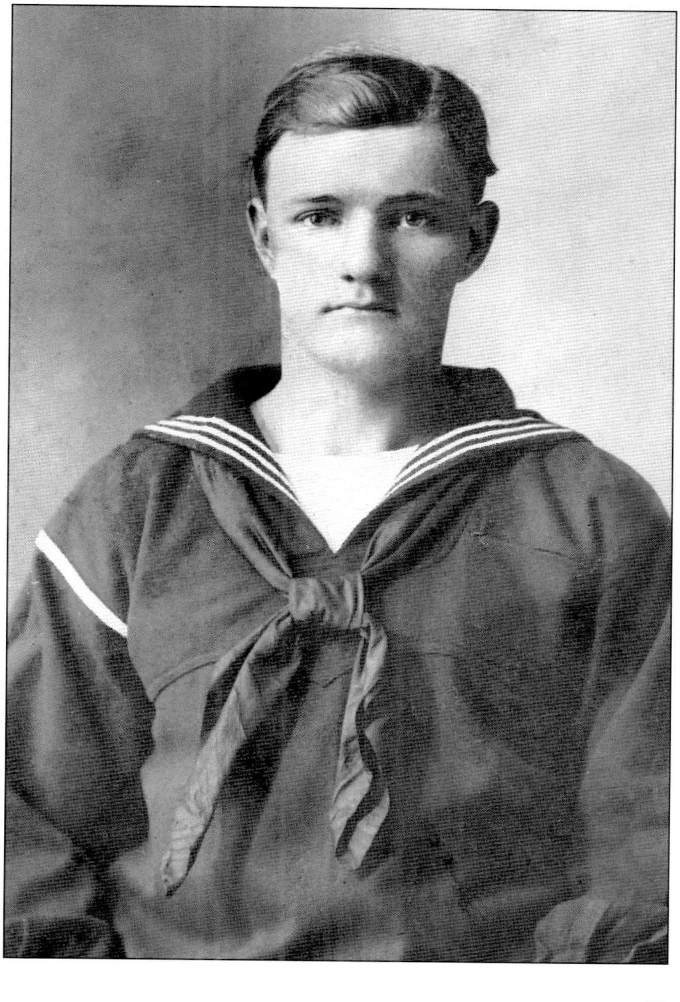

Ernest Thelbert Rippetoe, shown here in his Navy uniform, was the son of William P. Rippetoe and Mary Ida Cooper. As a veteran of the US Navy and a member of Lodge 631 Free and Accepted Masons, he was laid to rest with a Masonic graveside service in the St. Paul Cemetery after his death on December 30, 1970. (Courtesy of James Haywood Julian.)

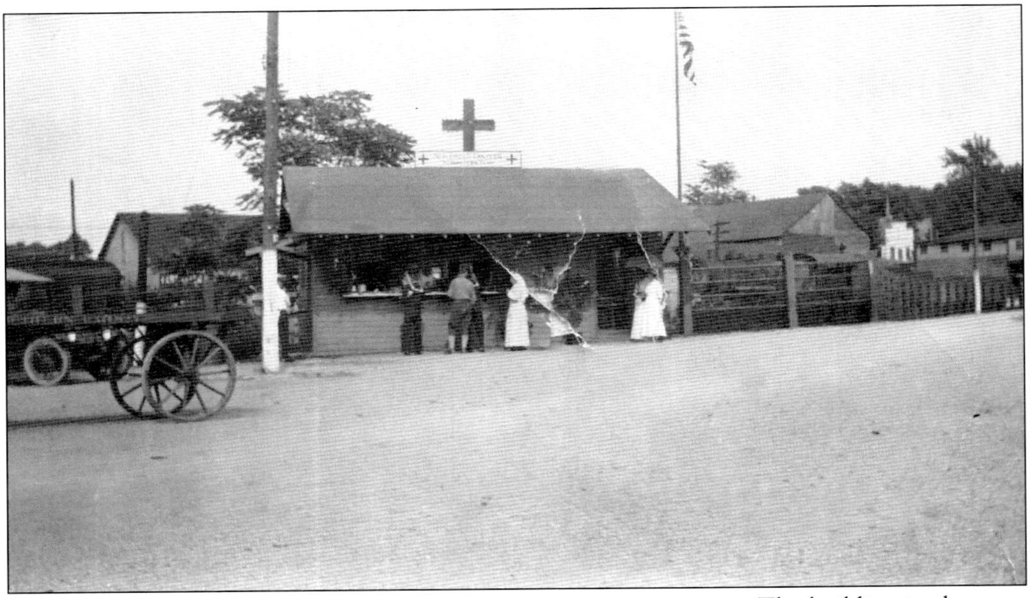

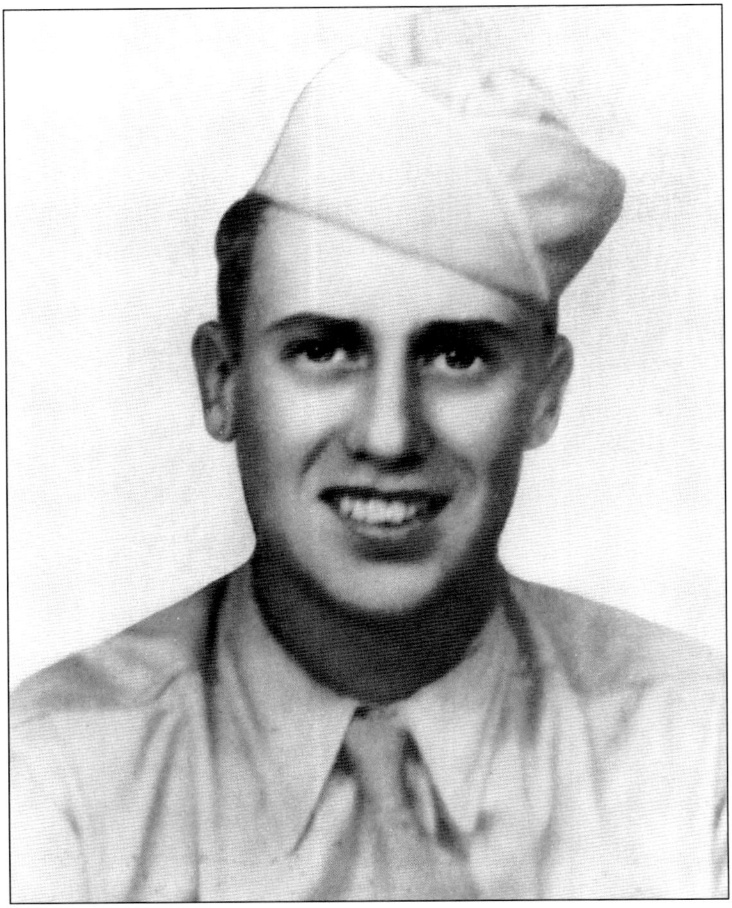

The building in the center is the Red Cross canteen that stood at the rear of Southern Railway passenger station from 1916 to 1918 during World War I. Within seven months in 1918, the local canteen and its volunteers fed over 100,000 soldiers. Figures like "Uncle Am" Stuart and Ben Noe were instrumental in helping recruit volunteers and scavenge for food throughout the community to keep the canteen supplied and soldiers fed.

PFC Benjamin Frank Wise was born on December 3, 1925, and was killed in the Black Forest of Germany on April 11, 1945, at the age of 19. He is buried in the village of Margraten in the Netherlands. (Courtesy of James D. Susong.)

Joining in 1952, Delmar L. Simmons served in the US Army until 1960 in locations such as Pusong and Taegu, South Korea. (Courtesy of Tina Simmons Wilson.)

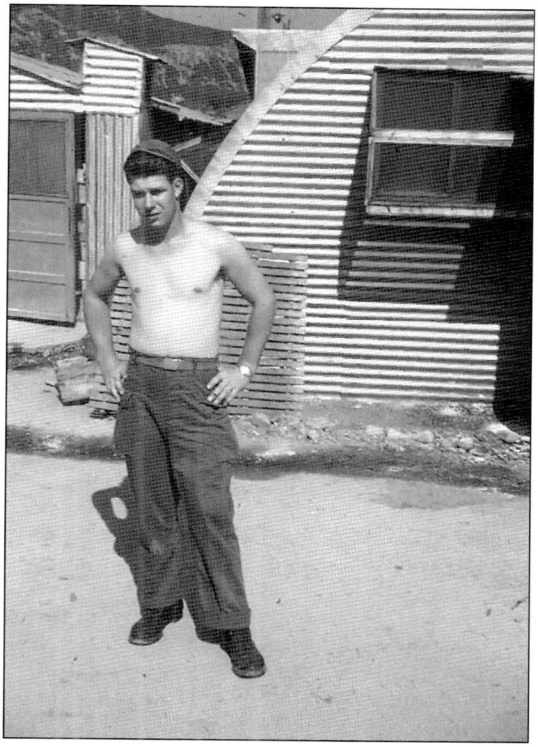

James Alex Susong, a World War II veteran, landed in France on D-Day and was taken as a prisoner of war. He later served in Korea. Serving in the Army for 12 to 15 years, James died at age 52 in a veteran hospital in East Orange, New Jersey. He was a first sergeant in Patton's army and was decorated many times. (Courtesy of James D. Susong.)

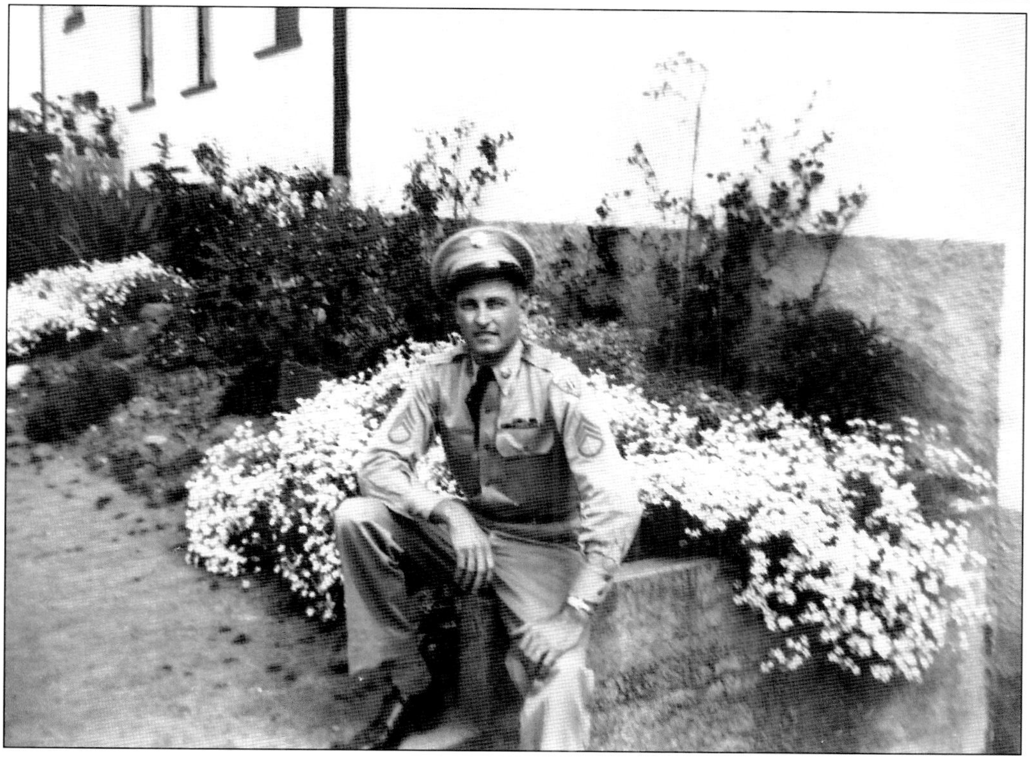

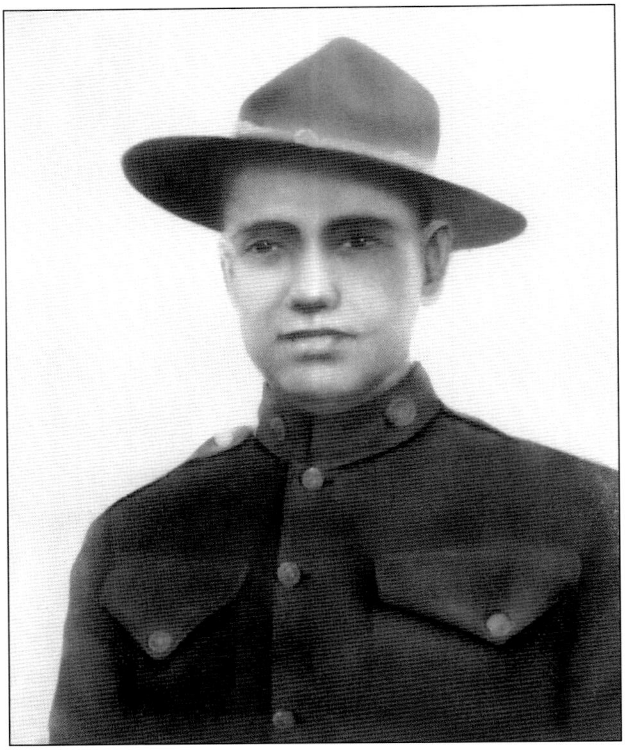

Calvin C. Ward, Congressional Medal of Honor recipient, entered active duty with the United States Army's 117th Regiment from the Tennessee National Guard during World War I. On October 8, 1918, he charged and captured the position of a Germany machine gun, freeing his company to advance against German lines in the last major offensive of the war, for which he was awarded the Medal of Honor and the Silver Star. Calvin ward died on December 15, 1967, and is buried in Glenwood Cemetery in Sullivan County, Tennessee.

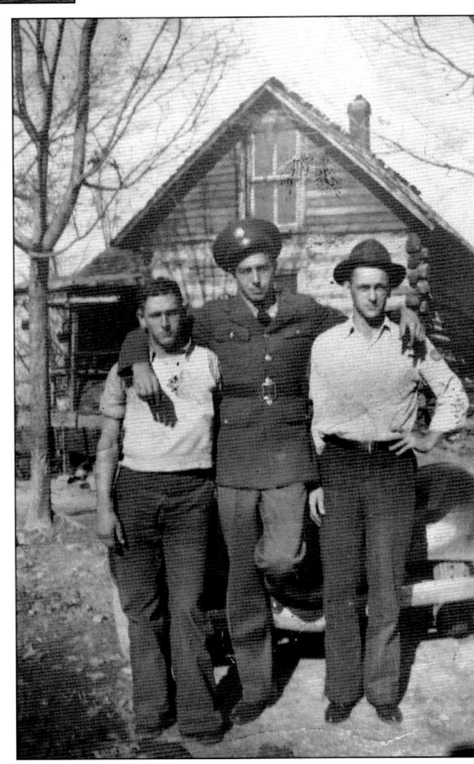

Walter Smith took some time off from his World War II Army duties. He is still in uniform with his arms around his brothers, ? Smith (left) and Jim Smith (right). The photograph was taken in 1942 at the family's home on Boatman's Mountain. (Courtesy of Billie D. Loveday.)

Sgt. Edward R. Talley joined the US Army from Russellville, and after completing recruit training, he was sent to France, where he distinguished himself in action near Pincheaux, France. He was a sergeant in Company L, 117th Infantry, 30th Division, when he was awarded the Medal of Honor for his actions on October 7, 1918, where he single-handedly silenced a German machine gun nest. Sergeant Talley died on December 14, 1950, and is buried at Bent Creek Cemetery in Whitesburg, Tennessee.

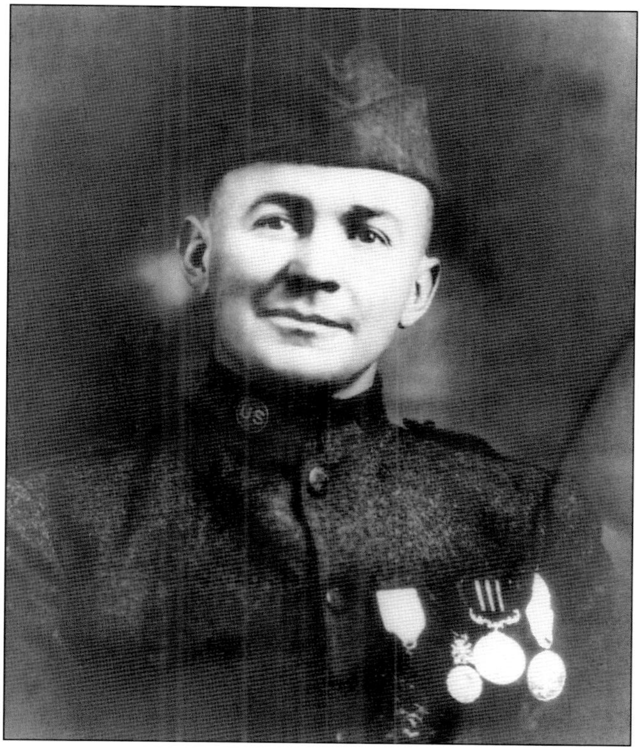

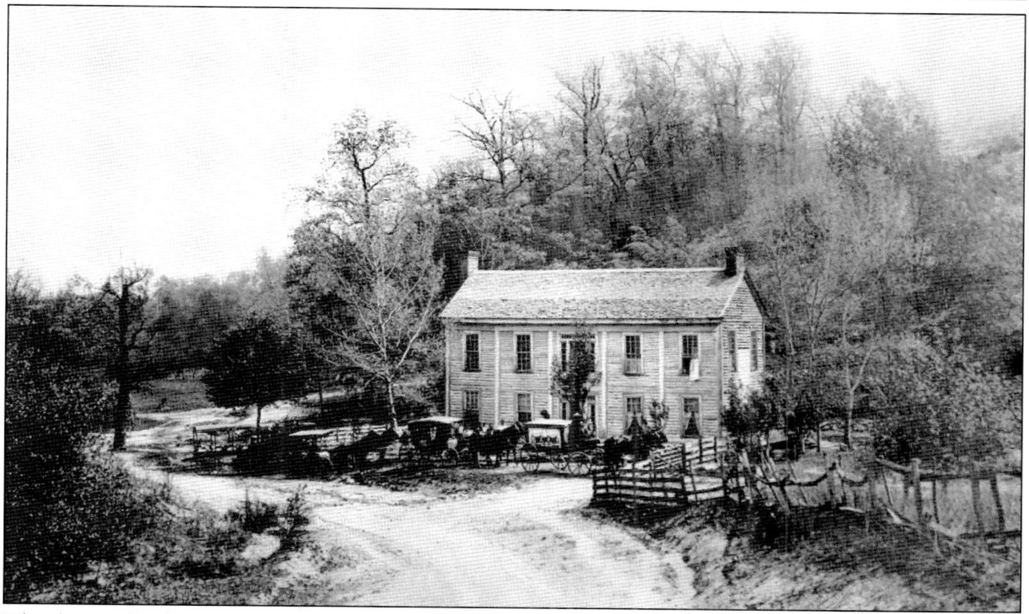

This home, built around 1825 by the Riggs family, has a colorful history. Located on the banks of Sulfur Springs near the pioneer Methodist Campground with its famous medicinal sulfur water, it served as a hotel, a Civil War hospital, and a tavern. It still stands at the intersection of Sulfur Springs and Fernwood Roads. This photograph is believed to have been taken at Colonel Riggs's funeral. (Courtesy of James D. Susong.)

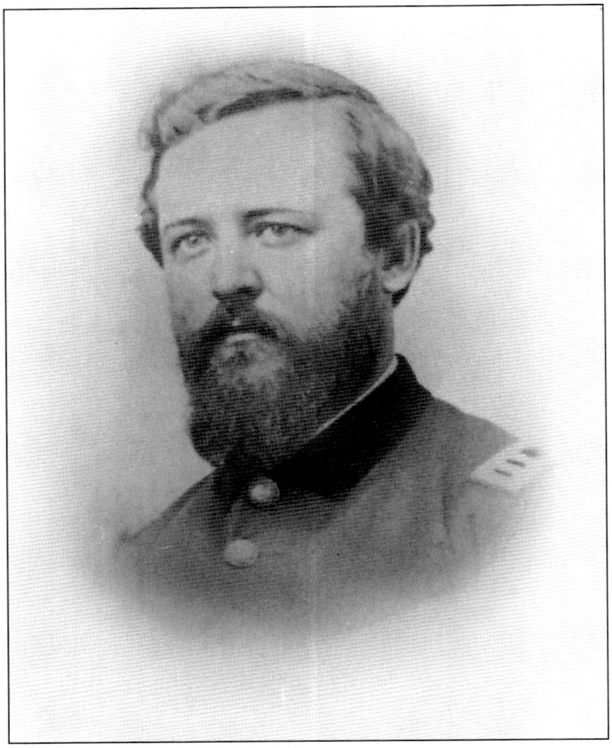

Born in Rhea County, Tennessee, in 1830, Dewitt Clinton Senter was a son of a Methodist minister. A staunch Union man, he was arrested in the spring of 1862 and held as a political prisoner for six months. Elected to both the Tennessee House of Representatives and the Tennessee Senate, where he served as speaker, Senter was later elected to fill the unexpired term of Gov. William Brownlow and afterward elected to a full term as governor in 1869. It was during his term as governor that Hamblen County was formed, and his signature can be found on all the official documents relating to the forming of the county. After his term as governor, he retired to his home in Morristown.

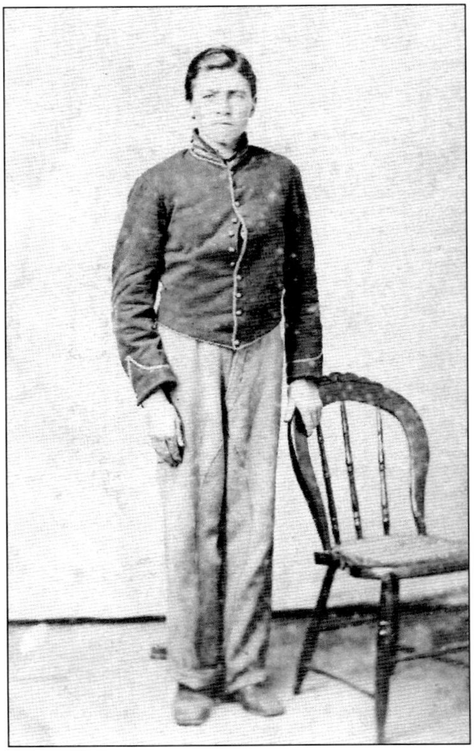

Col. James George Rose, shown posing in his Civil War uniform, was born in Tazewell, Tennessee, on September 1, 1835. During the Civil War, Rose become colonel of the 61st Tennessee Mounted Infantry. After a gallant record, he was captured near Bulls Gap and imprisoned on Johnson Island. Rose was nominated and elected to the state legislature and served as Hamblen County judge of the Second Judicial District. While serving as chairman of the Hamblen County School Board in 1892, Morristown's newest coeducational public high school was named in his honor; today, it is known as the Rose Center.

Robert McFarland IV (1832–1884) was the son of Robert McFarland III and Mary Ann Scott McFarland. He served in the Civil War by enlisting in the 31st Tennessee Infantry Regiment and becoming major of the 39th Tennessee Mounted Infantry. McFarland worked as an attorney and served as a Tennessee Supreme Court judge from 1871 to 1882. Poor health caused him to resign in 1882. A large brick residence on West Second North Street, later home to Sen. Herbert Walters and All Saints' School, was built by Judge McFarland and is still standing today. (Courtesy of Davy Anne Charles.)

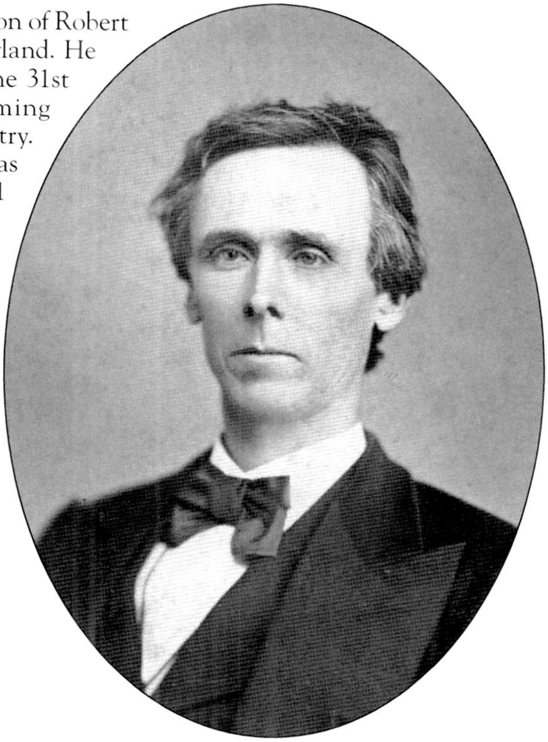

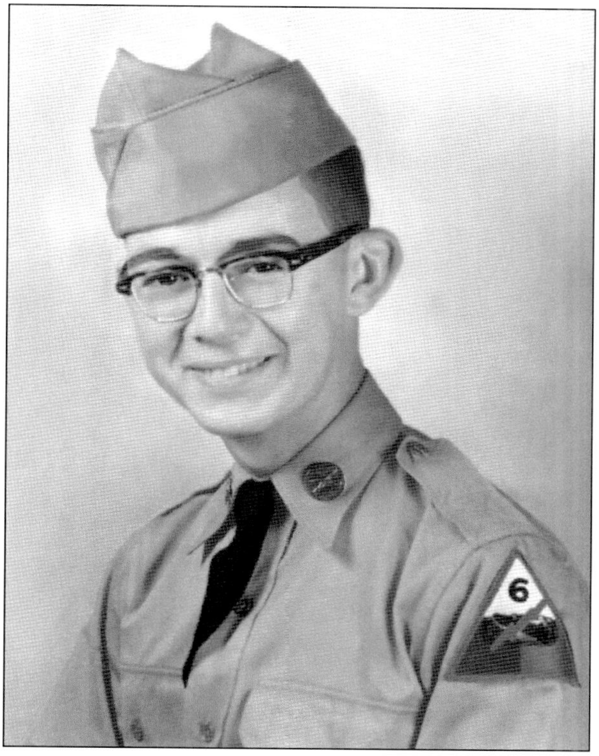

Douglas Raymond Bryan was born on October 3, 1938, and he entered the military on May 11, 1955, at the young age of 16. Bryan served over 11 years as a medical specialist and single-rotor helicopter specialist at Fort Campbell, Kentucky, and Fort Meade, Maryland. Bryan was honorably discharged from service on November 13, 1967, after suffering a heart attack.

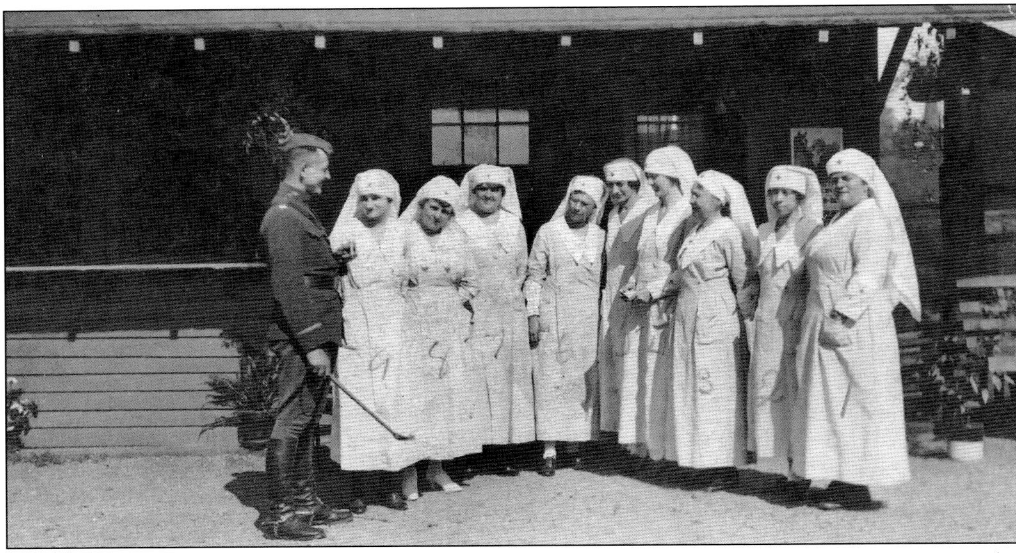

These women, local canteen volunteers of the Morristown Chapter of the Red Cross, provided food, drinks, and other comforts to the men and women coming through on troop trains during World War I. Approval for the local charter was granted on July 13, 1917, and a canteen was built in the "Y" at the Southern Railway Station, serving until May 1919. Canteen workers pictured, from left to right, are Purnie Pope Phillips, Myrtle Riggs Bassett, Annie Russell Hix, Nell Miller Pless, Marie Morris Henderson, Mary Hodge Dosser, Mattie Harle Legg, Ollie Rogers Pope, and Dora French Barrow.

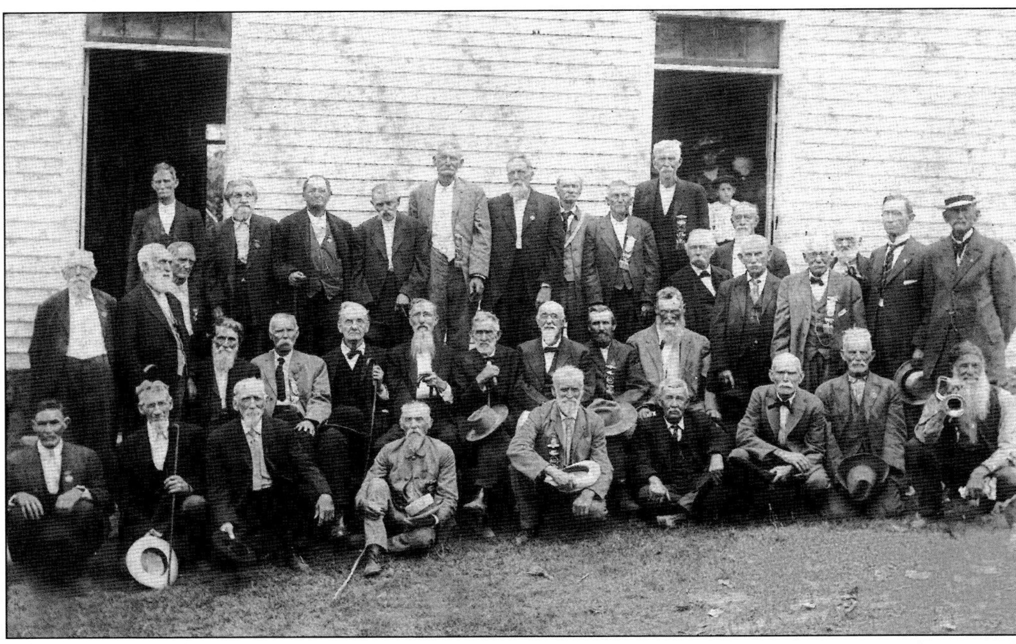

W.B. Tate Camp of the United Confederate Veterans gathered for a reunion at Liberty Hill Methodist Church around 1910. The camp was organized on August 24, 1894, and named in honor of William Brown Tate of Grainger County. The last Hamblen County Confederate veteran, James P. Graves, died at the age of 90 on September 30, 1937.

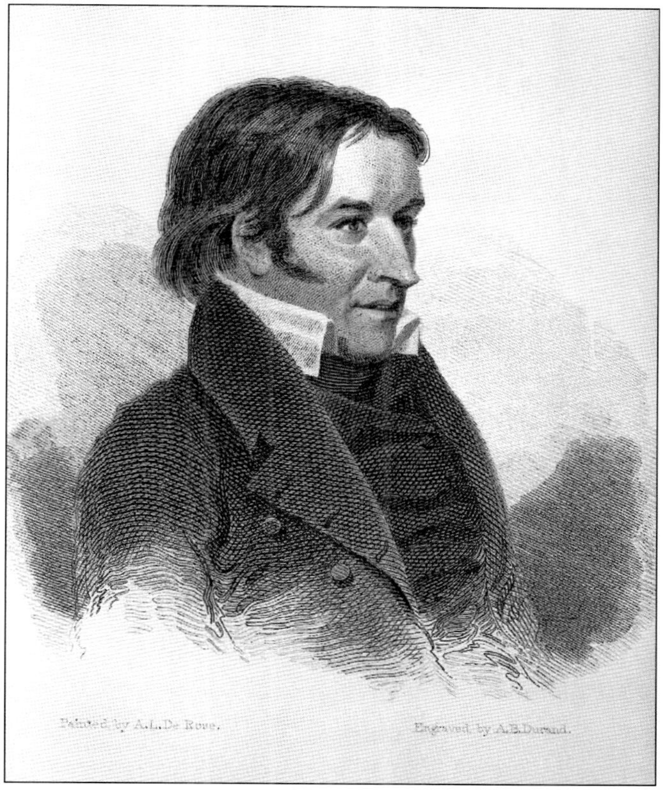

This image of Davy Crockett was painted by Anthony Lewis De Rose and engraved by Asher B. Durand. Davy Crockett, famous backwoodsman and Alamo defender, lived in Morristown with his parents until 1806, when he moved west. John Crockett, Davy's father, was among the first settlers in the area. Stories handed down say that Crockett honed his skill with a rifle while hunting on a local hill, now called Crockett Ridge. A replica of his boyhood home, the Crockett Tavern Museum, has been constructed on the original site of the family's tavern and home. (Courtesy of the Museum of Fine Arts of Boston.)

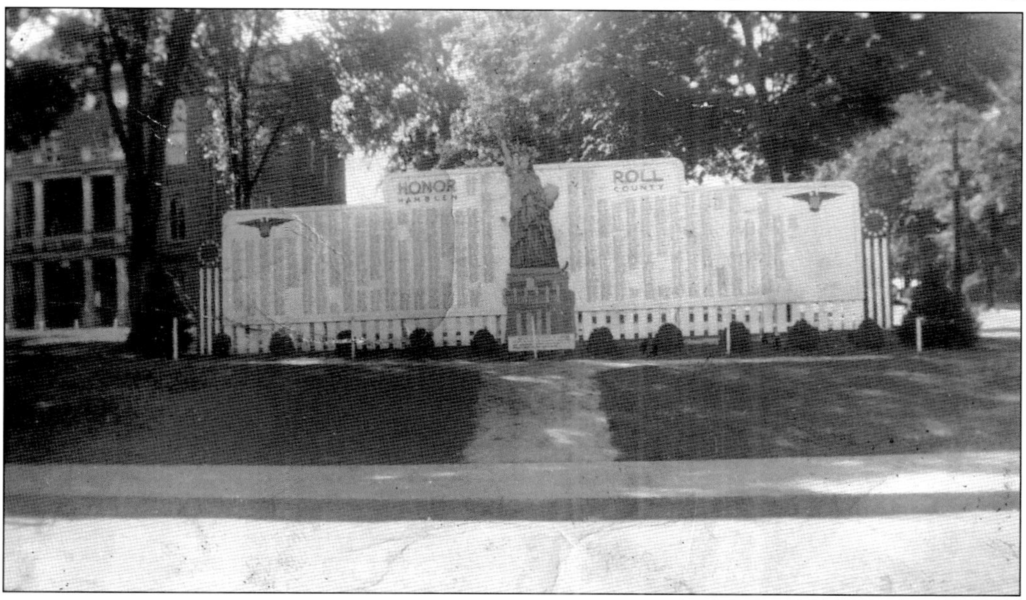

The Hamblen County honor roll from 1942 shows the names of local men and women from all four military branches that served during World War II. Once located on the Hamblen County Courthouse lawn, it attracted the attention of many people who wanted to find the names of friends and family. (Courtesy of Billie D. Loveday.)

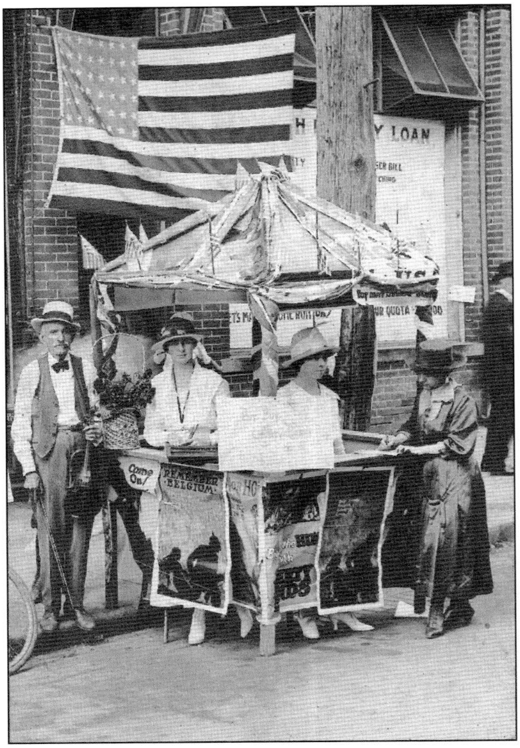

This booth was set up on Main Street during World War I to sell Liberty Bonds to passersby. Inside the booth on the right are Mary Hodge Dosser and Olive "Ollie" Rogers. Standing (left) is "Uncle Am" Stuart, who played his fiddle. A Liberty Bond was a war bond that was sold to support the allied cause in World War I. Subscribing to the bonds became a symbol of patriotic duty.

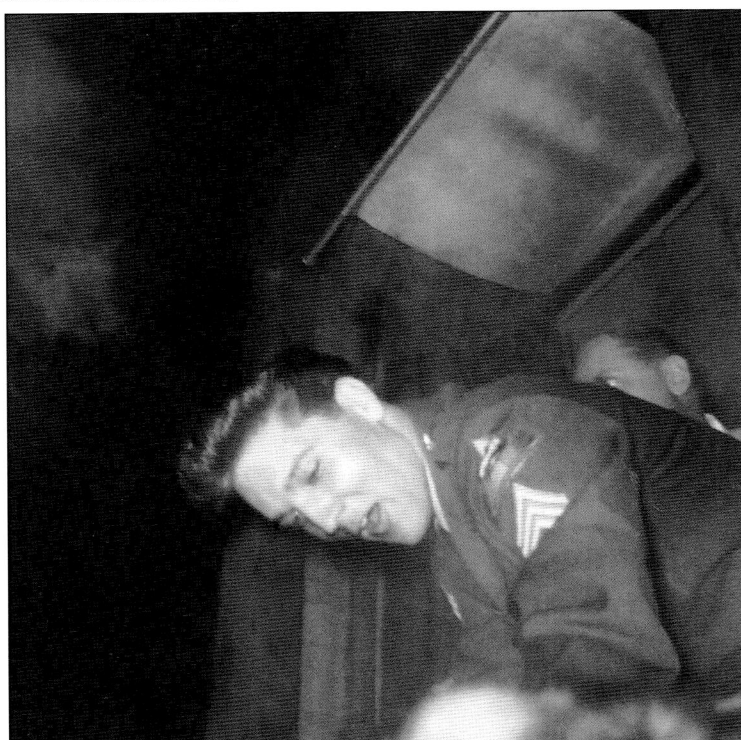

This image of Elvis Presley from April 1960 shows him traveling home after just being released from the Army. He was on his way home when the train stopped briefly at the Morristown depot and Elvis came to the back of the car, leaning over to greet and shake the hands of about a half-dozen girls who gathered at the back of his private car. Notice he was still wearing his military uniform. (Courtesy of Norma Samsel.)

Eight

Reading, Writing, and Recess

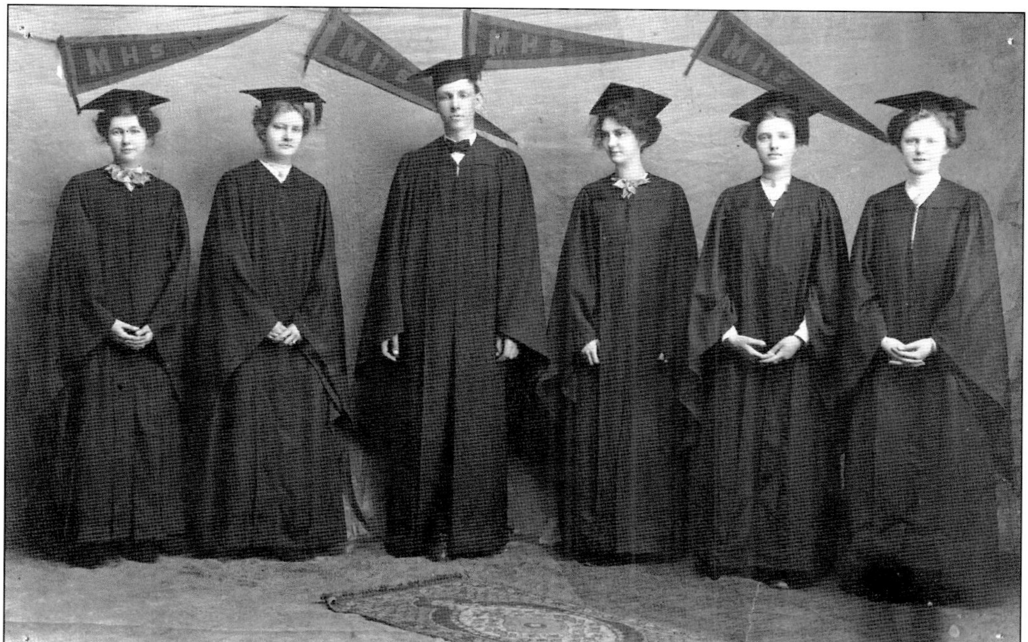

This is Morristown's graduating class of 1911. They are, from left to right, Clyde Porter, Bess Carmichael, Clifford Dyer, Pauline Bruner, Sidney Hisey, and Ruth Hale.

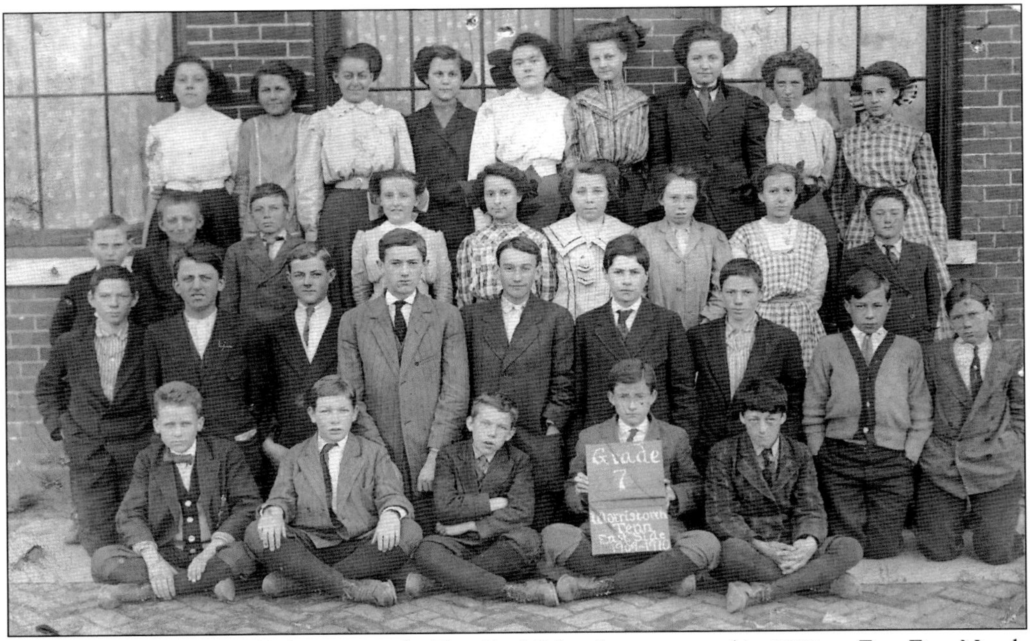

Roberts School, originally known as the East End School, was erected in 1901 on East First North Street. Pictured here is the 1909–1910 seventh-grade class. The students are, from left to right, (first row) Gaines Campbell, Robert Lotspeich, Harold White, Keith Burgner, and Elton Everett; (second row) Eugene Trobaugh, "Skin" Inman, Max Maloney, Charles Hodge, Paul Holley, Joe Richardson, Ernest Trobaugh, Frank "Scut" Smith, and Madison Eakes; (third row) Robert Toney, Harold McCorkle, Wayne Caldwell, Neva Hankle, Rose Rise, Anna Kate Smith, Annie Lora Craig, Naomi Trent, and Hal Noe; (fourth row) Olivia Smith, Addie Trueblood, Inez Stephens, Alma Mills, Almeda Carmichael, Irma Jones, Beatrice Smith, Juanita Miller, and Ellen Taylor.

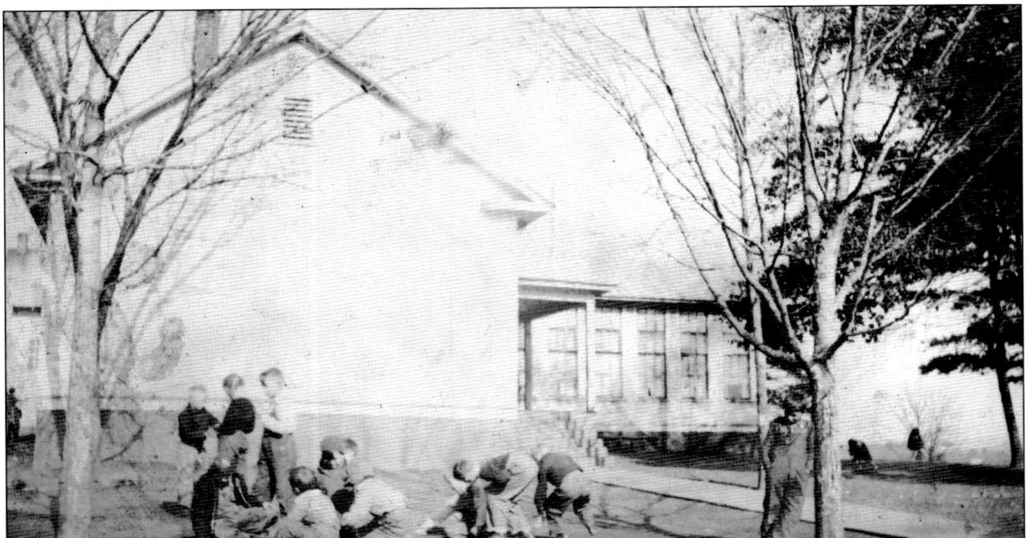

Russellville High School was built in 1911. It replaced Union College, which burned a year earlier. E.H. Moore was the first principal. (Courtesy of the late Frank Gracey Jarrell, WPA clerk.)

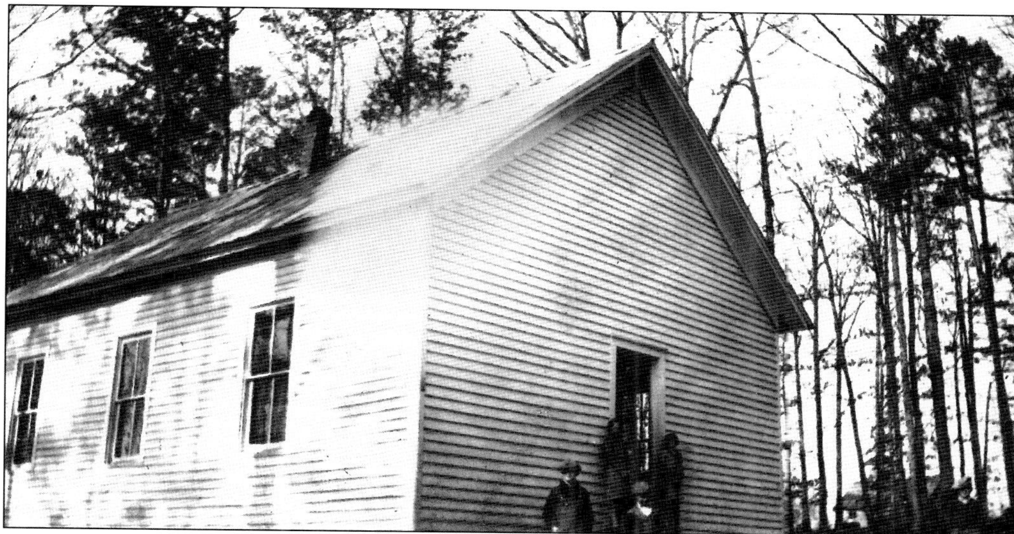

Talley's School was a poor one-room white school located in Russellville. Due to segregation, schools were either identified as being a white school or a colored school. It was not until the mid-1960s that Hamblen County schools were integrated. (Courtesy of the late Frank Gracey Jarrell, WPA clerk.)

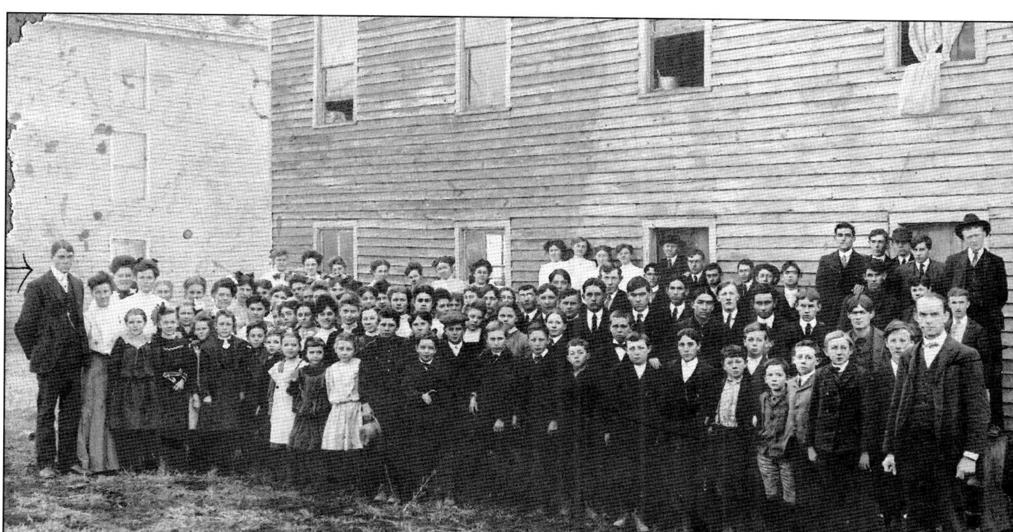

Union College, located in Russellville, was founded in 1891 under the name of Russellville High School. It became known as Union College in 1899. The school provided classes from first grade through high school and college. During the early years, it had an enrollment of 170 students. Fire destroyed the school on March 18, 1910.

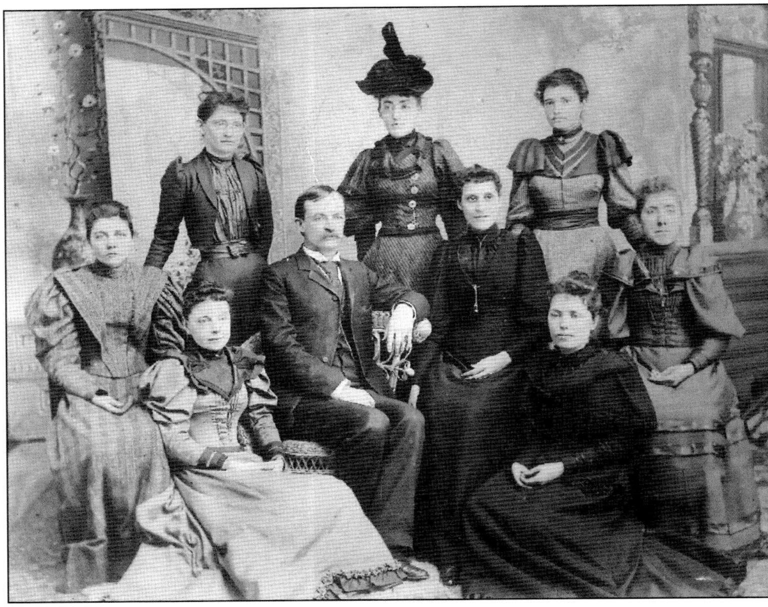

The Rose School was erected in 1892, and pictured here are the first faculty members of the high school. The members are, from left to right, (first row) Blanch Dick and Georgia Jarnagin; (second row) ? Wilson, Prof. Charles Mason, Kate Greenlee, and ? Wright; (third row) Sallie Loop, Meta Turley Bush, and Rozee Rankin.

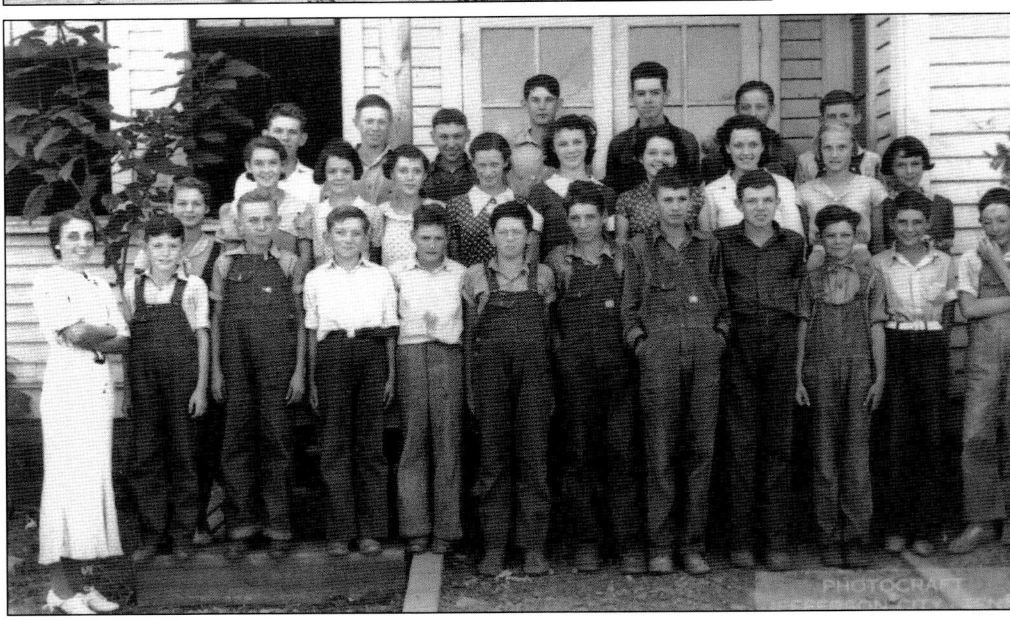

Manley School was named in memory of Hamblen County teacher Pleas M. Manley (1874–1909). His aunt, Harriet Tandy Senter, was the widow of Gov. DeWitt Clinton Senter, and she donated property from the Senter farm for Manley School and Manley Baptist Church. Pictured here are Manley School's seventh- and eighth-grade classes from 1935 to 1936. They are, from left to right, (first row) Louise Noe Kesterson (teacher), Wallace Barrett, G.L. Carter, H.J. Bell, Fox Britton, Irvin Shaver, Jess Covington, Elwood Hastie, Earl Sluss, Cecil Rines, Quentin Seals, and Warren Cottrell; (second row) Margaret Rines, Nellie Cox, Alice Goforth, Ann Seals, Lucy Snyder, Martha Cannon, Martha Altorn, Elaine Hazelwood, Jossie Smith, and Ida Fay Cowan; (third row) Sam Brown, Hearl Robertson, William Wheeler, Robert Everett, Marshall Rines, Connie Haun, and Charles Gray. (Courtesy of Minnie Robertson.)

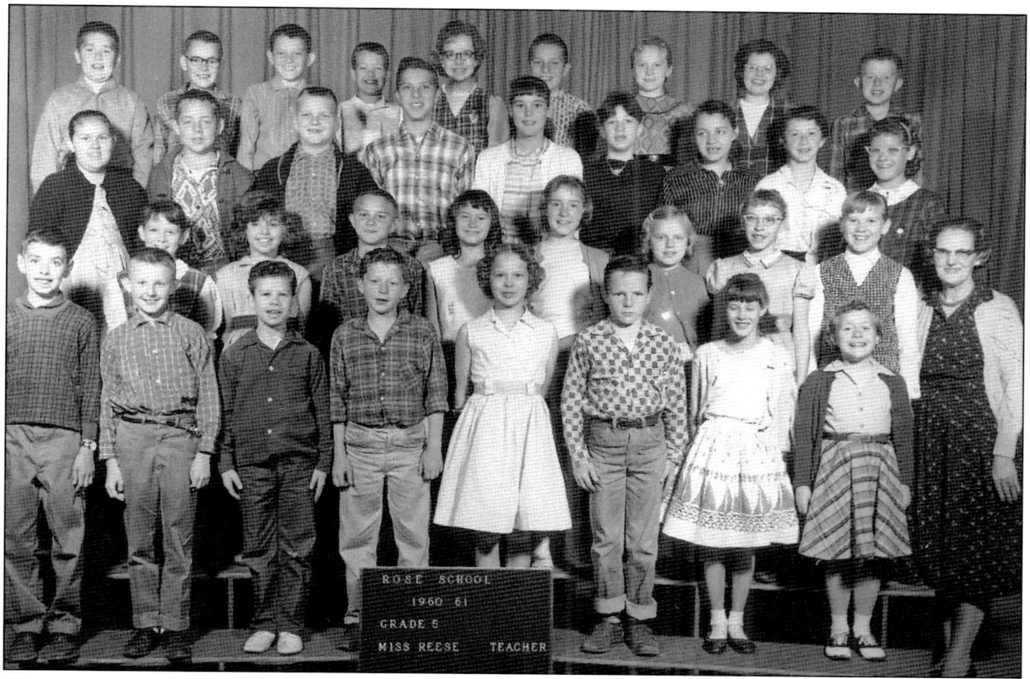

This was Rose School's fifth-grade class from 1960 to 1961. The teacher was Miss Reese (right), and the principal was Mr. Horner (not shown). (Courtesy of Billie D. Loveday.)

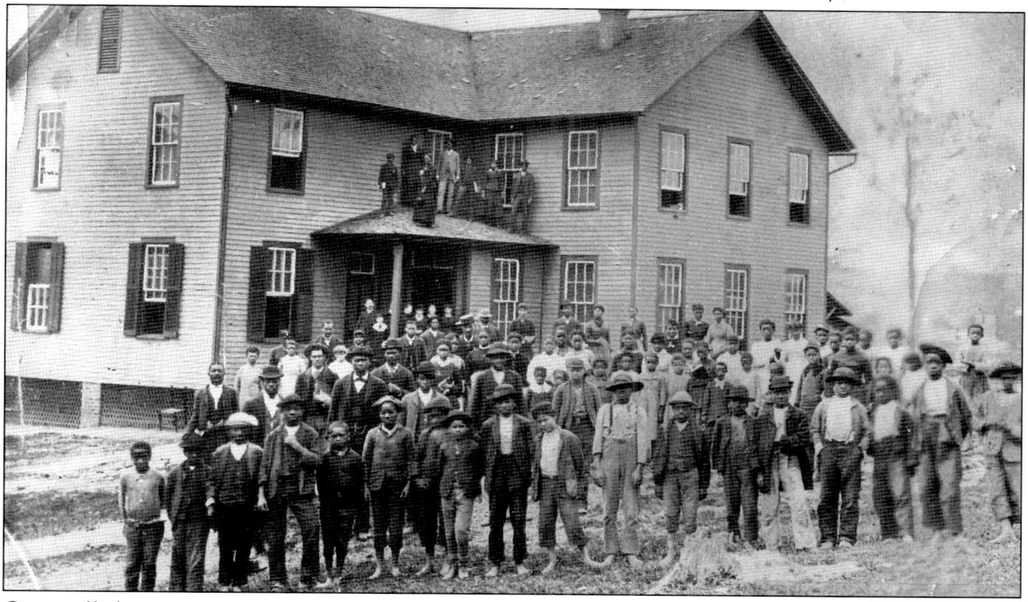

Originally known as Morristown Normal and Industrial College, Morristown College was founded in 1881 by Dr. Judson S. Hill. In the beginning, classes were held in an dilapidated old one-story building once used as a slave mart and as a hospital for smallpox victims and Civil War soldiers. Within 75 years, the college grew from the one building and one-acre campus to a campus with 12 buildings on 75 acres. It was a nationally known and respected institution. Dr. Hill, standing on the porch with his hand on the column, poses here with the student body of 1884.

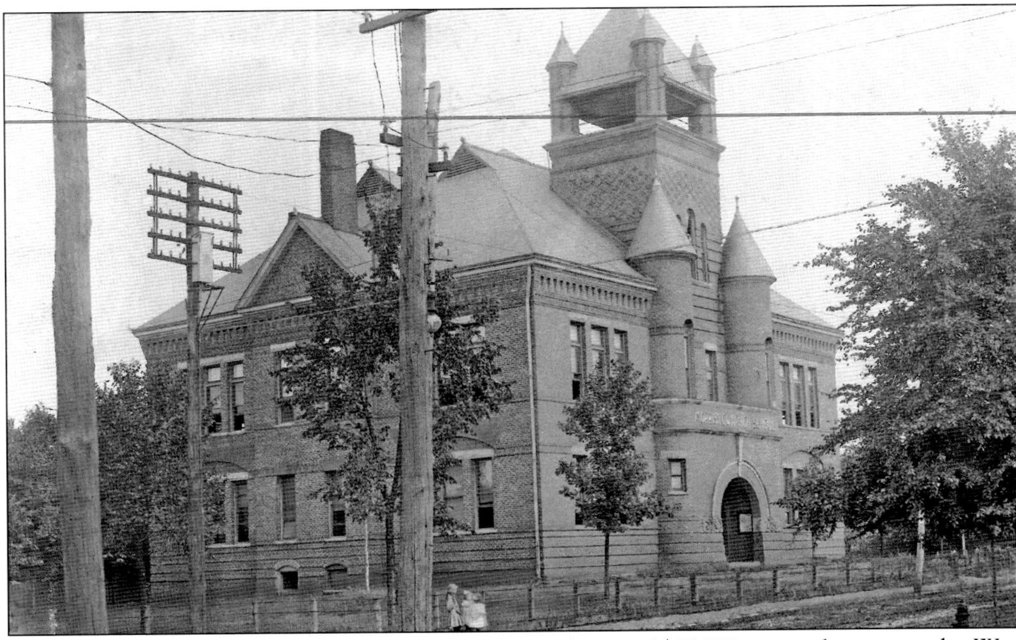

When the Rose Center was erected in 1892 at a total cost of $20,793, it was known as the West End School. It was a graded school teaching elementary through high school. In 1910, the Board of Education changed the name to Rose School, in honor of Judge James G. Rose, who was chairman of the Hamblen County Board of Education when the school was erected. Elementary classes were taught here until 1975. High school continued to be taught here until 1916, when it was moved to the newly built James A. Carriger building. (Courtesy of C.M. McClung Historical Collection.)

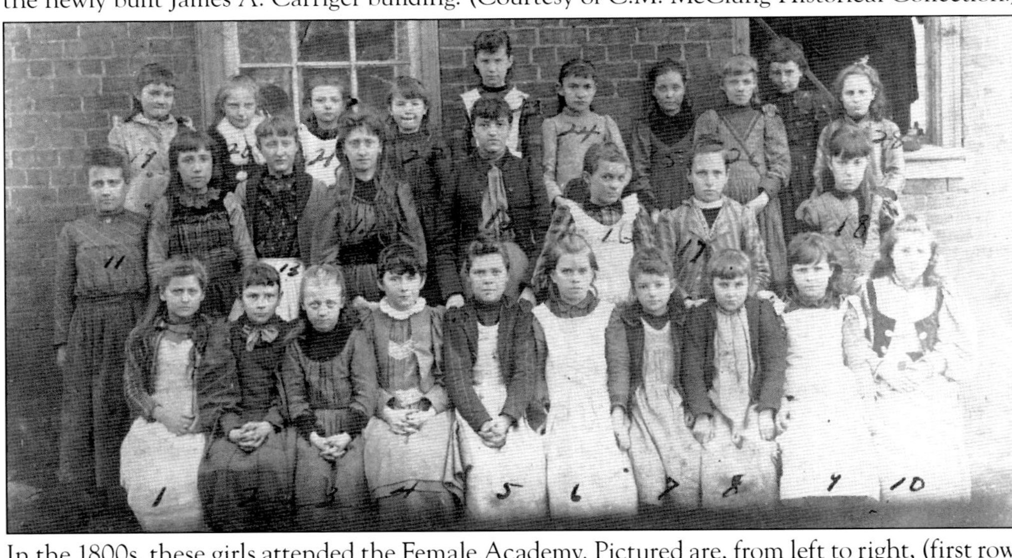

In the 1800s, these girls attended the Female Academy. Pictured are, from left to right, (first row) Effie Goodson, Ethel Murphy, Vera Wilkinson, Helen Turner, Nelle Allen, Nettie Sanders, Nelle Wilkerson, Bernie Miller, Jessie Holston, and Annie Back; (second row) Lelis Huffmaster, Gertie Cowden, Essie Hobbs, Mollie Hobbs, Addie Cooter, Ida DeSaussure, Kate Crouch, and Bess Mitchell; (third row) Leda Hensley, Kate Crump, Maude Wilson, Ethel Pendergrass, Nelle McCrary, Lora Riggs, Ollie Donaldson, Mary Kate Brown, Mamie McGhee, and Fannie Cartwright.

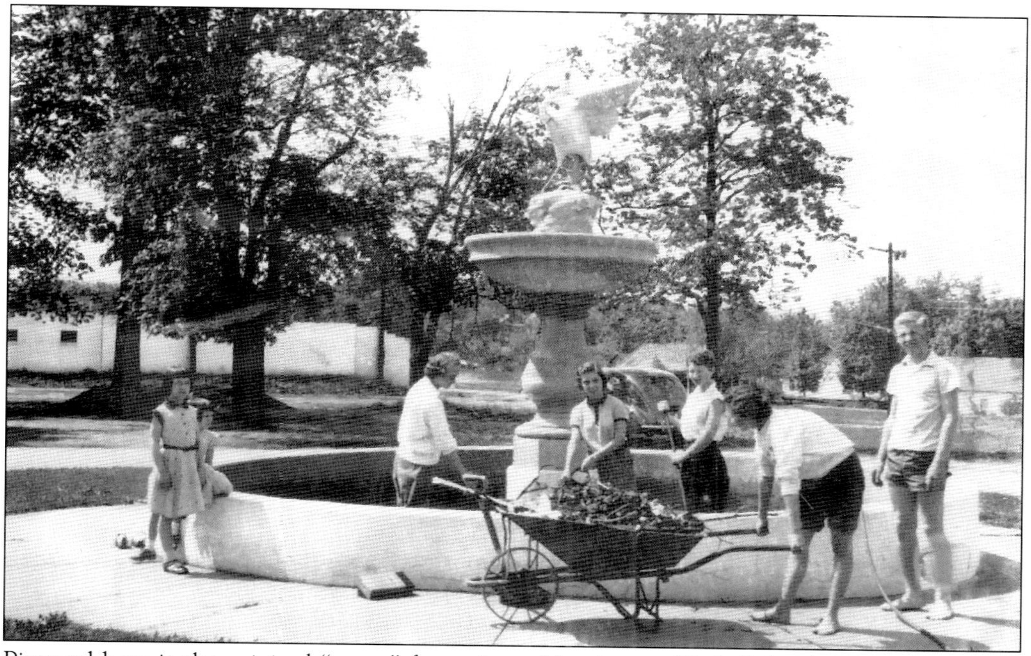

Pictured here is the original "goose" fountain at Morristown High School, now Morristown-Hamblen High School East. The fountain, which was donated by the Rowe family, was erected in 1926, and it became a popular meeting and picture taking spot. The "goose," as it is commonly called, is actually an ibis, and it mysteriously disappeared in the 1960s. It was not replaced until 2003. This 1953 photograph shows the Morristown Beautification Council busily cleaning the school grounds after entering the national Cleanest Town Contest.

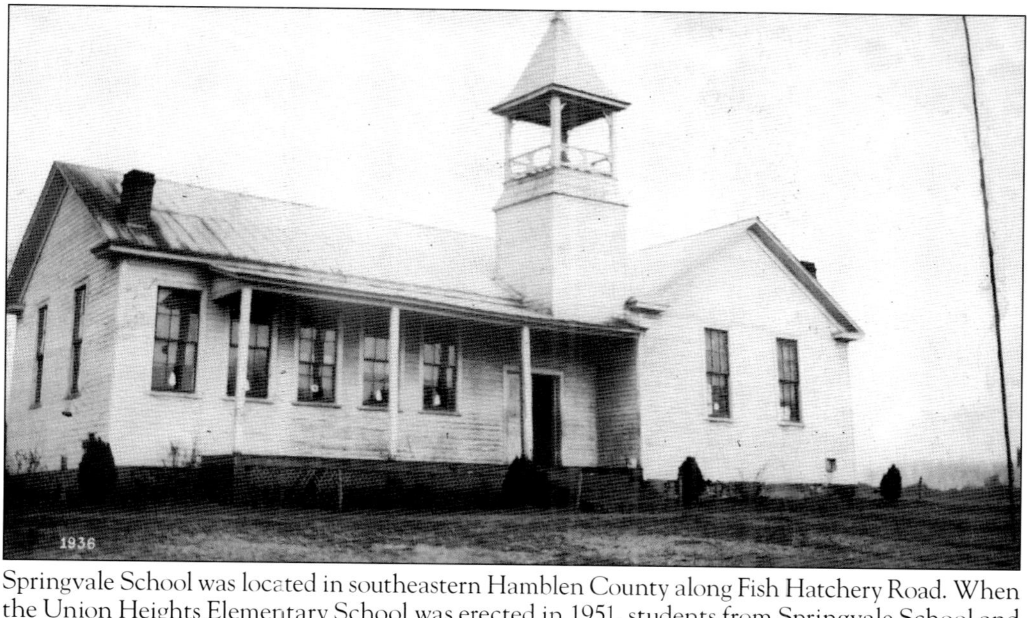

Springvale School was located in southeastern Hamblen County along Fish Hatchery Road. When the Union Heights Elementary School was erected in 1951, students from Springvale School and Lowland School merged into the new school. The old Springvale School building was thereafter used as a private residence. (Courtesy of the late Frank Gracey Jarrell, WPA clerk.)

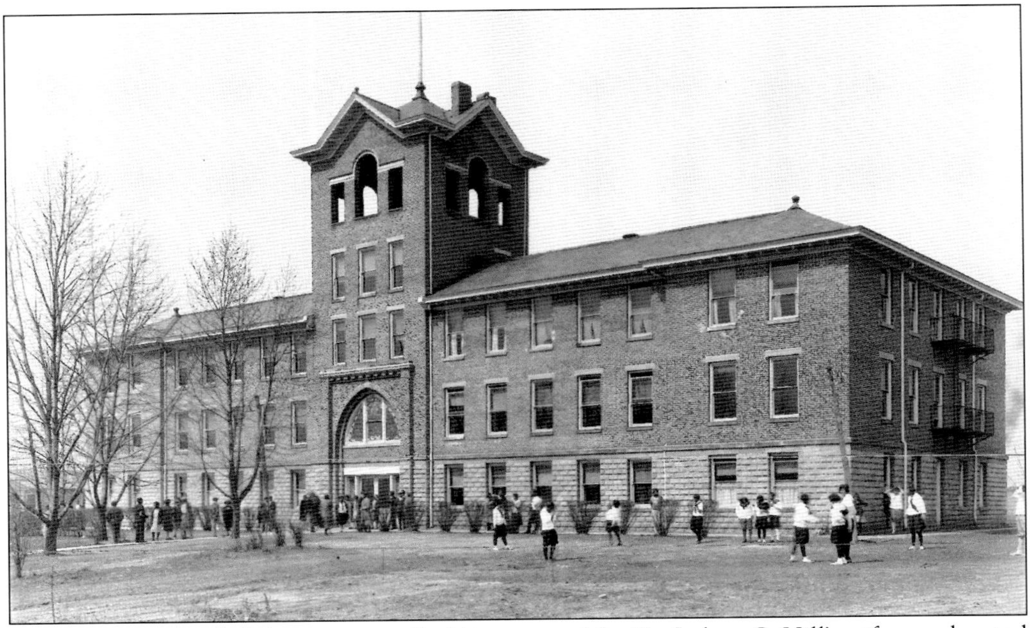

The Laura Yard Hill Administration Building, named for Dr. Judson S. Hill's wife, was located on the Morristown College campus. This photograph was taken in the 1920s. The building fell into disrepair many years later and was destroyed by fire on October 29, 2010. (Courtesy of C.M. McClung Historical Collection.)

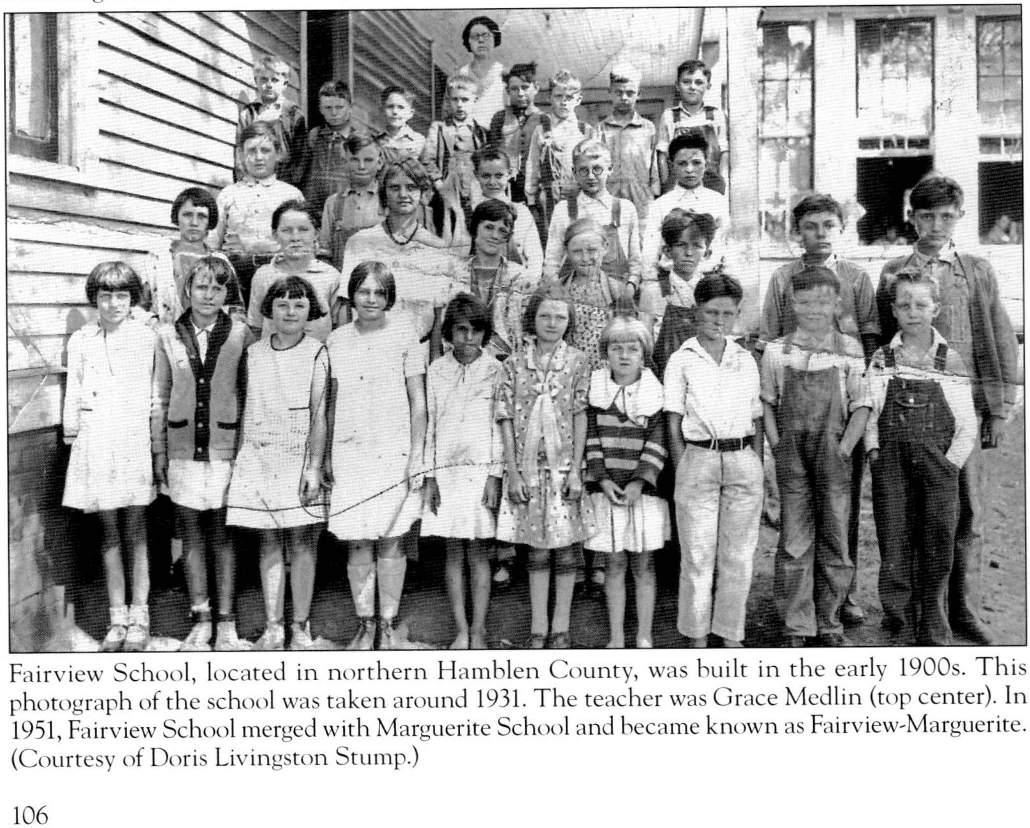

Fairview School, located in northern Hamblen County, was built in the early 1900s. This photograph of the school was taken around 1931. The teacher was Grace Medlin (top center). In 1951, Fairview School merged with Marguerite School and became known as Fairview-Marguerite. (Courtesy of Doris Livingston Stump.)

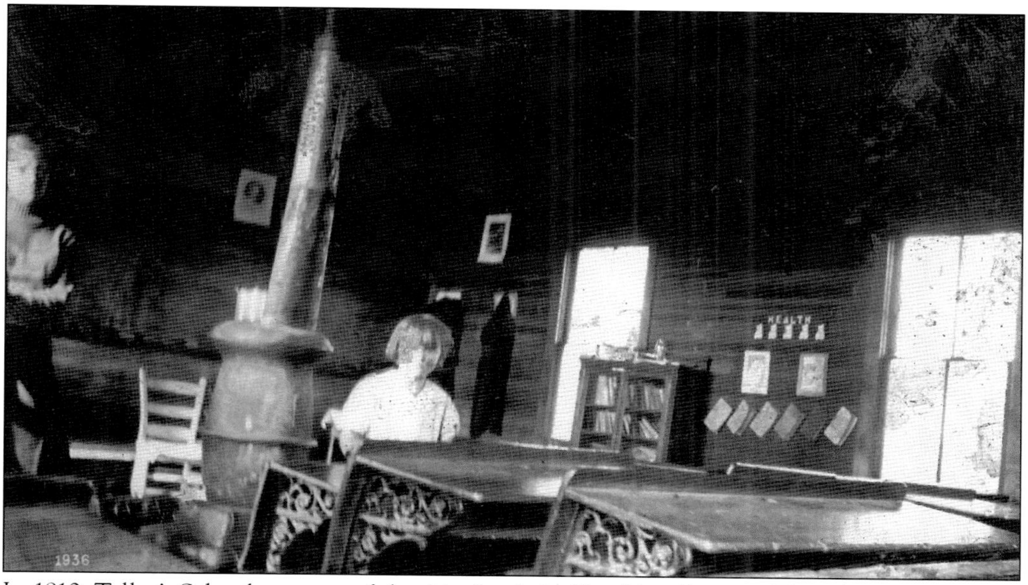

In 1910, Talley's School was one of the 44 schools in Hamblen County. This photograph shows the interior of the school. The potbellied stove in the center of the room was a familiar site in area schools during this time. (Courtesy of the late Frank Gracey Jarrell, WPA clerk.)

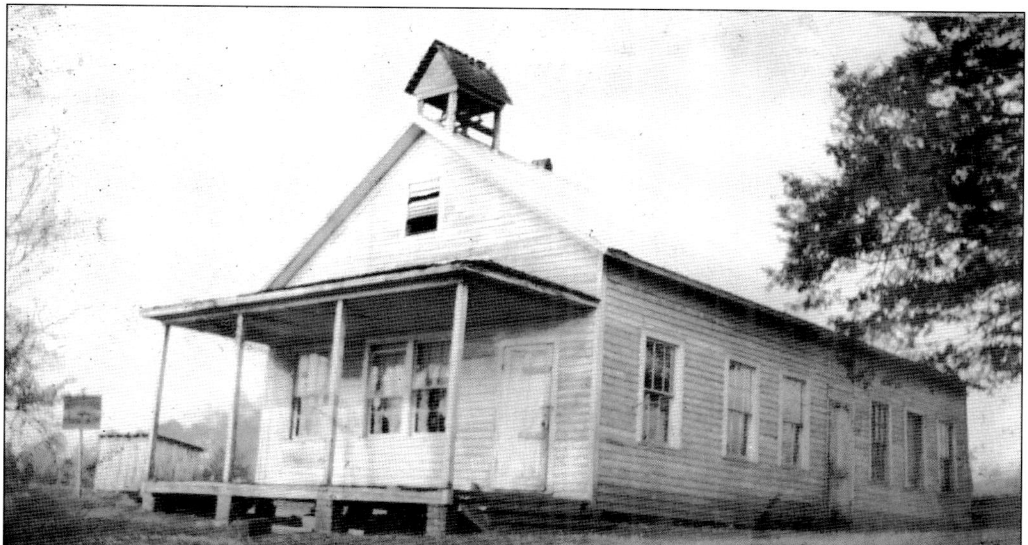

Cedar Grove School was a two-room, one-teacher school located in Russellville near the Silver City community. One room was used for the classroom, and the other room was used for the Works Progress Administration's (WPA) Hot Lunch Project. The building later served as the Cedar Grove Church. (Courtesy of the late Frank Gracey Jarrell, WPA clerk.)

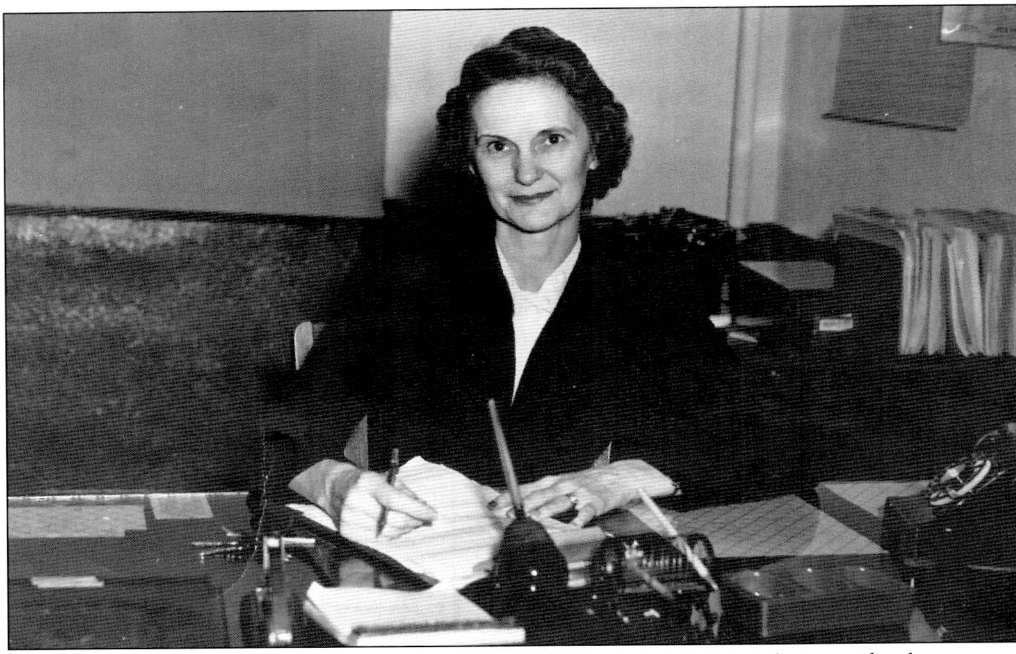

Jessie Mae Livingston Wallen McClister (1905–1980) served 40 years in education for the counties of Hamblen, Grainger, Unicoi, Hawkins, Greene, Jefferson, and Knox. She was a teacher, principal, supervisor, superintendent, and college professor. (Courtesy of Doris Livingston Stump.)

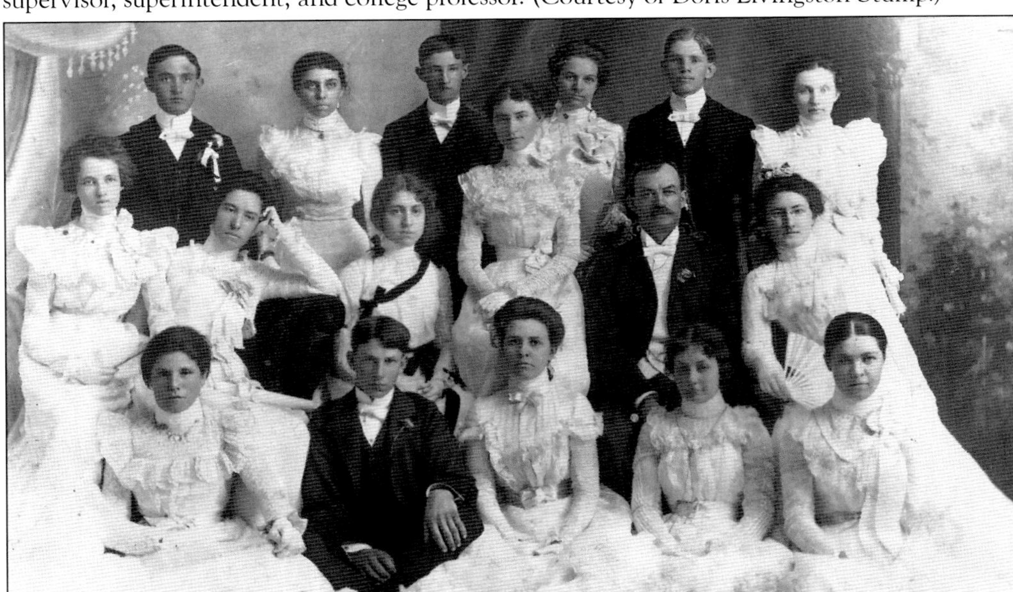

This is the Morristown High School senior class of 1900. Pictured are, from left to right, (first row) Maggie Young, Will Barnett, Annie Holston, Ollie Donaldson, and Nell Allen; (second row) Mary Kate Brown, Mae Holley, Annabel Essary, Nelle Loop, Prof. Charles Mason, and Gertrude Milholland; (third row) Clarence Rippetoe, Margaret Johnston, Will Mathes, Ida DeSaussure, Will Larkin, and Nell McCrary.

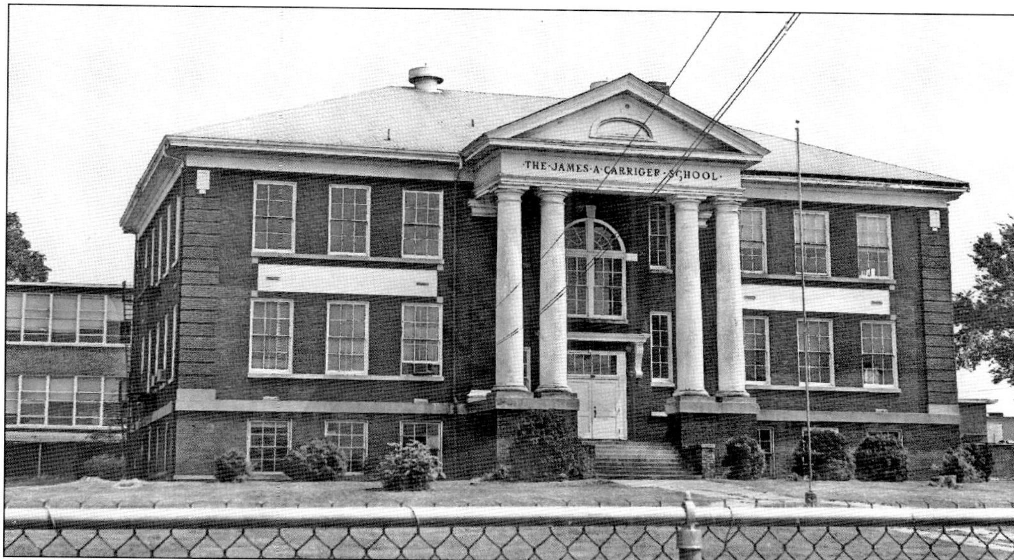

The James A. Carriger School was demolished in October 1978 and was located in what is now a parking lot in front of the Hamblen County Board of Education building. Built in 1915, it was home to Morristown High School from 1916 to 1923 and then home to the junior high school until 1975. James A. Carriger (1845–1930), the building's namesake, was a prominent citizen of his day. Some of his accomplishments were serving as the following positions: soldier in the Civil War, president of Merchant's Bank, organizer of Reagan High School for boys, mayor of Morristown, attorney, Hamblen County Board of Education member, and educator.

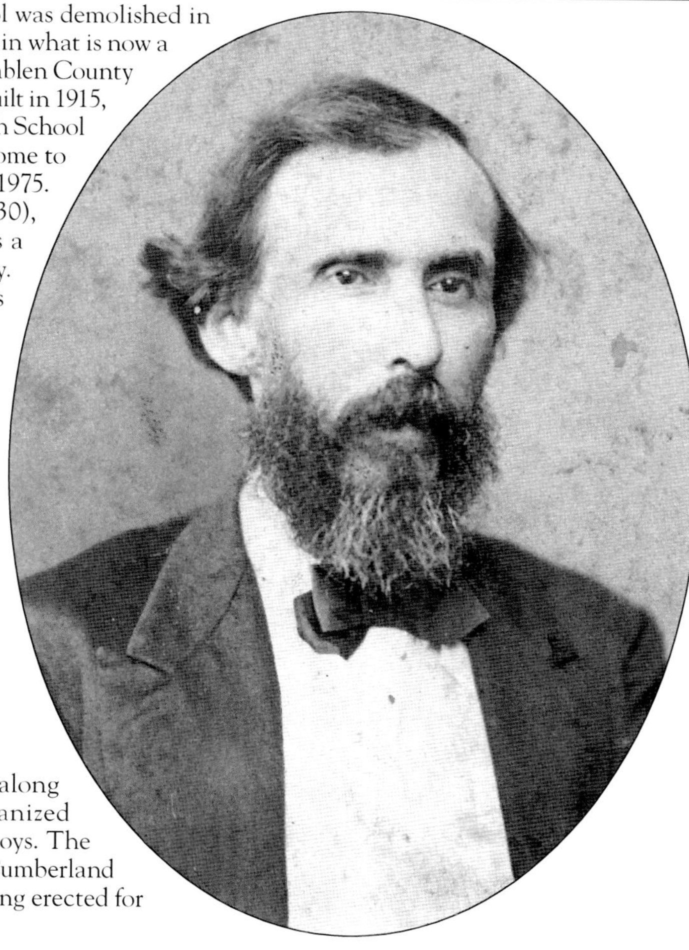

In 1867, Prof. A.W. Wilson, along with James A. Carriger, organized the Reagan High School for boys. The school was located on North Cumberland Street in a one-story log building erected for Bethel Baptist Church.

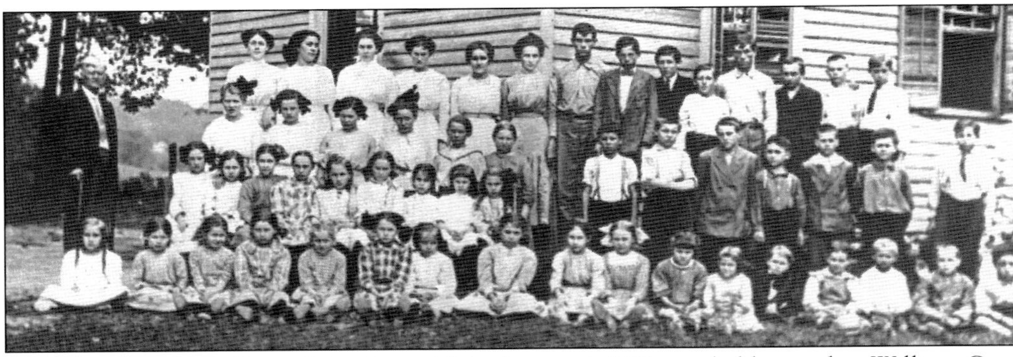

This class from New Hope School, established around 1910, was led by teacher William Cary. The students shown are, from left to right, (first row) Edith Fulton, Pearl Miller, Kate Robertson, Etta Blakley, Mary Robertson, Lona Garretson, Charlcie Purkey, Ada Purkey, Laura Miller, Edith Ryle, Mary Morgan, Minnie Morgan, Robert Miller, Jesse Ryle, Clyde Blakley, Willie Combs, and Charles Fulton; (second row) Cosby Cochran, Nannie Morelock, Clara Miller, Myrtle Inman, Ruth Fulton, Nettie Shipley, Cassie Shipley, Lucy Clevenger, and Annie Bettis; (third row) Flora Lou Noe, Virgie Rhea, Anna Miller, Annie Fulton, Eula Purkey, Emma Blakley, Jesse Morgan, Dave Robertson, John Combs, Ernest Morelock, Ernest Clevenger, Bascom Morelock, and Ernest Doyle; (fourth row) Mary Purkey, Minnie Purkey, Lula Miller, Nancy Cockran, Mary Fulton, Effie Purkey, John Shannon, Lewis Doyle, Everrette Purkey, William Fulton, Will Shannon, Henderson Purkey, Bryan Clevenger, and Ira Shipley. (Courtesy of Minnie Robertson.)

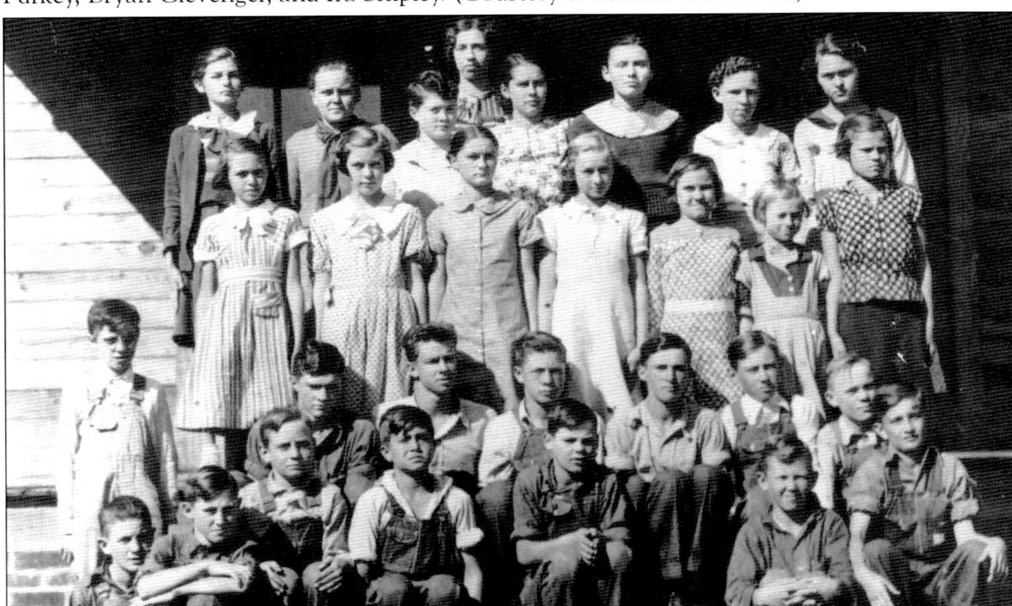

The students who were attending Marguerite School around 1936 are, from left to right, (first row) S.E. Fullington, Paul Inman, Arlie Purkey, Elmer Lampkin, James Stapleton, Malcolm Goforth, and Ralph McKinney; (second row) Hildred Hayes, Conrad Campbell, Albert Smith, Maurice Johns, Lewis Inman, Ralph Johnson, and Aden Brady; (third row) Mary Lillian Hoover, Lillie Mae Guffey, Mary Ruth Inman, Minnie Smith, Gula Hayes, Ruby Smith, and Beulah Stump; (fourth row) Willie Sue Turner, Lena Mae Purkey, Anna Lee Campbell, teacher Fay Templin, Elizabeth Morelock, Mildred Turner, Mary Brady, and Ruth Long. (Courtesy of Minnie Robertson.)

Nine

Faces and Family Portraits

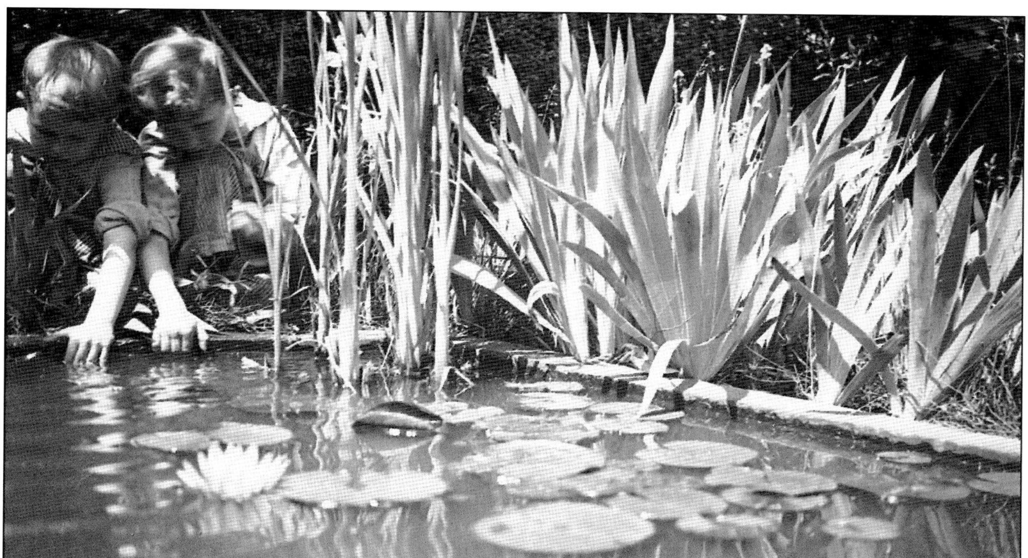

Leslie Beard Julian (left) and Edward Haywood Julian were the sons of Emma Beard Julian and Dr. Ralph E. "Doc" Julian (1886–1976). Their father was a pharmacist and co-owner of Roberts and Turner Drug Store in downtown Morristown. This photograph is a testament to his artistic photographic talents, as he was also a skilled photographer. Leslie followed in his father's footsteps and became a pharmacist after graduating from the University of Tennessee School of Pharmacy. Edward followed in his father's artistic footsteps. After becoming a decorated World War II veteran, Edward attended the Art Institute of Chicago. (Courtesy of James Haywood Julian.)

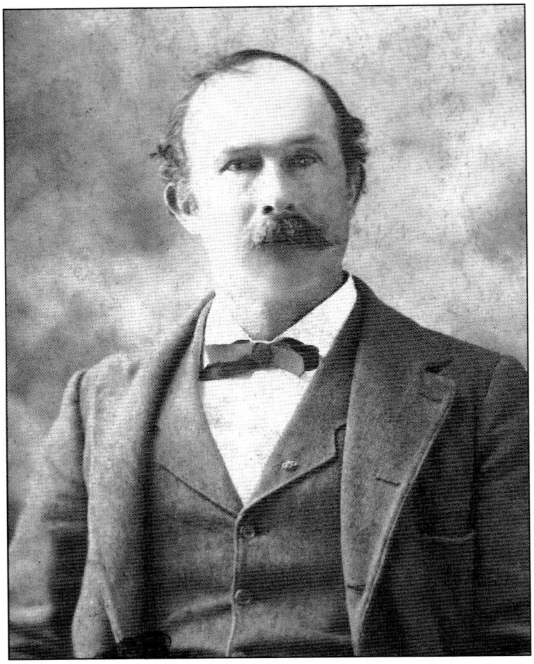

Robert McFarland Jones (1847–1922) was named after his uncle Maj. Robert McFarland. During the Civil War, when he was only 14 years old, he joined the 31st Tennessee Regiment. He was discharged one year later after serving at Vicksburg. Jarnagin Cemetery is his final resting place. (Courtesy of Davy Anne Charles.)

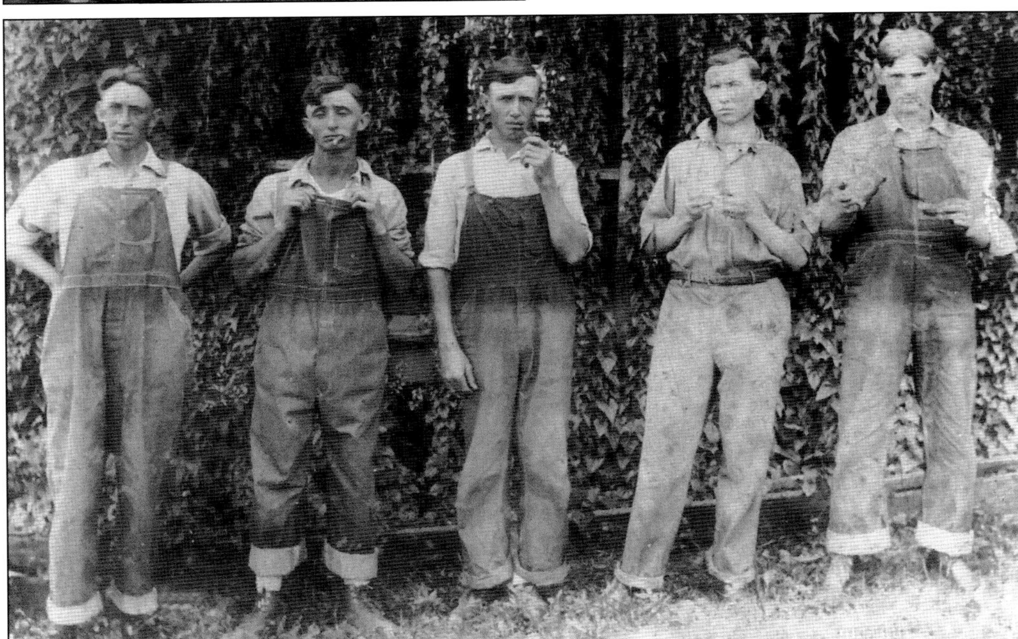

The four sons of James Charles A. Haun and Catherine Rebecca Courtney Haun pose here around 1915 to 1920 with their brother-in-law. Pictured are, from left to right, James Charles "Curt" Haun, Thomas Elmer Haun, Lewis Asberry "Berry" Haun, Leonard Sheraton Haun, and William "Will" Porter Saylor. Will Saylor married the brothers' sister, Della Haun. Catherine Nenney Baptist Church is the final resting place for many of the Haun family members. (Courtesy of Bobbie Finney.)

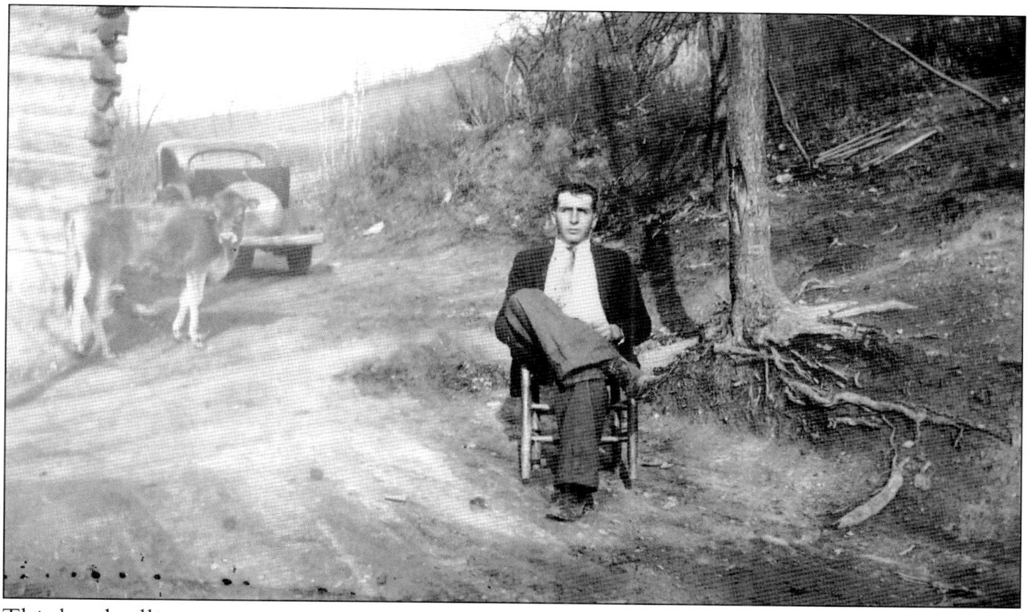

This log dwelling was the Smith homeplace on Boatman's Mountain. Henry Yank Smith takes it easy as his cow looks on. (Courtesy of Billie D. Loveday.)

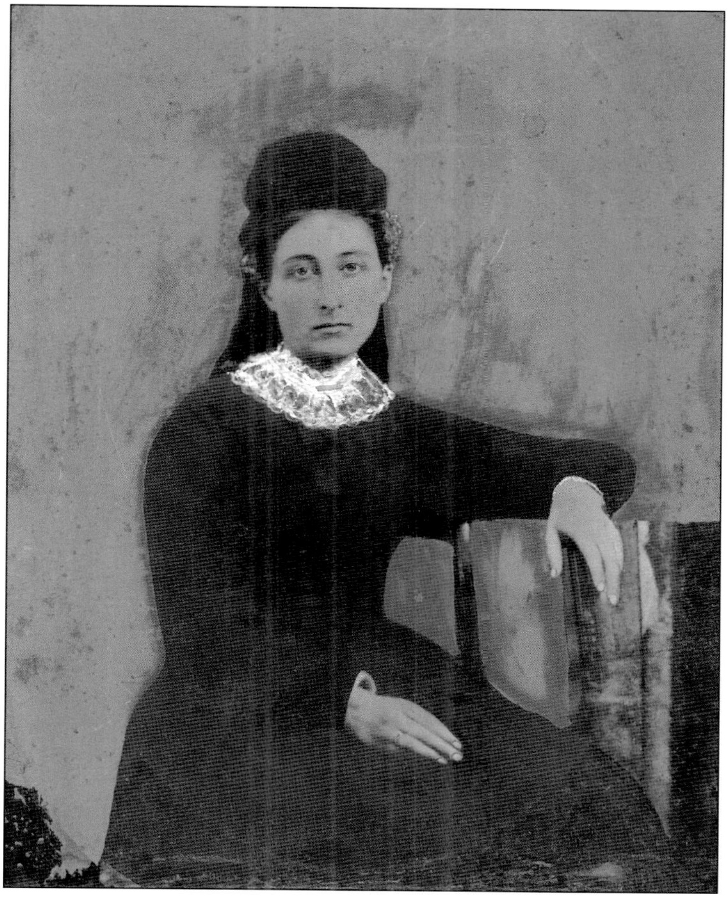

Flora Kathleen Livingston was born on May 20, 1885, and passed away on June 29, 1971. She is the daughter of James Finn Livingston and Charlotte Walker Livingston and married Edward Clyde Harris on April 17, 1901. Their two children were Harold W. Harris and Mae Harris Anderson. The original image from which this photograph was copied was a tintype. (Courtesy of Doris Livingston Stump.)

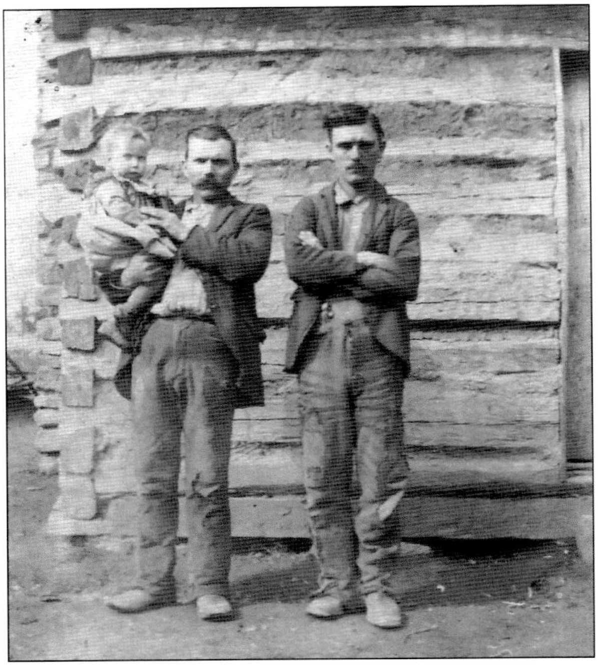

Half-brothers William Monroe "Row" Mayes and Andrew "Andy" Clinton Mayes are standing in front of Row Mayes's log cabin. Row Mayes is holding his son, James Ray Mayes. This photograph was taken around 1911, and the cabin still stands today on top of River Ridge between Kidwell's Ridge Road and Inman Bend Road.

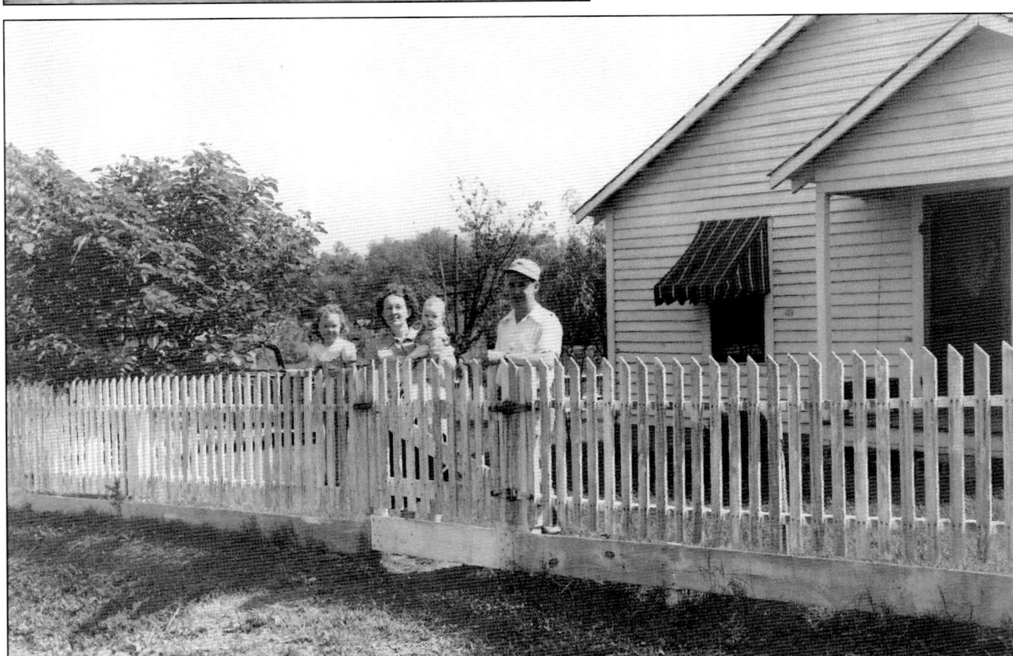

In the spring of 1952, the Roy Estelle Davis family posed in front of their home, located in the Witt community, for a magazine article featuring small tobacco farms. Pictured are, from left to right, Betty Davis Collake, Mary Kate Fowler Davis, Eddie Roy Davis, and Roy Estelle Davis. Young Betty Davis married Gary Ronald Collake in 1971, and young Eddie Roy Davis married Betty Buckner in 1976. Eddie Davis, county coroner, served as director of the Youth Emergency Shelter with his wife from 1979 until 2010. (Courtesy of Eddie R. Davis.)

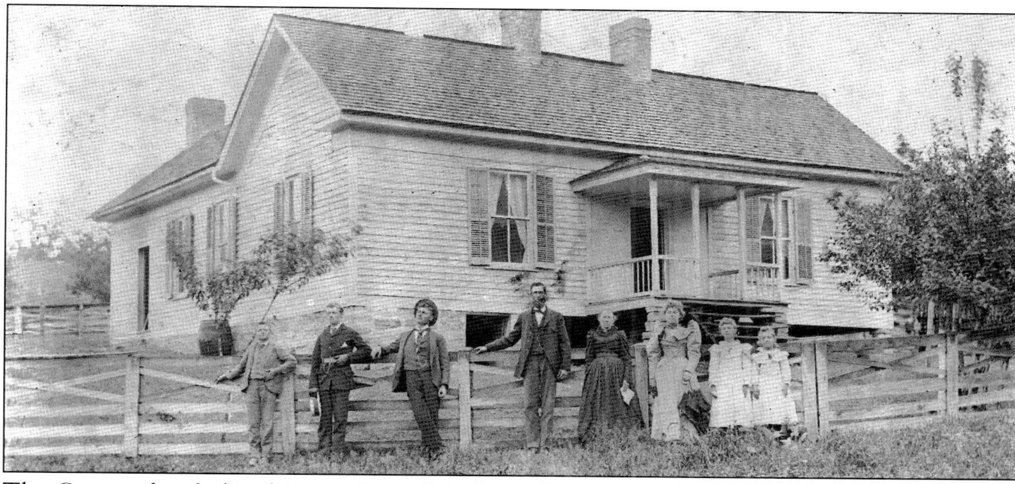

The Cooper family lived in southeast Hamblen County in what is known as the Springvale community. John Lockard Cooper (1842–1916) and his wife, Mary Angelina McDonald Cooper (1843–1906), standing in the center, raised nine children. This photograph was taken prior to Mary's death in 1906. It is believed their daughter, Ida Cooper Rippetoe, a widow of William P. Rippetoe, is standing next to her mother along with her four children: Ernest, Mary Ina, Joe, and Willie Mae. (Courtesy of James Haywood Julian.)

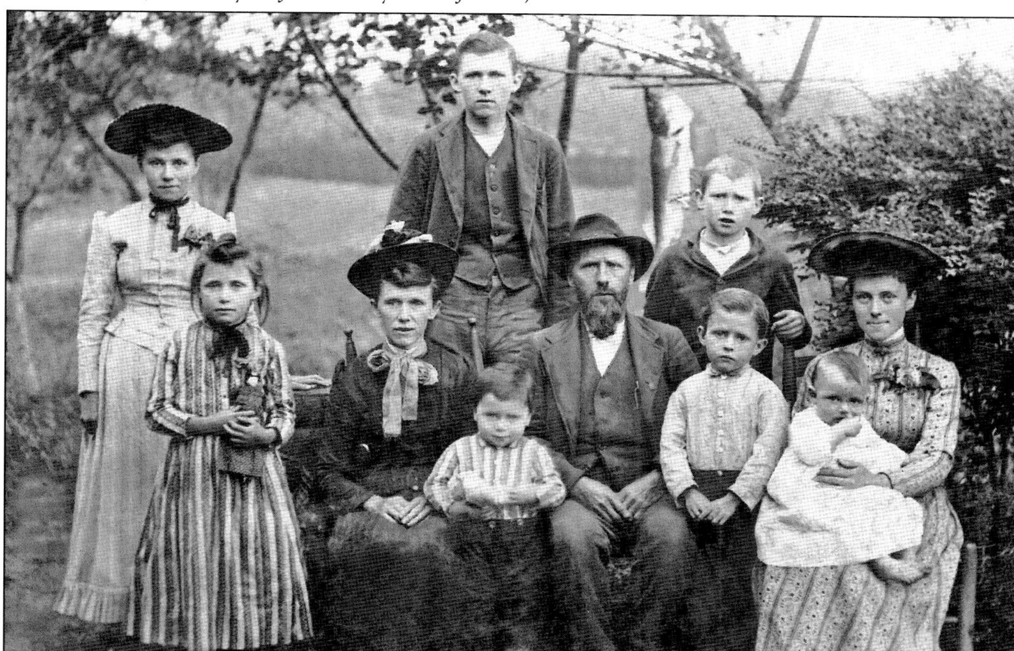

The family of James Polk Mayes and his wife, Maria Adeline Carter Mayes, posed for this photograph around 1893. During the Civil War, James served in Companies M and H of the 1st Tennessee Cavalry for the Union army. Pictured are, from left to right, (first row) Thompsie Mayes, Adeline Carter Mayes, Willie Mayes, James Polk Mayes, Ruben Tate Mayes, and Almeda Mayes Boatman holding her child, Burson Boatman; (back row) Lucy Mayes Winstead, Luther Mayes, and Garrett Mayes.

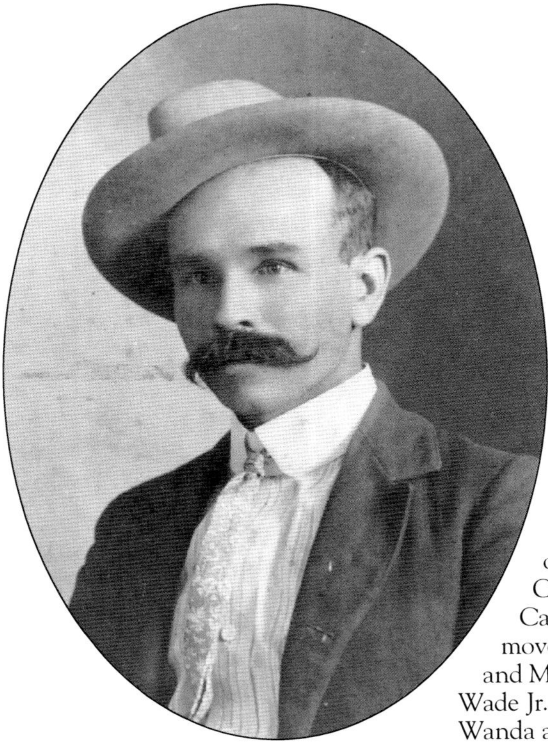

Wade Hampton Cowan Sr. and his wife, Minnie Ivy Cowan, were married in Hamblen County in 1912. They reared four sons and one daughter in a Civil War–era log cabin on a 50-acre hillside farm on Kidwell's Ridge Road. Minnie, born in 1892, was the daughter of John H. Ivy and Laura Smith Ivy. Wade Cowan, son of George W. Cowan and Nancy Cassell Cowan, was born in Virginia in 1875 and moved to Tennessee when he was a child. Wade and Minnie's children are Eugene, Cassell, Donald, Wade Jr. "Ginger," and Mildred Cowan. (Courtesy of Wanda and Ginger Cowan.)

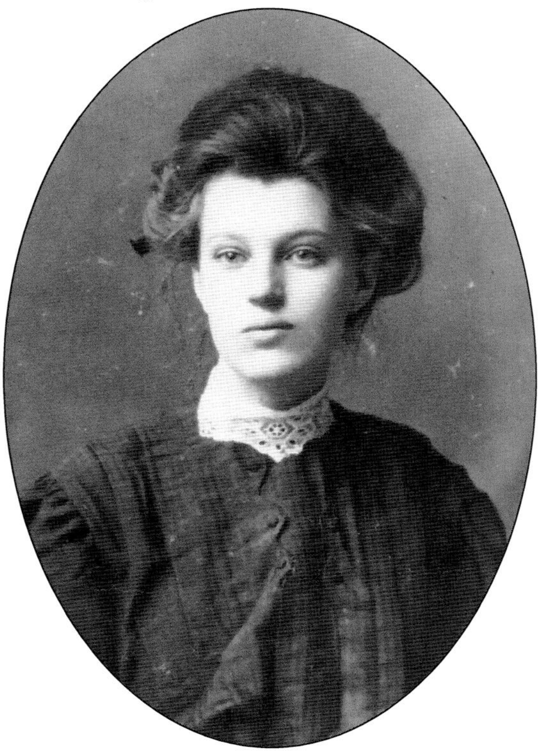

The Capps family came to Morristown from Russellville, Kentucky, in the late 1800s. John S. Capps and Elizabeth Strode Capps were parents to Mary Emma Capps (standing). The family owned and operated a popular boardinghouse known as the Capps House and a livery stable. The Capps House, once located at the corner of East Main and Hill Streets, was an impressive two-story brick Colonial that was used to board and feed the town's visitors for many years. Jarnagin Cemetery is the final resting place of the Capps family.

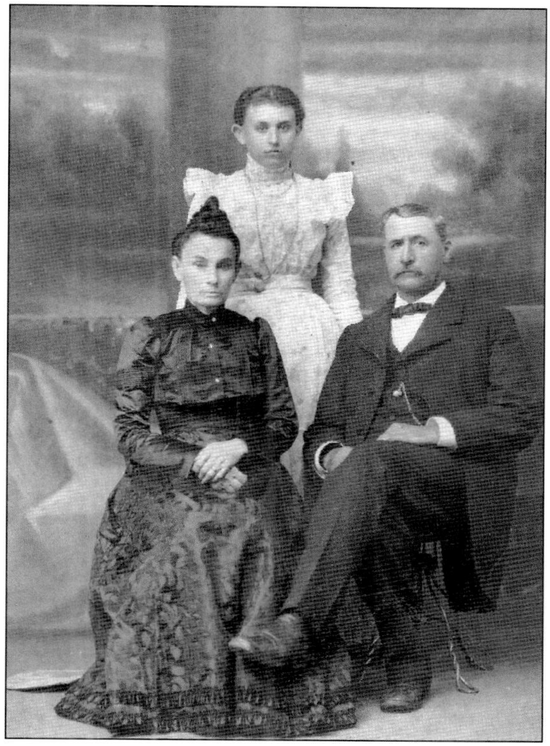

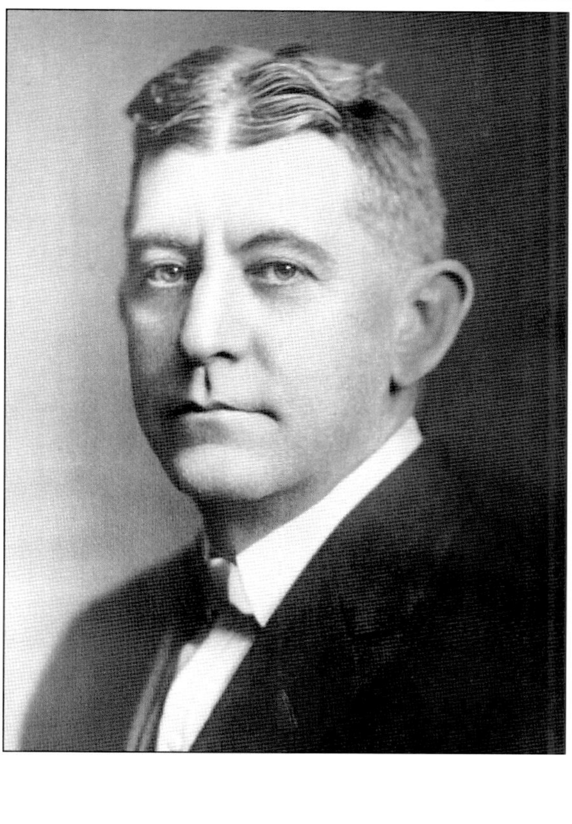

William Byrd Whittaker served one term as mayor of Morristown and also served as president of the Morristown Chamber of Commerce. He was instrumental in the fire department's purchase of the city's first motorized fire truck while serving as mayor, and the truck was later named in his honor. (Courtesy of the Morristown Chamber of Commerce.)

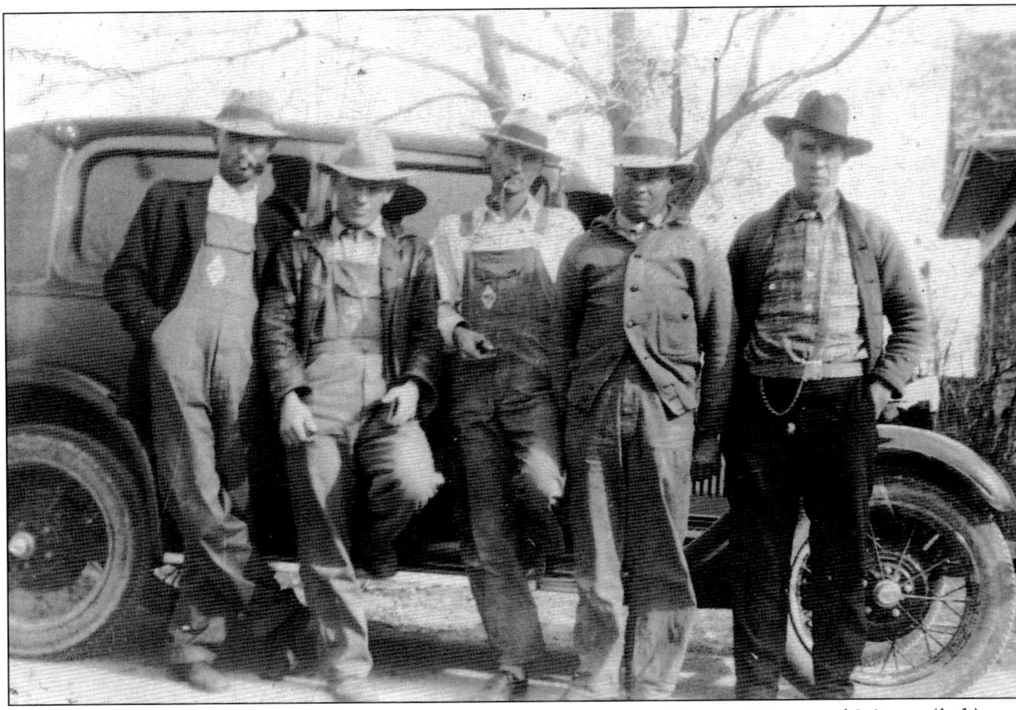

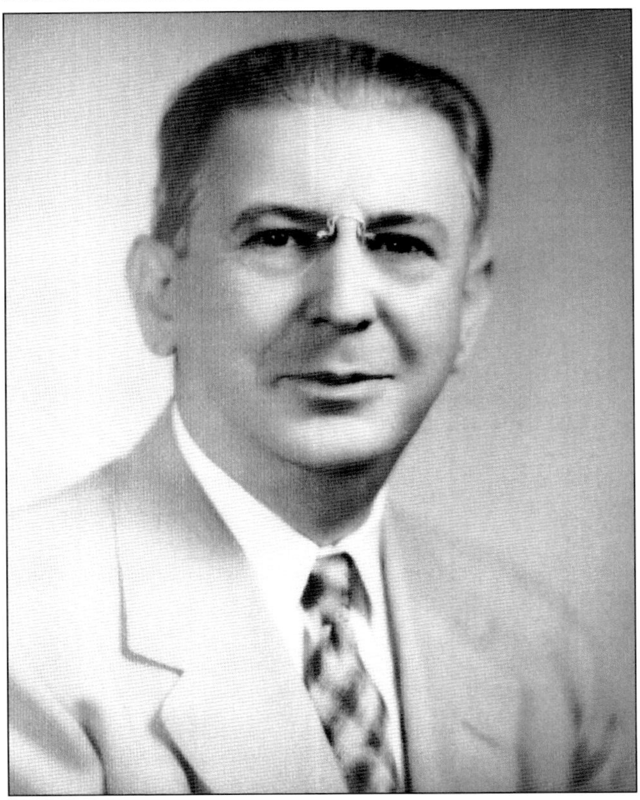

Horace Maynard Mayes (left) poses here with his brother G.B. Mayes (right) and with three other gentlemen They are, from left to right, Henry Jones, Oneal Hillin, and Logan Brand. (Courtesy of Billie D. Loveday.)

Frank Roger Miller was born in Morristown on May 1, 1886, to John Samuel and Orlene Miller. After marrying the famed author Helen Topping on June 15, 1910, in Hamblen County, the couple went on to have two children, John Wallace Miller and Frederick Eugene Miller. Former owner and operator of the *Morristown Republican*, Miller was serving as secretary of the Morristown Chamber of Commerce at the time of his death on the Miller farm, Arrowhill, in Talbott on January 26, 1944. (Courtesy of the Morristown Chamber of Commerce.)

Dr. Pleasant Littleton Henderson (1866–1944) received his medical degree from Bellevue Medical College in New York City and later moved to Morristown in May 1896. Leading the way in the organization of Morristown General Hospital, he served as its president for 16 years and as Morristown's mayor from 1927 to 1928. Henderson was instrumental in the creation of white light system and the completion of an efficient sewage system for the city. (Courtesy of the Morristown Chamber of Commerce.)

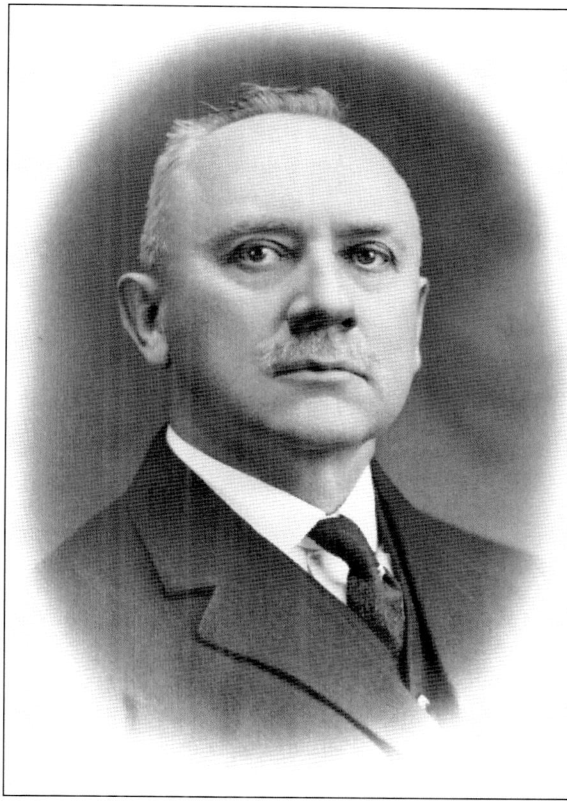

Benjamin Alexander Noe (1861–1929) and his wife, Jennie Elizabeth Pettigrew Noe (1863–1926), raised seven sons in the area of Noe's Chapel United Methodist Church, where most of them are now interred. Two of their sons are pictured here with friends on Cherokee Drive around 1910. They are, from left to right, Charles Spears, unidentified, Keith Noe, and Hal Noe. (Courtesy of Davy Anne Charles.)

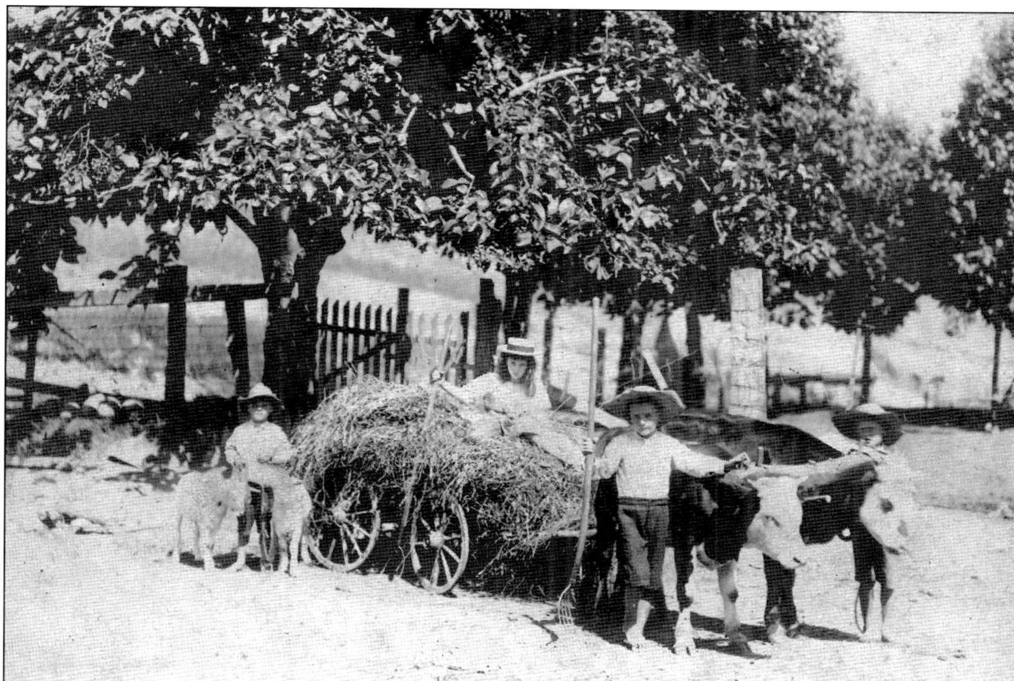

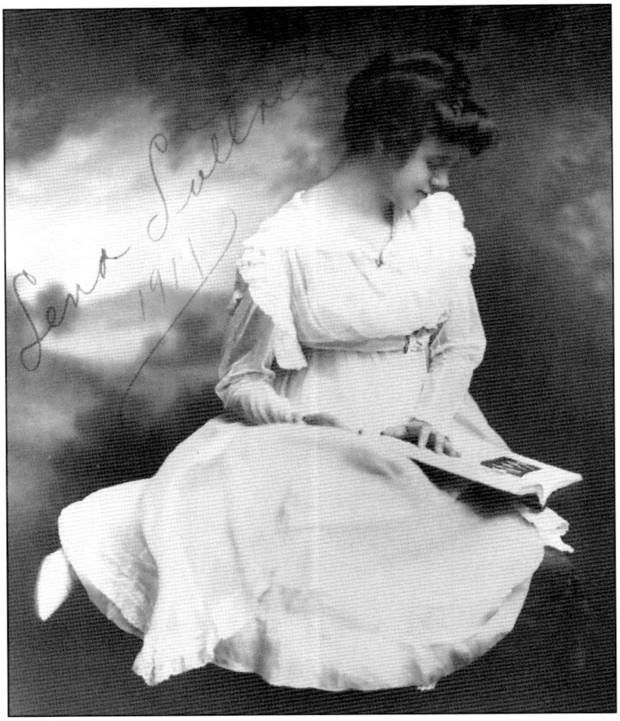

Lena Luttrell was about 21 years old when she posed for this 1917 photograph. She was one of five children of William Calvin Luttrell and Lillie Belle Fry Luttrell. Her father was a businessman and real estate investor. She is buried at Jarnagin Cemetery with her husband, Thomas H. Campbell.

Emma Smith Mayes married Crampton "Doc" Mayes in Hamblen County on July 27, 1887. The family had a large farm and was known for its peach orchards on top of River Ridge between Kidwell's Ridge Road and Inman Bend Road. This photograph, taken on the homestead, shows, from left to right, Lizy Clementin Mayes, Emma Smith Mayes, Bessie Mayes, Ben Harrison Mayes, and Hazel Mayes.

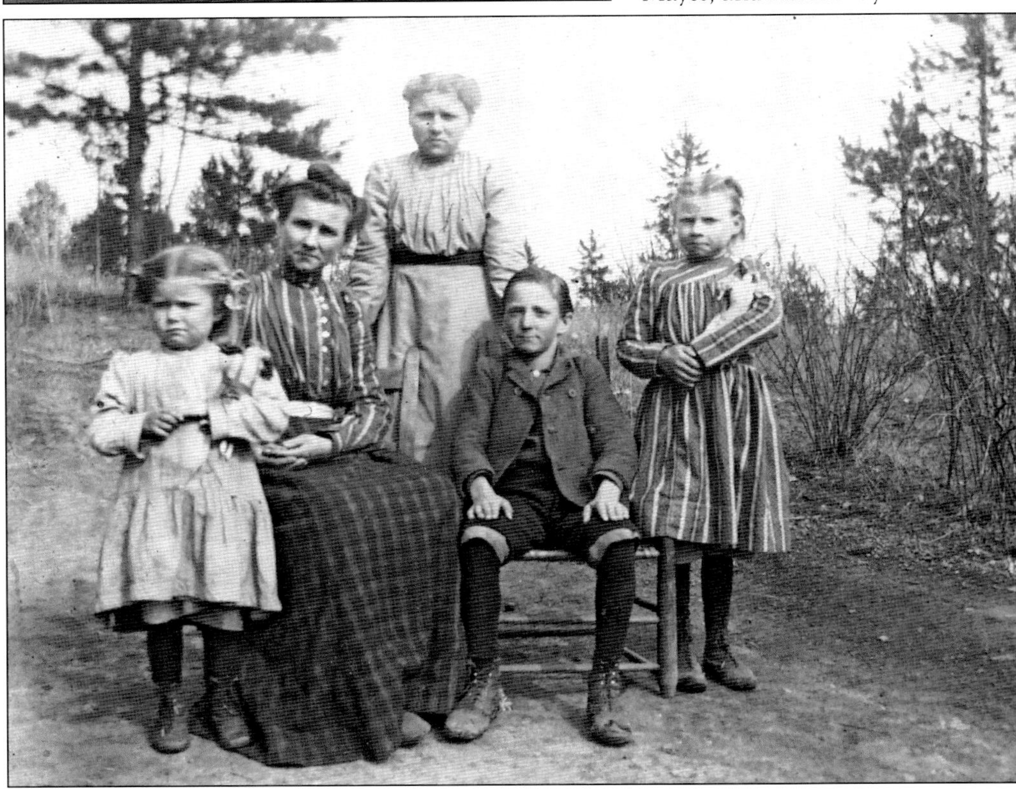

This couple posing for a portrait is Godfrey "Dick" Enoch and his wife, Hester Saylor. The couple married around 1890 and had four known children: Nannie, John B., William P., and Georgia Saylor. (Courtesy of Bobbie Finney.)

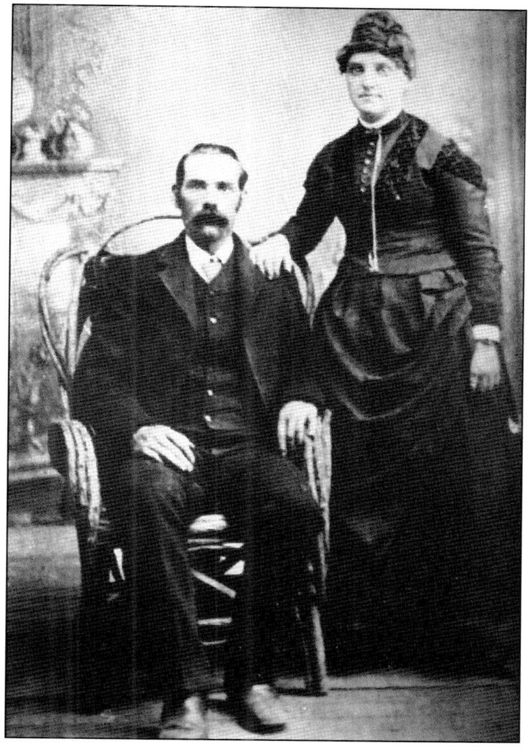

After settling into the area during the early 1800s, the Saylor family became substantial property owners in the Bent Creek area of Russellville. They donated property for the construction of the Salem Community School, more commonly known as the "Squeeze Tight School." There were six children born to this family, with three boys and three girls. Pictured is the Saylor family from around the late 1800s. From left to right are Georgia, William, Hester, Godfrey Enoch, John, and Nannie. (Courtesy of Bobbie Finney.)

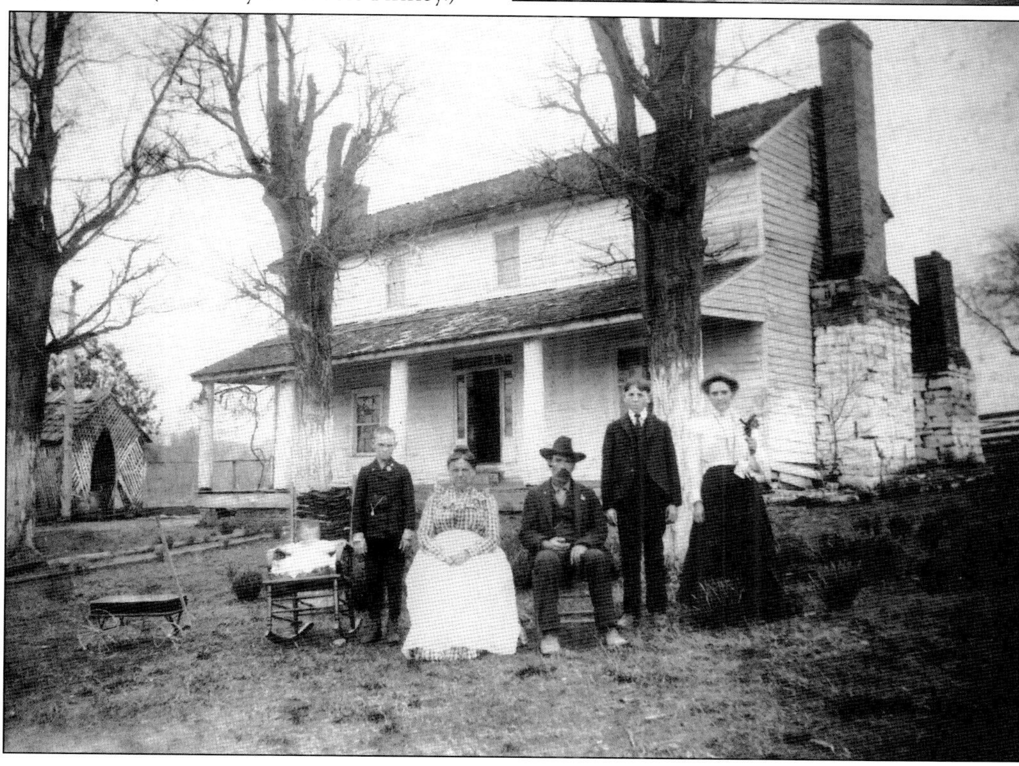

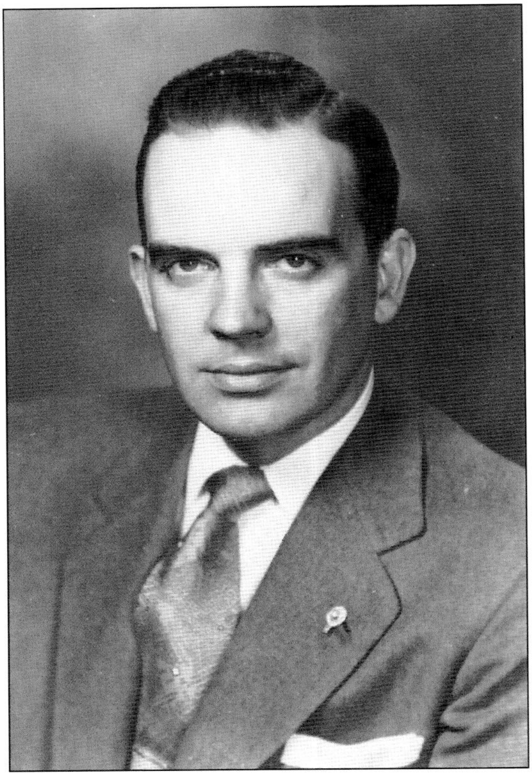

Frank Clement, seeking the position of Tennessee governor, had a rally in Hamblen County on Tuesday, August 5, 1952. Clement decided to challenge incumbent Gov. Gordon Browning in 1952 for the Democratic nomination for governor. Clement, only 32 at the time, became the youngest governor in the country when he upset Browning in the August primary and won the general election. (Courtesy of Doris Livingston Stump.)

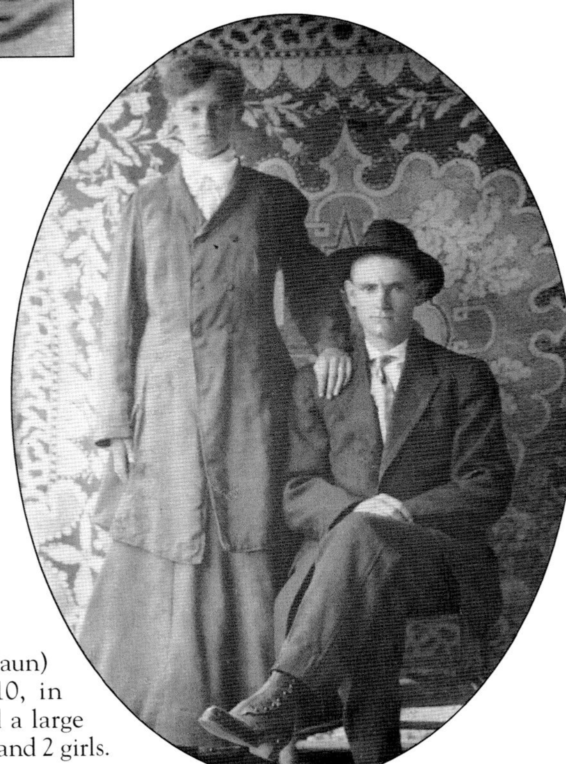

William Porter Saylor and Della Mae (Haun) Saylor married on December 24, 1910, in Whitesburg, Tennessee. The couple had a large family consisting of 12 children—10 boys and 2 girls. (Courtesy of Bobbie Finney.)

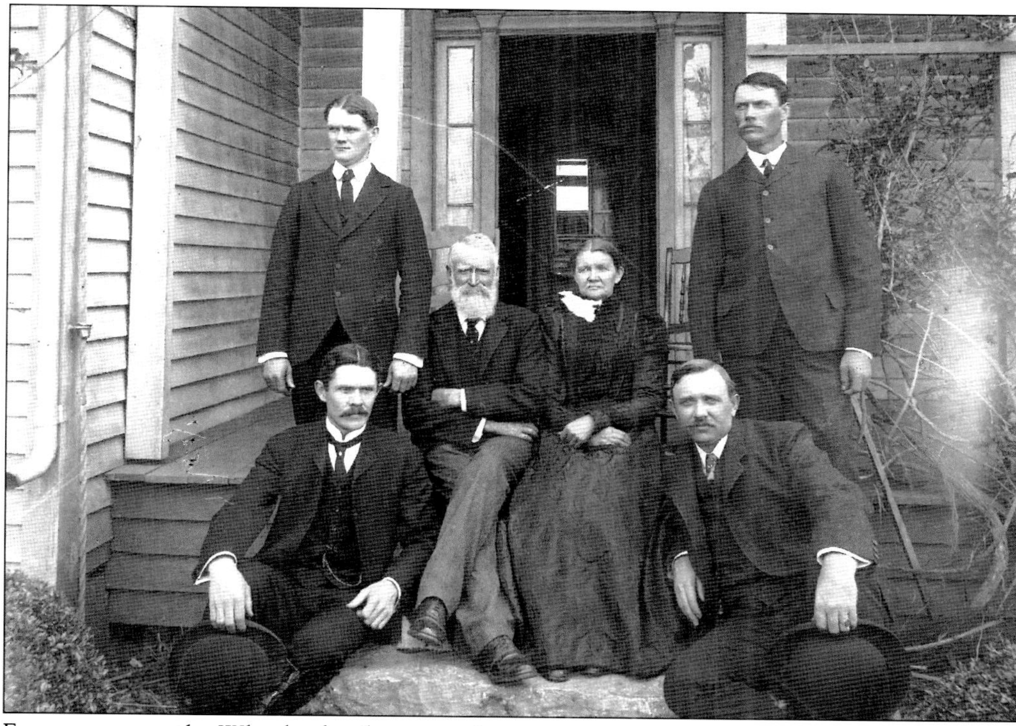

For many years, the Wheeler family operated the Wheeler Dairy Farm on Dover Road in southeast Morristown, the area today is known as Brockland Acres. Samuel and his wife, Mary, are posed with their four sons, from left to right: (sitting) Adm. Will Wheeler, Samuel Vincent Wheeler (confederate veteran), Mary Jane Baker Wheeler, and Adm. Charles Wheeler; (standing) Bob Wheeler and Bert Wheeler.

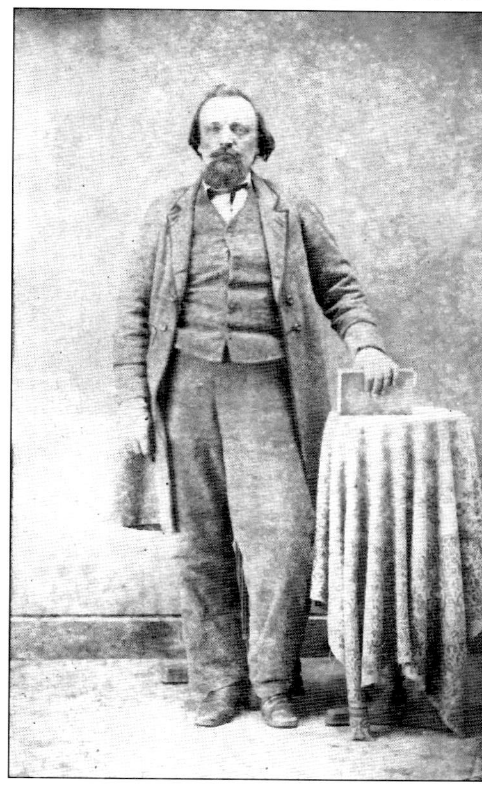

Edward Duffield Conway was born on July 29, 1873, to Joseph P. Conway and Sarah Senter Conway. He married Onice K. Buckner (1895–1964), and upon his death in Morristown on January 5, 1934, he was buried at St. Paul Cemetery. (Courtesy of James Haywood Julian.)

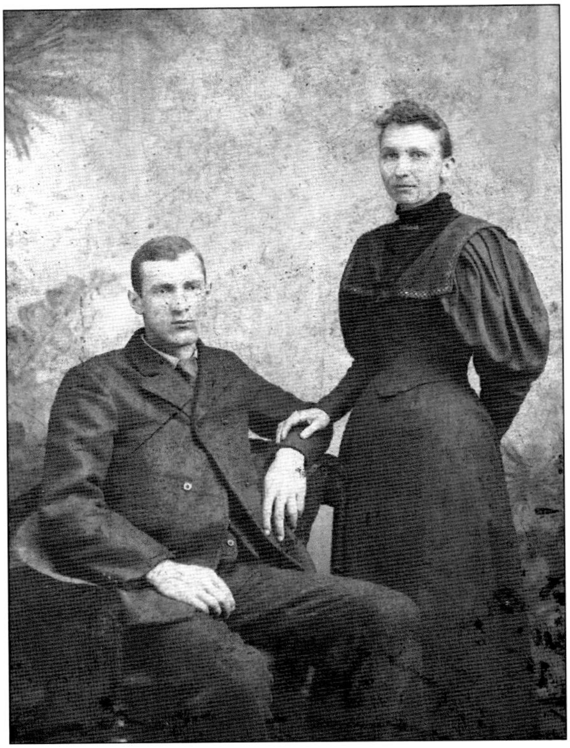

Frank Lonzo Mayes was born on December 25, 1875, to William Lafayette Mayes and Mary Darthula Ivey and married Ida Underwood Mayes in Hamblen County on March 14,1872. The couple was married for 56 years and had four children: Clara, Harry, Paul, and Hugh Mayes.

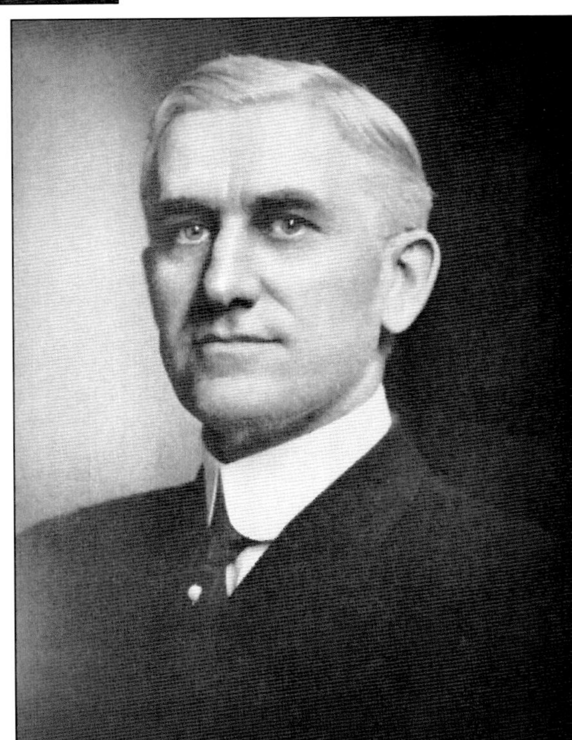

Jacob Nelson Fisher was the son of Daniel Fisher and Amelia Laudenslager. He was an active member of the First Presbyterian Church, serving both as elder and clerk for many years. He played an active part in the community, serving as president of City National Bank and general manager of the Augsburg Drawing Company. Fisher served as president of Morristown Produce and Ice Company and Morristown General Hospital until the time of his death on May 29, 1932. (Courtesy of the Morristown Chamber of Commerce.)

James Charles A. Haun (1863–1941) and his wife, Catherine Rebecca Courtney Haun (1869–1920), married in Hamblen County on September 12, 1887. The Haun family owned two large farms off Courtney Road in Whitesburg during the 1800s era. There were eight children born into the family, four boys and four girls. Some of their descendants still continue to live nearby, but the large farm tracts have been subdivided over the years and no longer exist. (Courtesy of Bobbie Finney.)

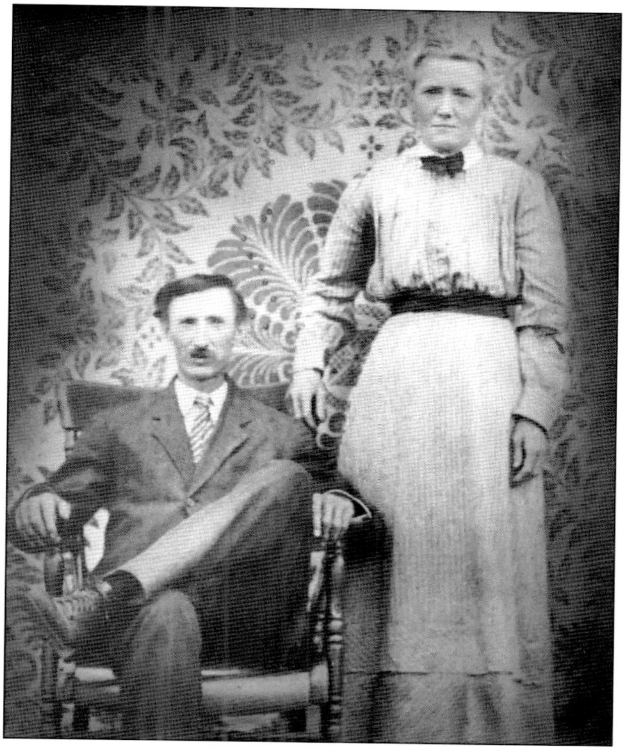

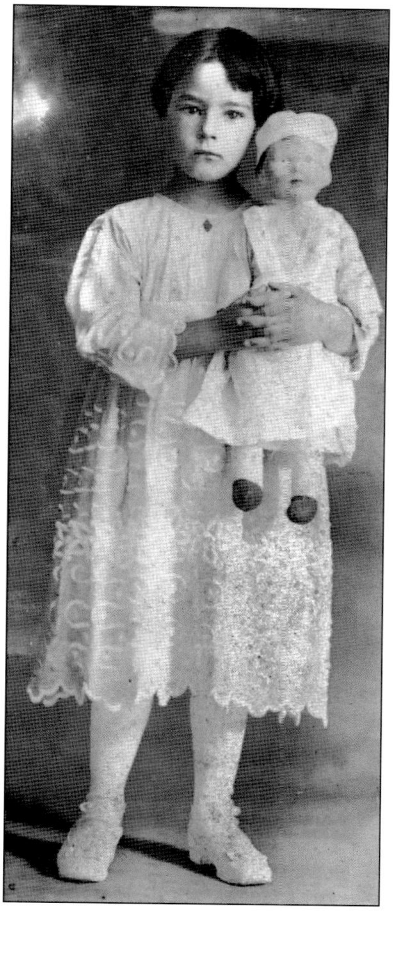

Mary Wilma Mayes Bryan, pictured here with her doll at a young age, was born in Hamblen County on August 28, 1911, to Andrew and Cassie Mayes. She married Henry Frank Bryan on May 18, 1933, in Hamblen County, and the couple had four children: Doris, Evadean, Raymond, and James Bryan. Mary died on July 14, 1998, and is laid to rest in Emma Jarnagin Cemetery.

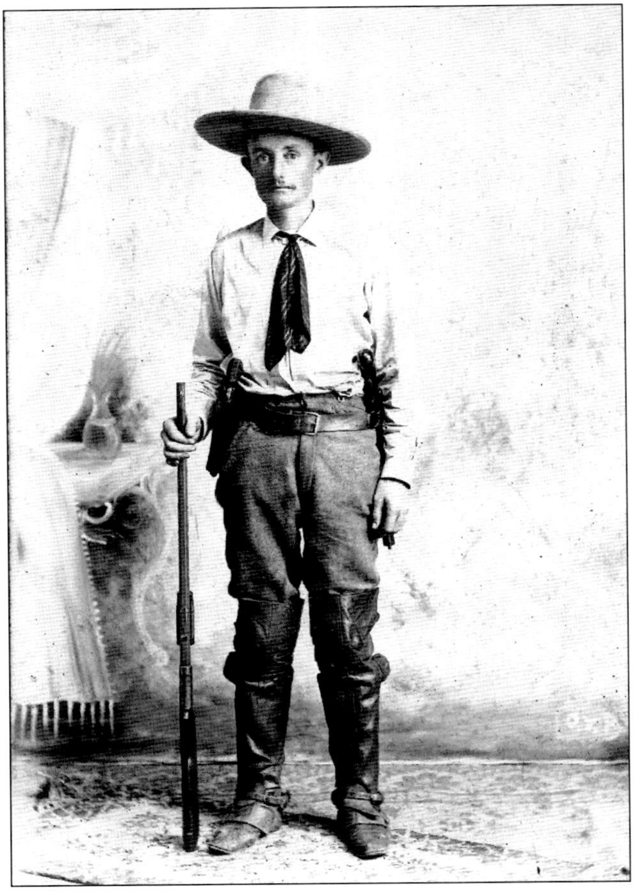

William P. Rippetoe was born on October 17, 1870, and married Ida Cooper on October 29, 1890, in Hamblen County. He served as the Hamblen County deputy sheriff, but he had a losing run for sheriff. He died on June 9, 1899, at 29 years of age from tuberculosis and is buried with his wife at Emma Jarnagin Cemetery. (Courtesy of James Haywood Julian.)

Five generations of the Livingston family pose for this September 23, 1928, photograph. They are, from left to right, (first row) Elizabeth Carlton Livingston and James Finn Livingston (son); (second row) James Leroy Livingston (grandson), Dorothy Livingston Farmer (great-great-granddaughter), and Randal Clifford Livingston (great-grandson). (Courtesy of Doris Livingston Stump.)

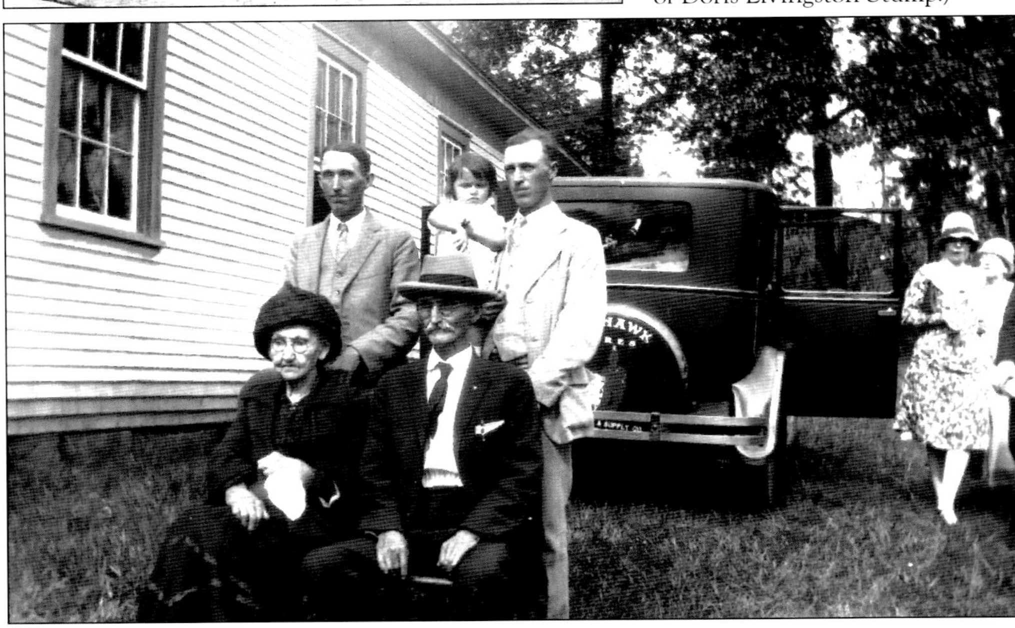

Bibliography

Brooks, Cora Davis. *History of Morristown, Tennessee.* Nashville: Nashville Historical Records, 1940.

Census on microfilm for Hamblen County, 1870–1880, 1900–1930.

Claborn, Jim and William Henderson. *Hamblen County, Tennessee: A Pictorial History.* Virginia Beach: Donning Publishing, 1995.

Citizen Tribune, 1975–2012.

Hale, S. George. *Hamblen County Chapter American Red Cross, 1917–1980.* Not published, 1981.

Hamblen County Genealogical Society. *Cemeteries of Hamblen County, Tennessee.* 3 vol. Morristown, TN: Hamblen County Genealogical Society, 1989, 1996.

Hamblen County Heritage Book Committee. *A History of Hamblen County, Tennessee and Its People.* Waynesville, NC: Don Mills, 1996.

Howell, Dr. W.E. *As I Remember Morristown.* Not published, 1951.

Itakha (Morristown High School yearbook), 1938–1950.

Moore, Lillie. *Around the Area: January to June Columns.* Charleston, SC: BookSurge Publishers, 2005.

———. *Around the Area: July to December Columns.* Charleston, SC: BookSurge Publishers, 2007.

Morristown Centennial Committee. *Historic Hamblen.* Morristown: TN: Hamblen County Centennial Program, 1970.

Morristown City Directory. Morristown, TN: 1922, 1928, 1944, and 1950.

Morristown Centennial Program. Morristown, TN: Centennial Committee, 1955.

Morristown Gazette/Daily Gazette & Mail, 1868–1975.

Powers, Leeper Lee. *Captain Thomas Jarnagin, 1746–1802.* Lake Lure, NC: L.L. Powers, 1985.

About the Organization

The Hamblen County Archives was officially established in February 2002 with the purpose and mission of preserving Hamblen County's legal records. With an annual budget of $5,000, space in the courthouse basement, and a group of volunteers, the Hamblen County Archives immediately began the important and very dirty work of cleaning and filing records.

The archives received the genealogical resources from the Morristown-Hamblen Library in 2005 and continues to receive resources from generous donors.

Without volunteers, the Hamblen County Archives would not exist today. From 2002 to 2011, they have logged more than 22,000 hours. Helen Danison, who served as director from 2002 until her sudden passing in January 2009, spearheaded the setup and operation of the archives office. Volunteers continue the important work she helped to begin.

The Hamblen County Archives would like to thank Larry Hobby for his hard work and perseverance in putting together this wonderful book about Morristown. With his gracious spirit and generous soul, his support is greatly appreciated by everyone at the Hamblen County Archives.

The archives is open to the public. For additional information go to: www.HamblenCountyArchives.blogspot.com. For current hours, call (423) 586-1961 or email: archives@co.hamblen.tn.us.